CASA Y COMUNIDAD

CASA Y COMUNIDAD

Latino Home and Neighborhood Design

Henry G. Cisneros
and John Rosales, Editors

Casa Y Comunidad: Latino Home and Neighborhood Design

BuilderBooks, a Service of the National Association of Home Builders

Christine B. Charlip	Publisher
Doris M. Tennyson	Senior Acquisition Editor
Courtenay S. Brown	Book Editor
Torrie Singletary	Production Editor
Manuel Garzon	Cover and Page Design
Circle Graphics	Composition
Automated Graphic Systems	Printing
Gerald M. Howard	NAHB Executive Vice President and CEO
Mark Pursell	NAHB Senior Staff Vice President, Marketing & Sales Group
Lakisha Campbell	NAHB Staff Vice President, Publication & Affinity Programs

Disclaimer

This publication provides accurate information on the subject matter covered. The publisher is selling it with the understanding that the publisher is not providing legal, accounting, or other professional service. If you need legal advice or other expert assistance, obtain the services of a qualified professional experienced in the subject matter involved. Reference herein to any specific commercial products, process, or service by trade name, trademark, manufacturer, or otherwise does not necessarily constitute or imply its endorsement, recommendation, or favored status by the National Association of Home Builders. The views and opinions of the authors expressed in this publication do not necessarily state or reflect those of the National Association of Home Builders, and they shall not be used to advertise or endorse a product.

Printed in the United States of America

10 09 08 07   2 3 4 5

ISBN-10 0-86718-613-5
ISBN-13 978-0-86718-613-0

Library of Congress Cataloging-in-Publication Data

Casa y comunidad : Latino home and neighborhood design / Henry G. Cisneros and John Rosales, editors.
      p. cm.
   Includes index.
   ISBN-13: 978-0-86718-613-0
   ISBN-10: 0-86718-613-5
   1. Hispanic Americans—Housing. 2. Hispanic American neighborhoods. I. Cisneros, Henry. II. Rosales, John, 1956– III. Title: Latino home and neighborhood design.

HD7288.72U5C37 2006
333.33'808968073—dc22

                                                            2006047569

For further information, please contact:

National Association of Home Builders
1201 15th Street, NW
Washington, DC 20005-2800
800-223-2665
Visit us online at www.BuilderBooks.com.

CONTENTS

FOREWORD

Crystal balls are often clear, but wrong. In 1989, an academic study forecast that residential real estate prices, "could fall as much as 3% a year in real terms or nearly 50% by the year 2007." The study was wrong. Instead, in these last 15 years, prices have soared, making this the most extended period of housing prosperity in our nation's history.

Academicians, commentators, and pundits were reading the right data—but not *all* the right data. What was missing from their models was the stream of foreign-born households. Most immigrants initially rent; but over time, they, like native-born Americans, want to buy homes. And so do their children.

Federal Reserve Chairman Alan Greenspan told the U.S. Congress in November 2001, "The underlying demand for new housing units has received support from an expanding population, in part resulting from high levels of immigration."

The stream of immigrants to the United States comes from throughout the globe and has contributed one-third of household growth over the past decade. Of this stream, Latinos are the fastest growing minority group. The Mexican-born population alone in the United States increased 21% to almost 11 million from 2000 to 2005.

Indeed, today most of the Latino population increase comes from births, not immigration. Even though Latinos represent less than 11% of all households, they accounted for 27% of net household growth from 1995 to 2005. In 2000, the foreign-born Latino share of households in California, Texas, and Florida ranged from 9% to 14%. Often those states mark immigrants' entry points, and from there families migrate north, south, east, and west. Census data show significant, and growing, Latino populations in New York, Hartford, Chicago, and Providence. The southern states saw the largest percentage increase in foreign-born Latinos.

The American-born children of Latino immigrants are writing their own Horatio Alger stories. These children represented 9% of the entire population aged 10–19 in 2005, and 12% of those under age 10. In terms of education and income, this U.S.-born second generation is on track to exceed the levels of their foreign-born parents. Between 1980 and 2000, the Latino share of the lower-middle income quartile increased from 6% to 10% and the upper-middle quartile grew from 5% to 8%.

So, it is no surprise that Latinos constitute a growing segment of the middle market for housing in the United States. Consider the common home buyer names. In 2000, Brown, Miller, and Davis were among the most common surnames. In 2005, they were replaced by Rodriquez, Garcia, and Hernandez.

The home-building industry, though, has often looked on this new, growing market of Latinos as an expansion of the regular home-buying market. Hiring Spanish-speaking Realtors and brokers and advertising in Spanish mark outreach to the market, but that in and of itself does not suffice.

The market of Latino home buyers does not necessarily replicate the larger market.

What are the characteristics of the Latino family? How do they live? What space configurations do they want in their homes? What neighborhoods do they consider most desirable? What are their financial barriers to homeownership, and how can they be overcome?

Henry Cisneros and John Rosales have edited an important book on this growing, yet often misunderstood, market. Their backgrounds in the public and private sectors provide an informed context to this discussion. Cisneros and Rosales are asking the right questions and illuminating a variety of answers. This compendium of insightful chapters goes beyond the surface numbers. Although many Latinos aspire to the American dream of homeownership, their aspirations do not merely parallel those of native-born Americans. Cisneros and Rosales have articulated a vision that emanates from the perspective of the Latino family itself. The book addresses questions that are critical to understanding the Latino home buying market.

Cisneros and Rosales have assembled a formidable team of housing practitioners—builders, designers, architects, public officials, and scholars—who examine the Latino housing market. Their conclusions demonstrate that this housing market is not just more of the same. Developers, builders, Realtors, and lenders are advised to heed the book's findings. The demographics are clear. Latinos are not a niche market but at the core of the entire housing market for many years to come. The impact of this market will shape our homes and our communities for the 21st century.

Nicolas P. Retsinas

Nicolas P. Retsinas is Director of Harvard University's Joint Center for Housing Studies, a collaborative venture of the Graduate School of Design and the Kennedy School of Government, which conducts research to examine and address the most critical housing and community development issues in America. He chairs Habitat for Humanity International and serves on the Board of Trustees for the National Housing Endowment and Enterprise Community Partners and is on the Board of Directors of ShoreBank, Community Development Trust, Inc., and the National Housing Conference. Retsinas is in the National Housing Hall of Fame and was named one of the most influential people in real estate by the National Association of Realtors, in home building by *Builder* magazine, and in multifamily housing by *Multi-Housing News*.

PREFACE

We knew we had the makings of this book during a presentation given by Henry Cisneros on December 10, 2004.

About 20 home builders, architects, interior designers, real estate agents, and city planners had been summoned to meet with the former HUD secretary at a secluded hotel in the Hill Country outside of San Antonio, Texas. They came from Chicago, Los Angeles, Minneapolis, Washington, DC, and other parts of Texas to participate in roundtable discussions, sponsored by the Freddie Mac Corporation, about their work as it related to the burgeoning U.S. Latino community.

Henry wanted their thoughts about the information gap between first-generation Spanish speakers hungry for their piece of the American dream—a house—and a predominantly non-Hispanic white housing industry, who, although willing to work with this consumer group, lacked knowledge about Latino culture. "We need practical solutions—not pie-in-the-sky remedies—to bring these groups together," he would repeat over the course of the symposium.

Participants were asked to make a 20-minute presentation in their area of expertise and then field questions. Every presentation ran over time. There was one presentation on Friday, the rest on Saturday, and by Sunday, participants were homeward bound.

After dinner, Henry began the first presentation, an overview about Latino history, values, and progress in this country. Somewhere in between cold statistics about demographic shifts and housing design, he brought the group together with an unexpected, almost trivial statement.

"According to recent polls, salsa has overtaken ketchup as the nation's number one condiment."

There were applause and laughter and some assurance that, in this small way, the United States from all points north and south had accepted without condition at least one tiny aspect of Latino culture. Across the nation, Latino culture in the form of a spicy blended tomato mixture was welcome in neighborhoods, even in those still without Latinos.

At around this time, reports from the 2000 Census showed changing population trends. For the first time, Latinos outnumbered African- and Asian-Americans in 26 of the 50 states. And although more than 50% of the nation's Latino population resided in California and Texas, it was the southern states—North and South Carolina to Arkansas and Alabama—that were experiencing the most Latino population growth.

Henry continued with his presentation by stating that Latinos were now the largest ethnic minority in over 20 states. He talked about employment opportunities for Latinos in places like Little Rock, which offered permanent jobs as well as social networks through Latino churches and nonprofit organizations. You could get a decent plate of arroz con pollo in Little Rock. But it was the low housing values in Little Rock and other places such as Memphis and Birmingham that were the main draw. Latinos in great numbers were relocating to Dixie to work, pray, raise families, and buy houses.

"This is a unique time in history and a unique time for us in the housing industry to reassess the relationship between home builders and Latino home buyers," Cisneros said. "It is a chance to reflect on the role of Latino culture in the 21st century and to understand the historical context behind the issues that exist."

The demographic shifts by natives of Mexico, Central and South America, and the Caribbean from gateway states—Texas, California, New York, Florida—to inner states is unprecedented. Although Latinos are now situating themselves in cities and towns where they might be the first Latino family on the block, home builders are stymied by how to sell them homes.

What else can be expected? It is difficult on the surface, at least, to know how to sell a house to a family that may not have a bank account or credit history, the case with many first-generation Latino families. A language barrier might also exist.

Then there are cultural preferences that many Latinos share, for example, when it comes to interior colors, stove type (only a gas oven works well for tortillas) and garage style, which is most attractive when it has potential to be converted into an apartment for the possible influx of in-laws, aunts, and nephews from the native country.

This isn't new. It has been happening for generations to immigrant groups from Asia, Europe, and Africa as well as Latin America. But each group has its special needs based on cultural habits and even quirks about kitchen and bedroom décor and natural or artificial lighting. Every world culture seems to have its own version of Chinese feng shui.

The fact that the Hill Country gathering occurred around the Christmas holidays was testament to the respect the guests have for the former San Antonio mayor and Clinton Cabinet official. Henry had moved into the property development and home building businesses. He knew most of the group from 30 years of working in government, business, and academia and with nonprofit organizations. He remains a national media commentator and keynote speaker on urban development, architectural, demographic, and Latino cultural trends. These activities afford him the opportunity to have conversations with the best thinkers in the country about topics like home building.

As host and emcee of the San Antonio symposium, Henry put his speechmaking on hold and just listened. For most of the event, he let his guests talk, and talk, and talk, which was good for me.

I was there to take notes. The discussion went everywhere and sometimes in circles. From urban sprawl in Los Angeles and nightmare commutes in Virginia to Latino religious beliefs, political and banking habits, high school dropout rates, immigration trends, neighborhood gangs, low-rider car clubs, and the price of tortillas in Houston. The discussion was scattered and unfocused at times, a sign that bottled-up knowledge was being uncorked. But if anyone knows how to stay on target, it's Henry. "They say I'm good at herding cats," he commented at the end of the symposium.

By then, it was clear that participants were excited about how 21st century home builders and planners would interact with first-generation Mexicans, Puerto Ricans, Cubans, El Salvadorans, Chileans, and other Latinos. They were also concerned about the information gap that exists between these groups and housing industry officials.

Participants weren't calling for a new orthodoxy or anything earth shattering. As is clear from passages throughout this book, home builders need a deeper sense of involvement with Latino clients if they want to close deals. Home builders, real estate agents, and government officials who care about the way Latinos live in this country must be willing to advocate for them. It is an extra step in the sales process, perhaps, but one that will reap dividends.

The Hill Country symposium was the culmination of a research project that I had been working on with Henry since May 2004. It started over lunch at a hotel located across the street from the National Association of Home Builders. Over that summer, after visiting book stores, interviewing housing authorities, and scanning Internet sites for articles, we learned that there was no single, in-depth publication that addressed this ever-widening space between hungry Latino consumers and willing housing providers. How these forces can come together more effectively was the theme that emerged in San Antonio and that lies at the heart of this book. In his or her own way, each contributor in this book suggests new ways of doing business with Latinos while examining old methods that should be revamped. Our target audience is home builders, architects, interior designers, city planners, and students of urban affairs. Although much of the information is technical and "how-to," readers will also be rewarded with a feast of insights about Latino food, music, and art.

As fortune would have it, we engaged the perfect publisher: BuilderBooks, the imprint of the National Association of Home Builders (NAHB). Their members are our primary audience. We began to talk and learned that NAHB had been grappling with the same questions about how to reach Latino families. It was clear that NAHB possessed the same spirit of investigation as those whom Henry had gathered in Texas. As an added bonus, the formidable Freddie Mac ("We Open Doors") joined the team, providing financial support and expertise.

A higher goal for this book, beyond building and selling houses, is to show how we can help Latino families feel welcome enough in this country to establish roots, raise their children, and contribute, in their own way, toward healthy communities across America.

What began as an informal symposium with about a dozen participants volunteering (or in some cases being cajoled) to contribute a chapter to this book has ended almost two years later. *Casa y Comunidad: Latino Home and Neighborhood* begins with an overview of the Latino community and housing industry. It is written by the person who started it all over a dinner, Henry Cisneros.

John Rosales

John Rosales is a former newspaper reporter at the *San Antonio Light* and an executive with Cisneros Communications of San Antonio, Texas—his hometown. He worked at the Department of Housing and Urban Development from 1993 to 2001, serving as a Special Assistant to the Secretary in the Office of the Executive Secretariat. He is currently writing and editing publications for the National Education Association, Washington, DC.

ACKNOWLEDGMENTS

Many people across the country talked to us about how to design houses, neighborhoods, and communities that would appeal to Latino families. Some helped while we were researching ideas for this book. Others were sounding boards regarding those ideas.

From the very start, two staff members from the Freddie Mac Corporation believed enough in the premise of this book to help fund a weekend symposium that brought together architects, city planners, interior designers, real estate developers, social historians, and other housing taste makers. Without the support of Jim Park and John Sepulveda, formerly of Freddie Mac, there might not have been a symposium in December 2004 in San Antonio, Texas. They understood the breadth of our mission from the start.

Most of the authors who contributed chapters to this book attended the symposium and gave audaciously comprehensive presentations. From then on, there was no doubt that we would publish this book. In addition, other presenters and participants at the symposium provided generous assistance and guidance, among them Jeff Bosse, Allen Ghormley, Carlos Meijia, Choco Meza, Saul Ramirez, and Jesus Serrato. Although they did not contribute chapters, they added to the vital spirit of mission that saw us through this two-year project.

We thank Gloria Paniagua-Rodriguéz, Sylvia Arce-Garcia, and Lisa Andrade for their organizational and public relations skills. They helped keep the administrative wheels turning.

Great thanks to our publisher Christine Charlip and her team of editors at BuilderBooks. They helped shape a wordy and sometimes meandering manuscript into a cleanly structured, fluent, and brisk book. They have a good ear for everyday speech and an eye for details . . . in text, photos, and the ever-shifting pulse of the housing industry.

"At the Birthday Party." Painting by Joe R. Villarreal. www.joetheartist.com.

CHAPTER 1

The Rise of the Latino Home Buyer

Henry G. Cisneros

The Latino population in the United States is growing rapidly via both immigration and the birth of new family members. These forces are quickly creating an expanding Latino housing market that requires all types of new housing—single-family and multifamily, rental and purchased homes, urban and suburban, affordable and upscale. This new home construction is occurring in areas across the country, as Latino families settle in large numbers within established Latino communities in large coastal cities and border regions, as well as in interior cities and rural areas that are experiencing relatively recent Latino expansion.

This new and growing demand for homes will require that

- home builders design homes and neighborhoods that satisfy the space needs of and appeal to Latino families
- housing finance experts tailor mortgage instruments to this group
- industry marketers imagine and implement new sales strategies
- the housing sector in general institutionalize practices that will better serve the nation's burgeoning Latino population

The volume of housing construction generated by Latino growth will be significant. Between 2000 and 2010 alone, an estimated 2 million more Latino families will be in the market for housing (Table 1.1). Virtually every projection of the demand for housing makes note of

Table 1.1 Projected Owner-Occupied Household Growth 2000–2010
(in millions)

Total	African American	Hispanic	Asian/Other	Total Minority
10.9	1.8	2.2	1.0	5.0

Source: 1998 Current Population Survey.

the role of Latinos, including immigrants, as major forces in the growth of the housing sector. Careful attention to the traditions of ethnic households will increase in importance as builders think through the practical implications of providing homes that respect cultural heritages.

A Portrait of America's New Largest Minority Group

Latinos are the fastest growing segment of America's population and accounted for 40% of the total U.S. population increase from 1990 to 2000. Recent Census Bureau updates conclude that Latinos are now the largest minority group in the country, and every projection indicates that the momentum of that population growth will continue. Census Bureau projections from 2000 to 2050 make clear that the fastest growing segment of the nation's population across that period is expected to be the Latino population (Table 1.2). During a time when the white non-Hispanic population will grow by 18 million people, the African-American population by 25 million, and the Asian population by 27 million, the Latino population in America will grow by 63 million.

Table 1.2 Actual and Projected Population Distribution by Ethnicity, 2005–2050 (in millions)

Year	Total	White/Non-Latino	Latino	African American	American Indian	Asian American
1995	262,820	193,566	26,936	31,598	1,931	8,788
2000	281,422	194,553	35,306	34,658	2,476	10,243
2020 E	324,926	207,145	55,156	44,735	3,207	19,589
2050 E	403,686	212,990	98,228	59,239	4,405	37,589

Source: U.S. 2000 Census & U.S. Census Bureau Population Division, Population Projections of the U.S., Total Population by Race, Hispanic Origin, & Nativity. E, estimated.

There are two fundamental reasons for the Latino population surge. First, Latino families are larger than the average American family. The average American household has about 2.6 people, whereas the average Latino household has more than 3.5 members. In demographic terms, this is a large difference; it means that Latino households are fully 35% larger. Another statistic illustrates the larger size of Latino families: Fewer than 8% of non-Hispanic white American families live in a household of 5 or more people, but almost 24% of Latinos live in a household with 5 or more people (Table 1.3).

Table 1.3 Household Size by Race and Ethnicity, 2002

Number in Household	Total Households	Hispanic	White (Non-Hispanic)	Non-Hispanic Other
1	26.3%	13.2%	27.9%	26.9%
2	33.2%	22.2%	35.8%	27.5%
3	16.2%	19.9%	15.2%	18.7%
4	14.5%	21.1%	13.4%	15.3%
5	6.4%	12.8%	5.4%	7.1%
6	2.2%	6.1%	1.6%	2.8%
7	1.2%	4.8%	.7%	1.7%
		= 23.7	= 7.7	

Source: U.S. Bureau of Labor Statistics, Current Population Survey, March 2002.

The second underlying dynamic is that Latino families are considerably younger. The population of the United States shows dramatically different pyramids of age distribution for non-Hispanic ethnicities and for Latinos (Figure 1.1). Clearly, a greater percentage of the Latino population is at the younger ages. As these younger Latinos advance in years, this factor will dramatically change the distribution of population in the nation. Today's Latino children will, over the next decades, form their own households, have their own families, and spur the momentum of demographic transformation.

In addition to its rapid population growth, the Latino community in the United States is also making remarkable economic strides. It is, for example, the fastest growing segment of the middle class in the United States. The convergence of demographic and economic trends—a large population that is increasing its earning power, improving its educational attainment, advancing within business and

Figure 1.1 According to population age demographics, the Latino population is younger than other ethnicities in the United States.

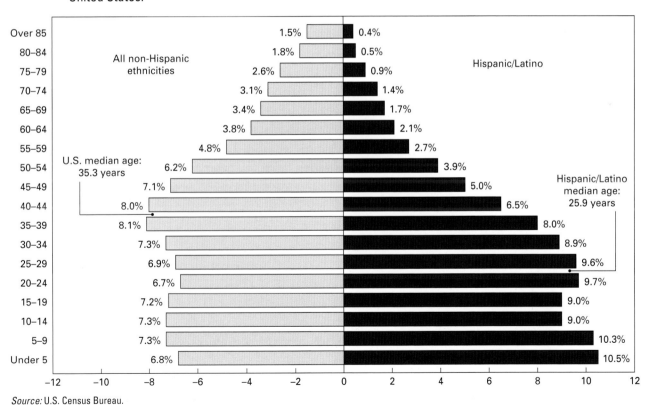

Source: U.S. Census Bureau.

corporate organizations, and characterized by a strong work ethic—assures that incomes will be rising rapidly as well.

Hispanic households will increase from over 10 million today to 13.5 million by 2010. They will control $670 billion in personal income by 2010. The implications for the housing sector are direct. For example, during the 1990s, when the nation achieved its highest homeownership rate ever, rising from 66% to 68%, the Latino homeownership rate rose from 42% to 48%. This 6% increase was the fastest rate of increase for any population segment in the country during the last decade. Perhaps most important to note is that Latino homeownership has a long way to go to approach the national average (Figure 1.2).

Many studies have shown that Latino families define their measure of advancement in our society, "the American dream," as revolving around homeownership. Homeownership consistently ranks as one

Figure 1.2 Comparison of Latino and U.S. average homeownership rates shows that Latino rates of homeownership have risen faster than the U.S. average since the mid-1990s.

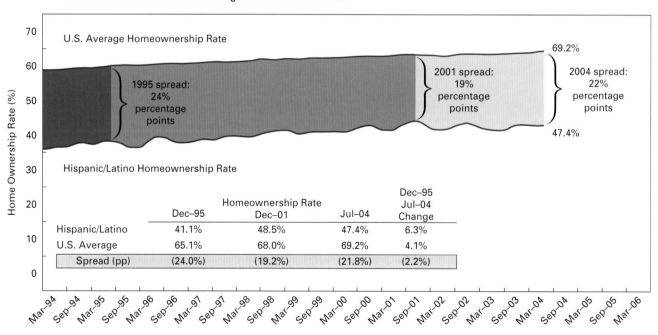

| | | Homeownership Rate | | Dec–95 Jul–04 |
	Dec–95	Dec–01	Jul–04	Change
Hispanic/Latino	41.1%	48.5%	47.4%	6.3%
U.S. Average	65.1%	68.0%	69.2%	4.1%
Spread (pp)	(24.0%)	(19.2%)	(21.8%)	(2.2%)

Source: U.S. Census Bureau.

of the highest priorities for Latino families. By recognizing the importance of homeowner-ship to Latino families, it is clear that Latino housing needs represent an opportunity for sustaining the growth of America's housing sector.

Latinos: Diverse and Growing Across the Nation

Immigration, both legal and illegal, is a major factor that also impacts the swelling ranks of American Latinos. Spanish-speaking immi-grants come to the U.S. from every nation to the south (Table 1.4). Several hundred thou-sand Spanish-speaking individuals are admit-ted annually through formal immigration processes, with about 60% from Mexico, fol-lowed by Cubans, Dominicans, El Salvadorans, and Columbians.

It is also estimated that there are as many as 12 million individuals who have migrated without documents living in the U.S. They have accumulated over many years—some arrived as long as 40 years ago—and repre-sent more than a quarter of the nation's overall Latino population. The largest percentage of these undocumented immigrants are from Mexico. The size of the undocumented population makes it a sub-stantial economic force, including in the housing markets. As legisla-tion is enacted to create guest worker programs or to establish pathways to legalization, the financial capacities of these immigrants will provide a powerful impetus to growth in the housing markets of the U.S.

But beyond absolute population numbers, it is important for housing leaders to understand the differences between Latinos who trace their heritage to Mexico, to Central and South America, and to the Caribbean. Although they share a common language, Latinos are as diverse as the Irish, the Scottish, and the English. Latino heritage is derived from every nation in Latin America (Figure 1.3).

Table 1.4 Legal Immigration by Country of Birth, 1997

Country of birth	1997		
	Number	Percent	
Mexico	146,865	18.4%	**Over**
Philippines	49,117	6.2%	
China	41,147	5.2%	**249,000**
Vietnam	38,519	4.8%	
India	38,071	4.8%	**— 31% —**
Cuba	33,587	4.2%	
Dominican Republic	27,053	3.4%	
El Salvador	17,969	2.3%	**come**
Jamaica	17,840	2.2%	
Russia	16,632	2.1%	**from**
Ukraine	15,696	2.0%	
Haiti	15,057	2.0%	**Spanish-**
Korea	14,239	1.8%	
Columbia	13,004	1.6%	**speaking**
Pakistan	12,967	1.6%	
Poland	12,038	1.5%	**countries.**
Canada	11,609	1.5%	
Peru	10,853	1.4%	
United Kingdom	10,651	1.3%	
Iran	9,642	1.2%	
Total	**798,378**	**100.0%**	

Source: U.S. Dept. of Justice, Immigration and Naturalization Service Annual Report, January 1999.

Figure 1.3 Latinos in the United States in 2002 were primarily of Mexican origin.

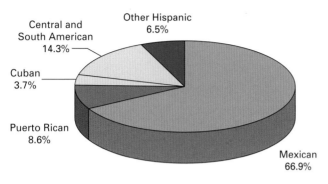

- Other Hispanic 6.5%
- Central and South American 14.3%
- Cuban 3.7%
- Puerto Rican 8.6%
- Mexican 66.9%

Source: 2002 Census.

Where Latinos Live

The juxtaposition of geography and national origin in Latino settlement patterns has relevance for housing practices. Figure 1.4 shows the major concentrations of Latino populations across the nation. Overall, California and Texas have the lion's share of Latino families (Table 1.5), but important new trends have emerged since the 1990s.

Most growth in absolute numbers over the last decades has occurred in so-called "gateway cities." In those cities and surrounding regions, we see massive immigration from Spanish-speaking countries to receiving neighborhoods where opportunities exist. The primary gateways

Figure 1.4 Latino populations by concentration in the United States, 2002, are no longer concentrated in large urban areas.

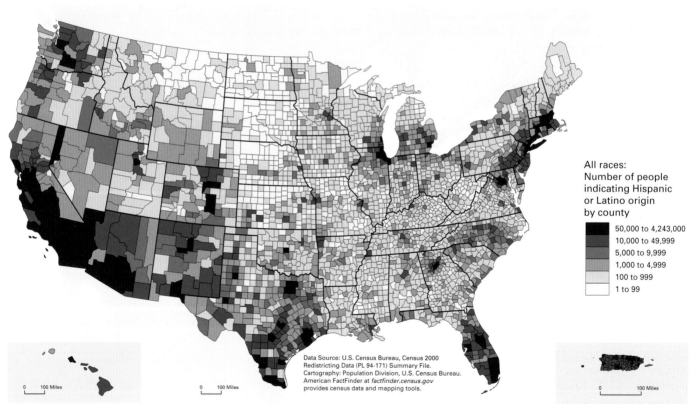

All races: Number of people indicating Hispanic or Latino origin by county

- 50,000 to 4,243,000
- 10,000 to 49,999
- 5,000 to 9,999
- 1,000 to 4,999
- 100 to 999
- 1 to 99

Data Source: U.S. Census Bureau, Census 2000 Redistricting Data (PL 94-171) Summary File. Cartography: Population Division, U.S. Census Bureau. American FactFinder at *factfinder.census.gov* provides census data and mapping tools.

0 — 100 Miles

Source: 2002 Census.

are New York (where approximately 14% of all immigrants per year choose to live), Los Angeles–Long Beach (8%), Miami (6%), and Chicago (4%), all of which are attractive destinations with established Latino communities of Puerto Rican, Cuban, or Mexican heritage (U.S. Department of Justice, Immigration and Naturalization Service *Annual Report*, January 1999).

One of the most interesting aspects of Latino progress in the United States over the last decade has been the emergence of new concentrations of Latino population. New or growing Latino communities are now found in states that have not been traditional Latino destinations. Perhaps the most useful way to understand the patterns created by the convergence of population growth, national origins, and housing needs is to imagine a trip across the nation.

The Northeast. If we began such a journey in the Northeast states, we would find growing concentrations of Latinos in New York, New Jersey, Connecticut, Massachusetts, and Pennsylvania.

Stereotype to the contrary, the Latinos in New York City are not exclusively from Puerto Rico. Although people of Puerto Rican heritage are the largest Latino population on the East Coast, numbering 1.2 million households, there are more than 1 million Latinos in the New York area who trace their heritage to the Dominican Republic heritage. The nearby New Jersey concentration of Latinos in Hudson County includes a large population of Cuban Americans, and the area's Mexican-origin population is swelling as immigrants are drawn to work in the region.

Cities in the region experiencing strong Latino growth include Boston, Providence, Hartford, Lowell, Worchester, Bridgeport, Camden, Philadelphia, and Allentown. The combination of strong demand for workforce housing and the difficulties of amassing land for reasonably priced housing in dense urban areas requires that creative financing and production strategies be forged in the Northeastern states.

The housing stock occupied by Latinos in the Northeast includes both traditional high-rise apartments and neighborhoods of owner-occupied homes evident in places such as Charlotte Street in the Bronx (Figure 1.5). Latinos have helped transform the Bronx into a vibrant area and are investing massively in housing, rebuilding entire neighborhoods of formerly vacant and burned out blocks.

Table 1.5 States with Largest Numbers of Latino Households, 2000

State	Number of Hispanic Households	Share of Total U.S. Hispanic Households*
California	2,566,688	27%
Texas	1,789,623	19%
New York	832,915	9%
Florida	846,907	9%
Illinois	370,552	4%

Source: U.S. Census, 2000.
*National Council of La Raza calculations.

Figure 1.5 Housing stock in the Bronx, such as the redeveloped Charlotte Street area.

Source: Suarez Photography and Video.

Florida and the Southeast. Florida has the next largest concentration of Latinos on the East Coast. Although conventional wisdom would identify this group as exclusively Cuban American, there are in fact now more non-Cuban Latinos in Florida than Cuban Americans. The population of Puerto Ricans in the Tampa and Orlando areas has grown dramatically, as have the number of Latinos of Mexican heritage in Homestead and other agricultural regions of the state. Nicaraguans, Columbians, and other Central and South Americans have also flocked to South Florida.

Despite these new trends, the dominant patterns of Latino housing in Florida have been established over the last 50 years by the Cuban migration. Homes in the Little Havana neighborhood of Miami are examples of classic housing types in South Florida (Figure 1.6). Homes reflect the lifestyles and taste preferences of Latinos of Cuban and Caribbean heritage in South Florida. Many homes in the region incorporate features such as outdoor patios and lush foliage, utilize the brighter color palette of the Caribbean, employ building materials that enhance comfort in the heat and humidity of South Florida, apply architectural themes with masonry and tile features to reflect the Spanish heritage of the residents, and are frequently modified to accommodate extended-family living arrangements.

As Latinos move into the middle class in massive numbers and into high-paying professional careers, more expensive high-quality homes are being constructed (Figure 1.7). They take into account the architectural preferences, lifestyles, and space needs of Latino homeowners in South Florida.

In the Southeastern United States, states such as Georgia, South Carolina, North Carolina, and Tennessee are seeing

Figure 1.6 A home in the Little Havana Neighborhood of Miami.

Source: Alberto E. Tamargo.

Figure 1.7 A high-quality home in South Florida, typical of homes in demand as Latinos move into the middle class.

Source: Alberto E. Tamargo.

a rise in the number of Latinos (Table 1.6). In each of these states, Latino workers are attracted to jobs in industries such as textiles, lumber, food production, and construction. This influx is establishing new concentrations in large cities, outer suburbs, and rural areas. From the rapidly growing Latino neighborhoods in Atlanta's suburbs to Raleigh's Mexican barrios, the need for housing for Latino families is growing at an unprecedented rate in the Southeast.

Texas. Texas has the second largest population of Latinos in the nation, 90% of whom are of Mexican heritage. Nearly 1 million Latinos reside in the Rio Grande Valley from Brownsville to McAllen, and another 1 million live along the U.S.–Mexico border from Laredo to El Paso. The major cities of interior Texas—San Antonio, Austin, Dallas, and Houston—have long-established and rapidly growing Latino populations. Vast areas within the larger cities of Texas are characterized by traditional Latino barrios, where redevelopment

Table 1.6 States with Rising Numbers of Latino Households, 2000

State	Hispanic Population Increase: 1990 to 2000	Total Population Increase: 1990 to 2000
North Carolina	393.9%	21.4%
Arkansas	337.0%	13.7%
Georgia	299.6%	26.4%
Tennessee	278.2%	16.7%
Nevada	216.6%	66.3%

Source: U.S. Census, 2000.
*National Council of La Raza calculations.

opportunities are abundant. Many older homes in neighborhoods such as Prospect Hill in San Antonio show pride of ownership (Figure 1.8). Newer patterns of Latino housing in those cities are spurring the growth of new suburban communities.

The many Latinos in Texas of Mexican heritage are often second- and third-generation Americans. The Sunbelt region as a whole is home to many younger, upwardly mobile Latino families who want the features associated with modern suburban homes. Significant percentages of the new homes being built in most Texas cities are sold to Latino families who are frequently first-time home buyers. They proudly regard a new home as a symbol of their own social progress and acculturation. At the same time, they frequently enjoy attributes and accessories in the home that allow them to recognize their own uniqueness, demonstrate their pride of heritage, share

Figure 1.8 A well-maintained bungalow in a Latino neighborhood in San Antonio, Texas.

Source: Gloria Paniagua-Rodriguéz, CityView.

the warmth of their Latino culture, and celebrate their own personal journey of achievement. These ideas are often expressed as attention to interior décor, types of landscaping, color choices, architectural themes, and exterior touches and in the treatment of social spaces. The Los Jardines community in South Austin is an example of new suburban-style homes being offered adjacent to an established Latino neighborhood (Figure 1.9).

The Heartland. Substantial growth in Latino populations is evident in cities of all sizes in Oklahoma, Kansas, Nebraska, Iowa, and Arkansas (Table 1.7). Latinos find employment opportunities in central U.S. states at poultry plants, feed lots, farms, and construction sites. Arkansas had the fastest percentage of growth in Latino population of any state in the U.S. in the 1990s, an increase of more than 400%. In many parts of the central United States, Latinos account for the principal growth occurring in communities that would otherwise be showing overall population losses.

Heartland communities whose traditional populations are aging rapidly are experiencing an infusion of young Latino families with children, which assures those communities of growth prospects into the future. But new families require new housing. This has become one of the pressing challenges confronting smaller communities from Rogers, Arkansas, to Dodge City, Kansas, to Bridge City, Nebraska.

The Upper Midwest. There are well-established communities of Latinos in the Midwest. More than 1 million Latinos, predominantly of Puerto Rican and Mexican heritages, live in the Chicago metropolitan area. Many reside in Chicago's central neighborhoods of Pilsen and Humboldt Park, where housing is at a premium. However, growing numbers of Latinos are living in suburban settings throughout the Midwest. Figure 1.10 shows a home typical of the inner-ring suburb of Cicero, outside of Chicago, where Latinos are now the majority population.

Wisconsin, Minnesota, Michigan, Ohio, and Indiana also have growing Latino populations. These newcomers are creating strong demand for both rentable workforce housing and homes for aspiring home owners in each of these states.

Rocky Mountain West. Located in the Rocky Mountain region is the state with the largest percentage population of Latinos—New Mexico. Latinos comprise 40% of the state's population. Traditions in New Mexico are rooted in 400 years of Spanish heritage. Cities such

Figure 1.9 The Los Jardines community of new homes, built adjacent to an established Latino neighborhood in South Austin, Texas.

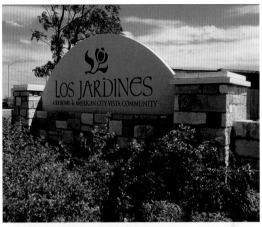

Source: Andrea Pérez.

Table 1.7 Projected Residential Unit Demand Ranked by the Percent of Housing Units Needed Between 2000 and 2030

Geographic Area	Housing Units 2000 (000s)	Housing Units 2030 (000s)	Growth-Related Units (000s)	Units Lost 2000–2030 (000s)	Units Needed 2000–2030 (000s)	Built After 2000 (%)	New Housing 2030 (%)
United States	115,905	154,756	38,852	20,087	58,939	50.9	38.1
West	24,378	5,922	11,544	4,585	16,129	66.2	44.9
South	42,383	60,174	17,791	7,954	25,745	60.7	42.8
Midwest	26,964	33,027	6,063	4,696	10,759	39.9	32.6
Northeast	22,180	25,594	3,414	3,053	6,467	29.2	25.3
Top 10 States							
1. Nevada	827	1,596	769	156	925	111.7	57.9
2. Arizona	2,189	3,863	1,674	412	2,086	95.3	54.0
3. Utah	769	1,327	558	145	703	1.5	53.0
4. Florida	7,303	11,397	4,094	1,373	5,467	74.9	48.0
5. Idaho	528	819	291	99	390	73.9	47.7
6. Colorado	1,808	2,792	984	340	1,324	73.2	47.4
7. Texas	8,158	12,457	4,300	1,534	5,834	71.5	46.8
8. New Mexico	781	1,163	382	147	529	67.8	45.5
9. Oregon	1,453	2,135	683	273	956	65.8	44.8
10. Washington	2,451	3,580	1,129	461	1,590	64.9	44.4
Top Ten Metro Areas							
1. Las Vegas	656	1,343	687	123	810	123.5	60.3
2. Austin	496	983	487	93	580	116.9	59.0
3. Phoenixz	1,331	2,417	1,086	250	1,336	100.4	55.3
4. West Palm Beach	556	980	424	105	529	95.1	54.0
5. Orlando	684	1,204	520	129	649	94.9	53.9
6. Raleigh-Durham	496	838	342	93	435	87.7	51.9
7. Dallas-Fort Worth	2,031	3,344	1,313	382	1,695	83.5	50.7
8. Salt Lake City	456	748	792	86	378	82.9	50.5
9. Sacramento	715	1,161	446	134	580	81.8	50.0
10. Charlotte	616	991	375	116	491	79.7	49.5

Source: Adapted from Nelson, Arthur C. *Toward a New Metropolis: The Opportunity to Rebuild America.* Washington, DC: The Brookings Institution, 2004, p. 10–11. http://www.brookings.edu/metro.

as Albuquerque, Santa Fe, Las Vegas, and Las Cruces were identified on the maps of the early Spanish explorers and missionaries.

New Mexico is the most "Spanish" of regions with large Latino populations. Although the majority of New Mexico's Latinos have roots in Mexico, the oldest and most influential families claim roots to the period of Spanish colonization more than 400 years ago. They are the direct descendants of explorers and colonists who brought with them the language, religion, and traditions and established the building types of "new Spain." Housing types in many New Mexico communities reflect that long history. The authenticity of the region's historic Spanish antecedents is visible in the floor plans, exterior elevations, and materials of traditional homes and of modern homes that fuse historic themes with contemporary functions. Preservation efforts there have encouraged builders to respect the themes of traditional housing styles. Homes of adobe-type materials and replicas of early architectural designs are evident in the most modern developments, such as in Santa Fe (Figure 1.11).

Throughout the Rocky Mountain West, in communities such as Pueblo, Denver, Fort Collins, Cheyenne, Boise, Salt Lake City, and Las Vegas, patterns of Latino migration are increasingly evident. In fact, the migration of Latino workers helped make Las Vegas the fastest growing American city in the decade of the 1990s and has redefined parts of the metropolitan area, such as North Las Vegas, as vibrant Latino enclaves. Long-standing Latino communities in Tucson and Phoenix demonstrate housing types that respect the desert topography in exterior themes and building materials. For example, in Phoenix, new homes have been built in a central city Latino neighborhood using native southwestern materials (Figure 1.12).

California and the Pacific Region. California is home to the largest number of Latinos in any state. More than 32% of California's approximately 36 million residents, or about 11.6 million, are Latino.

The history of Latinos in California spans more than 300 years. The

Figure 1.10 A home in an inner-ring suburb of Chicago, an area with a rapidly increasing Latino population.

Source: Michael Fortin, CityView.

Figure 1.11 A new home in Sante Fe exhibiting traditional New Mexico style, such as a flat roof and adobe-like exterior.

Source: KB Home.

Figure 1.12 A new home in central Phoenix constructed of local brick and stone.

Source: KB Home.

names of communities, from San Diego at the Mexican border to San Francisco in northern California, manifest the influence of Spanish missionaries and explorers. Sacramento, Los Angeles, San Luis Obispo, Santa Maria, Santa Barbara, Fresno, Modesto, San Jose, and dozens of other communities trace their first settlements to the early Spanish period.

Although housing types in California vary greatly, respect for the Spanish heritage has included mission themes since the earliest days. Modest homes from the post-war era of rapid suburban growth in the San Gabriel Valley suburb of Covina, for example, commonly reflect Spanish-style architectural themes. Newer homes in the rapidly growing "inland empire," Riverside and San Bernandino counties east of Los Angeles, continue to respect this influence of Spanish heritage and California mission themes (Figure 1.13).

The largest numbers of Latinos in Southern California are of Mexican descent, many of whom arrived in the immigration surge of the 1990s. As a result, many homes and neighborhoods across the region incorporate the bright colors and building materials of the villages and towns in Mexico from which the immigrants have come, especially in the home renovations and additions that they frequently undertake.

Latino communities are growing rapidly in the Pacific region beyond the borders of California, including sizable communities in Washington State and Oregon. Many of those communities have been the traditional destinations of migrant farm workers, such as the Yakima Valley of Washington (Figure 1.14). Most of the farm workers who have settled permanently in the Northwest are of Mexican heritage, and their homes and communities are modified to reflect the personal touches that recall their ancestral homesteads in Mexico or their home towns across the southwestern U.S.

Figure 1.13 Spanish-style architecture common in new homes in suburban Los Angeles.

Source: Author.

Where Latinos Are Moving: Suburbs and New Locales

Layered on this mosaic of diversity and geography are new trends that assure that today's patterns will change and that areas of the nation that have had no experience with Latino populations must seek to understand Latino housing needs. One trend worthy of note became evident during the 1990s: the movement of Latinos to suburban areas. The Latino population is rapidly suburbanizing within metropolitan areas, and large numbers of Latinos are moving into communities in which they have traditionally been a small minority. In effect, they are establishing beachheads in the suburbs and exurbs of metropolitan areas such as Chicago and Denver.

Analysis of Latino population growth by the Brookings Institution clearly shows the immense growth of the Latino population in the suburbs of areas defined as "established Latino metros" (Appendix A). In 13 of 16 metropolitan areas with established communities, Latino population growth in the suburbs between 1990 and 2000 was greater than the generally double-digit growth rates in the cen-

Figure 1.14 A workforce home in the Yakima Valley of Washington that may house year-round Latino residents instead of migrant workers.

Source: Larry Duren.

tral cities. In Chicago, for example, the absolute increase of Latinos in the central city, 218,329, was substantially less than the Latino population increase in the suburbs, 378,589. Similarly, in Denver, the 69,150 increase in the Latino population in the central city was less than the 119,822 increase in the suburbs.

The second largest group of Latinos is now found in "fast-growing Latino hubs," defined as metro areas that had significant Latino populations before 1990 but not major established concentrations (Appendix A). Between 1990 and 2000, these hubs experienced Latino metropolitan growth that in no case was less than a 50% increase. For example, the Latino population more than doubled in both the central city and the suburbs of Dallas; and in Phoenix, it more than doubled in the central city and almost doubled in the suburbs.

The Brookings report also highlights a second important trend: the increase in the Latino population in cities that have not had sizable Latino populations historically ("new Latino destinations"). In metro areas of North Carolina, such as Charlotte, Raleigh, and Greensboro–Winston Salem, Latino populations grew by more than 600% from 1990 to 2000 (Appendix A). Of the 51 destinations in this list, 34 have seen the Latino population double in 10 years. The growth of Latino populations in cities such as Las Vegas, Nevada; Birmingham, Alabama; Atlanta, Georgia; Columbus, Ohio; and Nashville, Tennessee is significant enough to identify undeniable and permanent new patterns of Latino settlement.

Finally, the Brookings report highlights communities far from traditional Latino patterns of settlement and generally in slow-growth metros where evidence of Latino population growth as a national phenomenon is discernable (Appendix A). These "small Latino places" are cities in which the Latino population has increased by more than 25,000 people and include Cleveland, Detroit, Newark, and Philadelphia.

These nationwide changes in Latino settlement patterns mean that housing sector leaders in every part of the United States will benefit by working with knowledgeable representatives to understand Latino housing needs and challenges. Looking ahead, another analysis from the Brookings Institution asserts that about 38.8 million units of housing will be needed by 2030 to accommodate new population (Table 1.7). Including the 20.1 million units that will have to be replaced, the Brookings report states that this nation will need to build about 58.9 million new housing units between 2000 and 2030. A review of the ten states and the ten metropolitan areas with the highest projected demand for new residential units shows that every one of these areas with high demand for residential construction is a location that has had strong Latino growth in recent years (Table 1.7). Builders can anticipate that significant shares of their future communities in important markets will be homes for Latino families.

The momentum of Latino population growth across our country and the economic progress of Latino families will shape the business decisions of home builders and drive housing production in many regions. Old-fashioned business attentiveness to this burgeoning market dictates that builders must rethink design and building features in order to produce housing products that serve this population. In addition to the physical attributes, however, builders must also calculate how Latino population and market growth will reshape their workforce composition, staffing practices, mortgage products, and marketing strategies.

Latino Family Attributes

Latino subgroups vary in how they have adapted to local history, geography, climate, and topography across the U.S. As such, housing types for Latinos will be diverse. But there are attributes that builders can take into account as they think through the challenges of building for the nation's fastest growing group of housing product consumers. Among the implications for builders are those that respond to the typical Latino family structure, lifestyle and activity patterns, and desired community amenities.

Family Demographics

The most important demographic attributes that characterize the national Latino population are the larger size and relative youth of families. For builders, those attributes will mean attention to the overall amount of floor space as well as thoughtful configuration of rooms. Communities should include homes of two, three, and four bedrooms. One attractive approach is building homes with more but smaller bedrooms, so that large families with children of different ages can be accommodated as they move from infancy to adolescence while the house itself remains as affordable as possible. Another approach is configuring the rooms so that parents can monitor the activities of children in their bedrooms and other areas of the house from a central activity space or from a master bedroom. Adding family social space, including study nooks and play spaces for children, will attract a large, active family.

Because of larger family sizes, many Latino families need more bedrooms but cannot afford a house with the necessary number of bedrooms. As family needs grow, many families convert their garages into an additional room. It is not unusual for an informal survey of a 10-year-old subdivision with a high proportion of Latino residents to show that about every other house has a converted garage. One pair of grandparents described their need to convert their garage into living space resulting from their enjoyment of having their growing number of grandchildren spend the weekends with them.

One answer is for builders to construct homes that trade the need for additional bedroom space for an enclosed garage. Such a home would have a less expensive carport or parking pad so that the additional bedroom could be provided. Another approach is to forego the extra bedroom at construction, but to finish the garage in such a way that it can be easily converted into an additional room as family needs dictate. This option might include a front elevation designed so that if the garage is eventually enclosed, it can be built to match the existing exterior façade.

Builders wishing to serve the needs of Latino home buyers must also consider the increased space requirements of multigenerational families. Many Latino households include elderly parents who live with the family. It is attractive to offer a bedroom that is physically separated from other bedrooms, so that a grandparent can have private space and individual use of a restroom. Designing such separation might extend to locating a room on the ground floor of a two-story home so that older family members with physical limitations do not have to climb a staircase to get to their bedrooms. Additional solutions are to provide more than one master bedroom, each with a private bathroom, or to size the family restroom slightly larger for use by more people, including live-in grandparents.

Because of the wear and tear associated with the active life of a larger family, it is advisable for builders to consider more durable materials. Fragile construction is, in the long run, a disservice to a family and to a neighborhood. One frequent request from Latino families is for solid floor surfaces, such as ceramic tile or vinyl, for ease of cleaning. Thoughtful attention to the durability of interior wall materials and carpet textures will sustain the appearance of a home over time. Other aspects of sustainability should include the use of energy-conserving materials and appliances.

Latino families tend to prepare food in their homes for a variety of reasons. For larger families, the cost of eating out is greater, and many families enjoy traditional recipes that may not be offered in restaurants. The result is that the homemaker may spend a good deal of time in the kitchen, and it becomes the center of the social space in the home. Builders will want to construct the kitchen in a way that assures ample space for a large family and is part of an open floor plan so that the homemaker in the kitchen can watch children at play. That would include creating sight lines to children in a family room as they do their homework, work at computers, or otherwise entertain themselves. Similar attention should be given to the configuration of outdoor play space so that large windows or doors make it possible for the person in the kitchen to keep an eye on children who are playing in the back yard or patio.

Although parts of the kitchen may extend into social space, other kitchen functions may need to be shielded from view by their placement among kitchen accessories. For example, some traditional Latino homemakers prefer washing dishes by hand instead of using automatic dishwashers, so dishes may remain in the sink until someone is free to wash them. To prevent the unsightly appearance of accumulated dishes, it may be desirable to position the sink so that it is not prominently visible from the social space. One desirable option may be to offer a sink of greater depth than usual.

Many foods in Latino recipes are best prepared over an open flame— tortillas, for example. Therefore, Latino home buyers in a new subdivision often express a preference for gas stoves over all-electric appliances for the kitchen. Whether to offer this feature is obviously a major decision for a home builder, because it dictates that gas lines be installed in the earliest stages of street and lot development. It is important to gauge the importance of this feature in your market when conducting predevelopment surveys of potential Latino home buyers.

Because of the larger average size of Latino families, builders should provide for ample storage space for family supplies, including pantries in the kitchen and closets in bathrooms. The number and ages of children also argues for positioning clothes washers and dryers near bedrooms for ease of doing laundry.

A conundrum for builders who try to provide for the space needs of Latino families will be to do so within the price constraints imposed by the economic circumstances of many Latino families. Latino families already dedicate large portions of their family budgets to housing and have a housing cost burden higher than the national average (Table 1.8). They often have limited abilities to pay more or are living in cities where housing costs are high because job magnets have created abnormal demand and price pressures. Although housing cost burdens of Latinos decreased mildly from 1991 to 2001, they are still substantially higher than the national average.

Builders can work within these constraints in several ways. One response is to include features that address space and the configuration of floor plans with an eye on affordability. Builders may also respond to family income limitations by applying a concept defined as "natural affordability." This describes rental or for-sale housing that is more affordable because it is smaller or is part of a higher-density grouping or compromises on certain features. Although this concept is not the universal answer to affordability concerns, particularly where larger families are involved, it often applies to the circumstances of singles, young couples, or retirees. In any case, smaller units at affordable prices have a place in mixed-income communities. Thoughtful incorporation of affordable features from the outset of design, making trade-offs with lesser priority accessories, and giving extra attention to price consciousness at every step, including land acquisition, will enable builders to create value.

Builders may also recognize that the Latino market for rental units, particularly apartments, is strong and growing.

Table 1.8 Housing Cost Burdens, 1991 and 2001

	Latino Families		National Average	
	1991	2001	1991	2001
Moderate Cost Burden 30–49% of household income goes toward housing costs	23.8%	23.2%	16.8%	16.5%
Severe Cost Burden 50% of household income goes toward housing costs	18.9%	18.6%	11.2%	13.2%
Total High Cost Burden	42.7%	41.8%	28%	29.7%

Source: National Council of La Raza calculations of U.S. Census Bureau, American Housing Survey, 1991 and 2001.

In many gateway cities, the combination of recent immigrant arrivals, the high cost of housing, and the unavoidable time lags involved with saving money and establishing credit dictate that many Latinos rent their housing for a considerable period. As the Latino population continues to expand, there will be a huge demand for decent family-sized, affordable apartments.

Both home builders and apartment developers can explore ways to reduce the cost of housing and to position their products within the price reach of Latino families. They can work with local governments to secure assistance with land assembly, infrastructure expenses, expedited approvals, and redevelopment incentives. More and more local governments are responding to the lack of available workforce housing. Many local officials recognize that a well-designed community of solid homes and stable families is the most durable form of redevelopment they can champion.

Builders can also pursue reasonably priced capital to finance workforce housing. Banks and other lenders have priorities that include Community Redevelopment Act considerations. Government-sponsored enterprises have development funds to support builders in their efforts to increase the supply of affordable housing. Pension funds and foundation investment funds are allocating capital to affordable housing partnerships. Increasingly, builders can identify capital to build housing at affordable prices, but the design of the financial architecture will have to be as conscious a process as the physical planning of homes to meet the needs of Latino families.

Lifestyles

Like many American families, Latino families tend to lead active lives that typically focus around family involvements. With their large, extended families, it is common to host gatherings that include not only the family members who reside in the home but also the host's siblings and their children plus grandparents, aunts, uncles, nieces, nephews, and in-laws. Special days on the calendar, such as Mother's Day and Easter and celebratory family days such as birthdays, baptisms, quinceañeras, and saints' feast days can generate a large number of family guests.

It is not unusual for Latino families to host social gatherings of 50 people, even in a small home. Fiestas can come together on a spontaneous basis, generated by nothing more than the televised football or soccer game of a family's favorite team. Builders will have

The Cazun Mijangos family of Lincoln, Nebraska. *Source:* Fernando Pagés, Brighton Construction Company, Lincoln.

to take into account how family space used during the week for children's activities can be flexibly converted into a social venue large enough for extended family gatherings.

One possible accommodation is to design space so that the flow of people from an inside social space is directed to an outdoor gathering or cooking space. Tens of millions of Latino families live in temperate climate—in Texas, Florida, Arizona, and California—so that even in the winter months, it is common to enjoy days in which a good deal of the social activity occurs outdoors. Latino family gatherings are frequently characterized by groupings of people in different spaces. The older men may sit outside near a barbecue pit while the señoras gather in the kitchen and the younger children play outside in the yard. Young men may be gathered around a television set watching a sporting event and the young misses talking in an adjacent bedroom. Builders planning for these frequent uses should consider not just interior layouts but also exterior spaces, including a barbecue pit, patio space, and play space for children. Because of the intensity of the sun in many of these areas, it may also be useful to provide outdoor covered spaces, perhaps with a ceiling fan, to create the feeling of an "outdoor room."

Another physical element might be space for plantings, because many Latino families enjoy brightening the outdoor scene with gardens of flowers and fruit trees. One of the more visible attributes of existing Latino communities is the obvious enjoyment of gardening. This perhaps harkens to traditions from agrarian or tropical origins or perhaps simply reflects a culture that values taking time to work with one's hands in the earth and nurture living things that add color. Plants have a place in most Latino homes. If grass is not included as a standard outdoor feature, then the use of outdoor space for an active family can be restricted. A backyard fence is also necessary to create usable family space and should also be considered as a standard feature.

A family's income-earning occupation may require storage of work-related tools and equipment. A thoughtfully created nook as part of a garage or tucked alongside a carport can allow for storage out of public sight and prevent unsightly accumulations of equipment and materials. In a similar vein, many Latinos whose jobs have sharpened their "handyman" skills use those abilities to improve their own homes. Therefore, thoughtful creation of work space, even outdoors, could discreetly separate it from recreational or social spaces.

Many Latino families at some point need space for a home-based business, such as day care or other businesses allowed within residential zones. This suggests that builders should consider during design how a home's social space might accommodate multiple purposes over time. It may also be useful when designing the floor plan and the exterior configuration to consider where a room could be added to the structure, should that eventually prove necessary.

Another dimension of the practical interplay between family activities and work obligations as they impact space requirements involves providing ample space for parking automobiles at each home. One of the more common complaints in existing communities experiencing an influx of Latino families, as well as in new communities not planned with Latino families in mind, is too many cars parked on the streets. Clearly, if a family requires multiple cars for its multigenerational members' transportation needs for work and school, then more parking for cars is needed.

Many Latino wage earners are entrepreneurs in occupations, such as construction, that require a pick-up truck or van. Building a home for Latino families that can accommodate only one car in a garage or on a driveway will generally prove to be inadequate. Recognizing the need for parking more vehicles, builders may provide an extended driveway or set the garage to the rear along the side of the house. In this way, the home has a driveway of greater length where multiple cars can be parked on the property instead of crowding the street.

Families in the phases of life that involve multiple workers within the household require vehicles to meet their obligations. If data collected in Southern California are indicative, no population in America has more workers per household than Latino families (Figure 1.15). In this study, the largest percentage of multiple-worker households was foreign-born Latino families, followed by foreign-born Asians and native-born Latinos.

Having more workers per household has obvious implications for the need to park vehicles at home. Add to this daily parking burden

Figure 1.15 Percentage of Households with Three or More Workers by Ethnic Heritage in Five Counties in Southern California, 1990

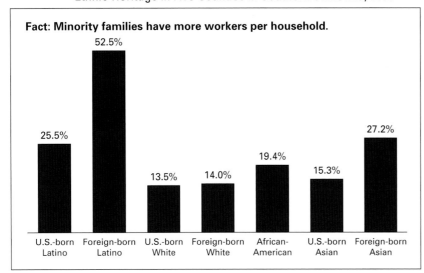

Fact: Minority families have more workers per household.

- U.S.-born Latino: 25.5%
- Foreign-born Latino: 52.5%
- U.S.-born White: 13.5%
- Foreign-born White: 14.0%
- African-American: 19.4%
- U.S.-born Asian: 15.3%
- Foreign-born Asian: 27.2%

Source: Rodriguez, Gregory. *The Emerging Latino Middle Class.* Malibu, CA: Pepperdine University for Public Policy, Davenport Institute, 1997, p. 12.

the large family gatherings on special occasions or events at more than one home on a popular social day, such as Thanksgiving, and neighborhoods will simply be overflowing with cars. Implications for the design of the street system are obvious. For example, cul-de-sacs do not provide enough parking area. Builders must address this dimension of Latino life in the design of the home and the community.

One solution is to build communities near public transit lines, thus reducing the need for multiple vehicles per family. This highly desirable solution allows the family to lower the overall monthly cost of shelter and transportation taken together, perhaps enough to allow a more ample home. That is the concept behind the "location efficient" mortgage, which qualifies a household for a greater home expenditure if it does not have expenses for additional cars, maintenance, or parking at work because family members can easily use public transit. However, as ideal as building near public transit hubs may be, as a practical matter, communities will continue to be built at greater distances from core cities to achieve affordability through lower land prices. In such communities, the need for more family vehicles is inescapable, and parking concerns must be addressed through community and home design.

Latino Community

When building communities in areas where Latino families are likely to be a large percentage of home buyers, builders should plan community facilities with family size and recreational preferences in mind. Because of the large number of children, it will be important to consider play space for children. The siting of homes within a community to allow for walking access to play areas through an interconnected network of sidewalks, bike paths, or trails is important. The type of play areas could also be important. It would be ideal to locate soccer fields or other ball fields within a larger community. In smaller communities, basketball courts, small parks, plazas for sitting in central locations, and barbecue pits for family gatherings can accommodate the community needs of Latino families.

A possible community attraction for Latino families is the incorporation of heritage themes. Consideration should be given to the respectful naming of the community and endowing it with theme elements that create a connection with the name. Color schemes and architectural details used on the individual houses can help create a larger community effect. A new community in Austin, Texas, developed on an infill site adjacent to an established Latino neighborhood by KB Home was named "Los Jardines" or "the gardens." It has a foliage-and-flowers identity from the entry monument to the street names intended to make Latino families comfortable (Figure 1.9).

Great care was taken to select names that may be recognizably Spanish in origin but that are easy for the non-Spanish speaker to pronounce and recognize. An example would be a name like "Victoria," which means "victory" in Spanish, connoting a celebration of personal accomplishment in the home purchase, and yet is a familiar word to the non-Spanish speaker. Another tactic is to use words that are common to both English and Spanish. For example, in a garden-themed community, builders might name a street "magnolia," which is spelled exactly the same and is the same variety of flower in both languages.

The selection of the exterior colors for homes can add to the attractiveness, sense of liveliness, and identity of an entire community. Many older Latino homes, whether in the Caribbean, in Mexico, or in the barrios and colonias of U.S. cities, are more brightly colored than typically found in American home painting palettes. It is not unusual to see homes painted in turquoise, sky blue, or peach in Miami's Little Havana and Tampa's Ybor City. And the west side of San Antonio and east Los Angeles are notable for homes and stores painted yellow, orange, and even light purple. Builders of modern subdivisions in areas of cities with large Latino populations have found that offering "brighter-than-pastel" colors seems to add fun and freshness as well as appeal to heritage and nostalgia.

A critical dimension of building in Latino communities will be attentiveness to the interaction with nearby schools. Builders need to be willing to create relationships that support existing neighborhood schools and commit to enhancing the quality of facilities, equipment, or resources in those schools. It is difficult to imagine attracting upwardly mobile Latino families to neighborhoods where the schools are perceived as unsafe, chaotic, or underperforming. Builders may want to join local efforts to provide computers, strengthen library resources, endow scholarships, or otherwise create positive momentum in established schools.

In completely new neighborhoods, builders will want to work with local governments and school districts to provide land for schools. In those instances where schools are planned from conception, it will be important to create effective interconnections between the community and the school. Schools can serve as important centers for the civic life of the community and share assets such as jogging paths, meeting spaces, recreational equipment, library resources, family centers, after-school programs, and computer labs and other facilities. Builders may be able to work with nonprofit agencies to share the costs of recreation centers and other public facilities. These collaborative uses can be preplanned in the community design process, creating invaluable connecting links through networks of sidewalks, parkways, and appropriately designed streets and through the thoughtful location of the school site itself.

When designing the street system and community amenities, builders should be attentive to security considerations. This includes designs that facilitate police patrols and neighborhood ingress and egress.

Conclusion

A vast variety of housing types and themes can be utilized in Latino communities. Reaching prospective Latino home buyers with the appropriate design for living spaces depends on the region of the country and the imperatives of climate, topography, and custom. Builders will want to take care to find local themes that satisfy traditional preferences in locations as varied as South Florida, the Chicago area, New Mexico, and Southern California (Table 1.10).

Each area has its own traditions and heritage of architecture, colors, and styles. But it is reasonable to anticipate that Latino families, who are increasingly manifesting pride in their heritage, will express that pride in the selection of distinctive exterior and interior colors, cultural touches, furniture selection, art, fabrics, plants, landscaping, and elevation details.

It is possible to focus too heavily on cosmetic characteristics. This may lead some home builders to believe that working for the Latino market means adding only architectural, color, or decorative dimensions. It is perhaps more important for builders to focus on creating floor plans and interior features that will support the lifestyle requirements of Latino families. It is necessary for builders to provide solu-

Table 1.10 Home and Community Design Considerations for Latinos

Design for the Larger Family Size and Relative Youthfulness of Latino Families	
• Assure that communities include homes of two, three, and four bedrooms. • To maintain affordability, more bedrooms may mean smaller room configurations, higher density of homes, and mixed-income groupings. • Configure rooms so that parents can monitor children's activities in study, work, and play spaces. • Finish garages to enable conversion into additional bedrooms or living spaces in future years, including front elevations that allow the conversion to appear seamless. • Trade off an enclosed garage for a less expensive carport or parking pad and instead offer another bedroom.	• Plan to house multigenerational families by offering a ground-floor bedroom with bathroom access for an elderly live-in grandparent. • Include ample storage space for family supplies such as pantries in kitchens and closets in bathrooms. • Provide a deeper kitchen sink for more dishes generated by larger families. • Position washer and dryer near the bedrooms for ease of doing laundry. • Use durable interior and exterior materials that withstand family wear and tear and are easy to clean and maintain.

Design for the Social and Work Characteristics of Latinos	
• Plan for the kitchen as the center of the social space. • Position the kitchen so that it is visually open to other family gathering areas and outdoor play spaces. • Consider providing gas stoves, which allow for open-flame cooking of traditional recipes such as tortillas. • Design family space to be interchangeably converted from children's activities to extended family gatherings, including easy flow to outdoor patios or yards through French or sliding doors.	• Accessorize exterior spaces with patios, barbeque pits, safe play areas, or covered "outdoor rooms." • Provide areas for gardening with flowers and fruit trees. • Create storage areas for work-related tools and equipment, such as a nook tucked alongside a garage or carport. • Design rooms that could eventually be used for home-based businesses, such as day care allowed in residential zones. • Provide driveway space for multiple vehicles to limit crowding of streets.

Plan Communities that Serve and Attract Latinos	
• Create opportunities for outdoor activity for children and adults, including play areas and shopping areas reached via networks of sidewalks, bike paths, or trails. • Design neighborhoods with public transit lines in mind, reducing transportation costs and the need for multiple vehicles per family and allowing a larger budget for home features. • Provide neighborhood basketball courts, small plazas for sitting, and barbeque pits for family gatherings. • Plan heritage themes to include respectful naming of the community, exterior colors for homes, and architectural details.	• Stimulate interaction with neighborhood schools by sharing assets such as jogging paths, playing fields, meeting spaces, recreational equipment, library resources, after-school programs, computer labs, and other facilities. • Keep safety in mind by including home security systems, access for police patrols, and practical neighborhood ingress and egress. • Build family-size rental units, an important part of the housing inventory in any area with a high rate of Latino population growth.

tions to challenges as basic as parking for the many Latino families who take great pride in gathering relatives and friends in their homes on special days. Builders who recognize the significance of Latino population growth for the housing market and the vast potential of Latinos as home buyers will sell more homes while contributing to the economic advancement of their communities.

Henry G. Cisneros is a former Secretary
of the Department of Housing and Urban
Development and former San Antonio
mayor. He is the founder and chairman
of CityView, a real estate development
company, located in San Antonio, Texas.

Appendix A Growth in Latino Population in 100 Largest Metropolitan Areas

Metropolitan Area	Metro Area			Central City			Suburb		
	1990	2000	% Chng	1990	2000	Chng	1990	2000	Chng
Established Latino Metros	10,286,158	14,119,006	110%	5,783,141	17,484,062	110%	4,503,017	16,634,944	147%
Albuquerque, NM MSA	217,340	296,373	36%	131,465	179,075	36%	85,875	117,298	37%
Chicago, IL PMSA	819,676	1,416,584	73%	535,315	753,644	41%	284,361	662,940	133%
Denver, CO PMSA	208,264	397,236	91%	106,554	175,704	65%	101,710	221,532	118%
El Paso, TX MSA	411,248	531,654	29%	355,260	431,875	22%	55,988	99,779	78%
Fresno, CA MSA	262,004	406,151	55%	102,930	170,520	66%	159,074	235,631	48%
Jersey City, NJ PMSA	181,222	242,123	34%	54,231	67,952	25%	126,991	174,171	37%
Los Angeles-Long Beach, CA PMSA	3,306,116	4,242,213	28%	1,470,354	1,884,165	28%	1,835,762	2,358,048	28%
McAllen, TX MSA	326,923	503,100	54%	64,572	85,427	32%	262,351	417,673	59%
Miami, FL PMSA	949,700	1,291,737	36%	233,438	238,351	7%	726,262	1,053,386	45%
New York, NY PMSA	1,842,127	2,239,836	27%	1,737,927	2,160,554	24%	104,200	179,282	72%
Oakland, CA PMSA	266,283	441,686	66%	49,267	87,467	78%	21`7,016	354,219	63%
San Antonio, TX MSA	624,941	816,037	31%	517,974	671,394	30%	106,967	144,643	35%
San Francisco, CA PMSA	226,734	291,563	29%	96,640	109,504	13%	130,094	182,059	40%
San Jose, CA PMSA	307,113	403,401	31%	204,012	269,989	32%	103,101	133,412	29%
Tucson, AZ MSA	161,053	247,578	54%	117,267	173,868	48%	43,786	73,710	68%
Ventura, CA PMSA	175,414	251,734	44%	15,935	24,573	54%	159,479	227,161	42%
	10,286,158	14,119,006	37%	5,783,141	7,484,062	29%	4,503,017	6,634,944	47%
New Latino Destinations									
Albany, NY MSA	14,440	23,798	65%	3,225	5,349	66%	11,215	18,449	65%
Allentown, PA MSA	26,697	50,607	90%	11,822	26,058	120%	14,875	24,549	65%
Atlanta, GA MSA	55,045	268,851	388%	7,640	18,720	145%	47,405	250,131	428%
Baltimore, MD PMSA	28,538	51,329	80%	6,997	11,061	58%	21,541	40,268	87%
Bergen-Pasaic, NJ PMSA	145,094	237,869	64%	*	*	*	145,094	237,869	64%
Birmingham, AL MSA	3,520	16,598	372%	1,175	3,764	220%	2,345	12,834	447%
Boston, MA-NH PMSA	130,896	202,513	55%	59,692	85,089	43%	71,204	117,424	65%
Charlotte, NC-SC MSA	9,817	77,092	685%	5,261	39,800	657%	4,556	37,292	719%
Columbus, OH MSA	10,003	28,115	181%	5,968	17,471	193%	4,035	10,644	164%
Fort Lauderdale, FL PMSA	105,668	271,652	157%	10,574	14,406	36%	95,094	257,246	171%
Fort Worth-Arlington, TX PMSA	147,431	309,851	110%	107,987	220,185	104%	39,444	89,666	127%
Grand Rapids, MI MSA	27,195	68,916	153%	8,447	25,818	206%	18,748	43,098	130%
Greensboro-Winston Salem, NC MSA	6,844	62,210	809%	2,415	25,785	968%	4,429	36,425	722%
Greenville, SC MSA	5,712	26,167	358%	567	1,927	240%	5,145	24,240	371%
Harrisburg, PA MSA	9,336	19,557	109%	3,738	5,724	53%	5,598	13,833	147%
Hartford, CT MSA	77,132	113,540	47%	43,372	49,260	14%	33,760	64,280	90%
Indianapolis, IN MSA	11,918	42,994	261%	7,463	30,636	311%	4,455	12,358	177%
Jacksonville, FL MSA	22,206	42,122	90%	15,572	30,594	96%	6,634	11,528	74%
Kansas City, MO-KS MSA	45,199	92,910	106%	27,154	55,243	103%	28,380	37,667	33%
Knoxville, TN MSA	3,433	8,628	151%	986	2,751	179%	2,447	5,877	140%

(Continued)

Metropolitan Area	Metro Area			Central City			Suburb		
	1990	2000	% Chng	1990	2000	Chng	1990	2000	Chng
Las Vegas, NV-AZ MSA	86,570	322,038	272%	31,249	112,962	261%	55,321	209,076	278%
Little Rock, AR MSA	4,741	12,337	160%	1,427	4,889	243%	3,314	7,448	125%
Louisville, KY-IN MSA	5,040	16,479	227%	1,490	4,755	219%	3,550	11,724	230%
Memphis, TN-AR-MS MSA	7,546	27,527	265%	4,011	19,317	382%	3,535	8,203	132%
Middlesex-Somerset-Hunterdon, NJ PMSA	70,021	131,122	87%	*	*	*	70,021	131,122	87%
Milwaukee, WI PMSA	48,276	94,511	96%	37,420	71,646	91%	10,856	22,865	111%
Minneapolis-St. Paul, MN-WI MSA	34,334	99,121	189%	17,627	51,890	194%	16,707	47,231	183%
Monmouth-Ocean, NJ PMSA	35,619	63,813	79%	*	*	*	35,619	63,813	79%
Nashville, TN MSA	7,250	40,139	454%	4,131	25,774	524%	3,119	14,365	361%
Nassau-Suffolk, NY PMA	157,118	282,693	80%	*	*	*	157,118	282,693	80%
New Haven, CT PMSA	30,629	53,331	74%	16,350	26,443	62%	14,279	26,888	88%
Norfolk-Virginia Beach, Newport News, VA-NC MSA	31,551	48,963	55%	23,930	34,280	43%	7,621	14,683	93%
Oklahoma City, OK MSA	32,851	72,998	122%	21,148	51,368	143%	11,703	21,630	85%
Omaha, NE-IA MSA	15,419	39,735	158%	9,703	29,397	203%	5,716	10,338	81%
Orlando, FL MSA	98,812	271,627	175%	14,121	32,510	130%	84,691	239,117	182%
Portland-Vancouver, OR-WA PMSA	49,344	142,444	189%	14,693	45,093	207%	34,651`	97,351	181%
Providence, RI-MA MSA	45,893	93,868	105%	23,744	52,146	120%	22,149	41,722	88%
Raleigh-Durham, NC MSA	9,923	72,580	631%	4,550	35,320	676%	5,373	37,260	593%
Richmond, VA MSA	8,788	23,283	165%	1,744	5,074	191%	7,044	18,209	159%
Salt Lake City, UT MSA	61,269	144,600	136%	15,220	34,254	125%	46,049	110,346	140%
Sarasota, FL MSA	15,186	38,682	155%	2,282	6,283	175%	12,904	32,399	151%
Scranton, PA MSA	3,239	7,467	131%	520	1,999	284%	2,710	5,468	101%
Seattle-Bellevue, WA PMSA	53,479	126,675	137%	19,097	35,546	86%	34,382	91,129	165%
Springfield, MA MSA	48,024	74,227	55%	25,642	41,343	61%	22,382	32,884	47%
Tacoma, WA PMSA	19,445	38,621	99%	6,270	13,262	112%	13,175	25,359	92%
Tampa-St. Petersburg-Clearwater, FL MSA	136,027	248,642	83%	49,699	78,778	59%	86,328	169,864	97%
Tulsa, OK MSA	14,498	38,570	166%	9,340	28,111	201%	5,158	10,459	103%
Washington, DC-MD-VA-WV PMSA	221,458	432,003	95%	31,358	44,953	43%	190,100	387,050	104%
West Palm Beach, FL MSA	65,028	140,675	116%	9,200	14,955	63%	55,828	125,720	125%
Wichita, KS MSA	18,437	40,353	119%	14,314	33,112	131%	4,123	7,241	76%
Wilmington, DE-MD PMSA	11,701	27,599	136%	4,809	7,148	49%	6,892	20,451	197%
	2,333,640	5,282,035	126%	745,144	1,612,249	116%	1,598,831	3,669,786	130%
Fast-Growing Latino Hubs									
Austin, TX MSA	174,482	327,760	88%	105,162	200,579	91%	69,320	127,131	83%
Bakersfield, CA MSA	150,558	254,036	69%	35,033	80,170	129%	115,525	173,866	51%
Dallas, TX PMSA	364,397	810,499	122%	204,712	422,587	106%	159,685	387,912	142%
Houston, TX PMSA	697,208	1,248,586	79%	442,943	730,865	65%	254,265	517,721	104%
Orange County, CA PMSA	556,957	875,579	57%	279,238	421,010	51%	277,719	454,569	64%

Appendix A 100 Largest Metropolitan Areas *(Continued)*

Metropolitan Area	Metro Area			Central City			Suburb		
	1990	2000	% Chng	1990	2000	Chng	1990	2000	Chng
Phoenix-Mesa, AZ MSA	374,275	817,012	118%	224,667	528,253	135%	149,608	288,759	90%
Riverside-San Bernardino, CA PMSA	675,918	1,228,962	82%	114,154	185,337	62%	561,764	1,043,625	86%
Sacramento, CA PMSA	140,153	234,475	67%	58,716	87,974	50%	81,437	146,501	80%
San Diego, CA MSA	498,578	750,965	51%	223,616	310,752	39%	274,962	440,213	60%
Stockton, CA MSA	108,987	172,073	58%	50,370	79,217	57%	58,617	92,856	58%
Vallejo, CA PMSA	59,576	99,014	66%	11,201	18,591	66%	48,3765	80,423	66%
	3,801,089	6,818,961	79%	1,749,812	3,065,335	73%	2,051,277	3,753,6726	83%
Small Latino Places									
Akron, OH PMSA	3,844	5,874	53%	1,503	2,513	67%	2,341	3,361	44%
Ann Arbor, MI PMSA	11,624	17,676	52%	2,629	3,814	44%	8,995	13,862	54%
Baton Rouge, LA MSA	7,280	10,576	45%	3,462	3,918	13%	3,818	6,658	74%
Buffalo, NY MSA	23,521	33,967	44%	15,287	22,076	44%	8,234	11,891	44%
Charleston, SC MSA	7,150	13,091	83%	504	1,462	190%	6,646	11,629	75%
Cincinnati, OH-KY-IN PMSA	7,639	17,717	132%	2,319	4,230	82%	5,320	13,487	154%
Cleveland, OH PMSA	49,617	74,862	51%	22,330	34,728	56%	27,287	40,134	47%
Columbia, SC MSA	5,740	12,859	124%	2,033	3,520	73%	3,707	9,339	152%
Dayton, OH MSA	6,612	11,329	71%	1,204	2,626	118%	5,408	8,703	61%
Detroit, MI PMSA	78,454	128,075	63%	27,157	47,167	74%	51,297	80,908	58%
Gary, IN PMSA	47,116	66,207	41%	6,282	5,065	−19%	40,834	61,142	50%
Honolulu, Hi MSA	54,680	58,729	7%	15,450	16,229	5%	39,230	42,500	8%
Mobile, AL MSA	4,353	7,353	69%	2,152	2,828	31%	2,201	4,525	106%
New Orleans, LA MSA	52,563	58,545	11%	15,900	14,826	−7%	36,663	43,719	19%
Newark, NJ PMSA	183,986	270,557	47%	69,204	80,622	16%	114,782	189,935	65%
Philadelphia, PA-NJ PMSA	165,844	258,606	56%	84,186	128,928	53%	81,658	129,678	59%
Pittsburgh, PA MSA	11,881	17,100	44%	3,415	4,425	30%	8,466	12,675	50%
Rochester, NY MSA	29,712	47,559	60%	18,936	28,032	48%	10,776	19,527	81%
St. Louis, MO-IL MSA	25,383	39,677	56%	4,850	7,022	45%	20,533	32,655	59%
Syracuse, NY MSA	8,882	15,112	70%	4,177	7,768	86%	4,705	7,344	56%
Toledo, OH MSA	18,675	27,125	45%	11,958	17,141	43%	6,717	9,984	49%
Youngstown, OH MSA	7,246	10,743	48%	3,596	4,282	19%	3,650	6,461	77%
	811,802	1,203,339	48%	318,534	443,222	39%	493,268	760,117	54%
Total (All Metro Area Types)	**17,232,689**	**27,423,341**	**59%**	**8,596,631**	**12,604,868**	**47%**	**8,646,393**	**14,818,473**	**71%**

*Metros with no central city. MSA, metropolitan statistical area; PMSA, primary metropolitan statistical area.
Italics denotes hypergrowth metros with Latino population growth over 300% between 1980 and 2000.
Source: Adapted from Suro, Roberto and Audrey Singer. *Latino Growth in Metropolitan America: Changing Patterns, New Locations.* Washington, DC: Brookings Institution, 2002, p. 15–17. http://www.brookings.edu/metro

Source: Christine B. Charlip.

CHAPTER 2

A Builder's Guide to Reaching Latino Home Buyers

Rick Schwolsky

Seeing the numbers representing the dramatic growth in the Latino population certainly confirms what many of us have known in our own communities for years. Latino culture has entered our daily lives from food to fashion and magazines to music, and a steady stream of radio and TV advertisements clearly targets this growing segment of our society. The building industry is not far behind.

For builders, a look at the workforce composition on our construction sites over the past decade or more has given us strong and early indicators of what the Census Bureau and private studies now report. There are few places where builders have yet to experience significant increases in the number of Latino contractors and crews on their projects, reflecting the growth in population. The difference now is that Latino hunger for homeownership is driving home sales in every major U.S. housing market, a trend that forms the basis for future growth and expansion in the housing industry.

Even markets that were below the radar until the late 1990s are now setting the pace for Latino household growth (see Chapter 1, The Rise of the Latino Home Buyer). Along with increasing populations and expanding markets, we can measure the surge in the Latino home-ownership rate that has grown from 40% in 1993 to its current level of 47.4% and is projected to increase to 53% by 2010, a boost of 2.2 million owner households in the next five years. If the trend continues as expected, according to the Tomás Rivera Policy Institute, Latino home owners will account for 19% of the total increase in home owners nationwide despite composing just 9% of households in the U.S.[1]

In California alone, Latinos will require 1.9 million new housing units by 2020, close to 50% of the total demand in that state.[2] This remarkable and sustained growth has everyone in the building industry pursuing this demographic as the next big wave of home buyers.

The Pew Hispanic Center reports that the Latino population in the United States increased by 14 million since the 2000 Census to reach 40.4 million in 2004 and projects that it will reach 47.7 million by the end of the decade and 60.4 million by 2020.[3] In traditional as well as transitional Latino markets, builders who can tap into this growth will harness a powerful force that will clearly drive new home sales for decades.

What does this mean for you and your business? First, if you sell homes to first-time and move-up buyers, you are well positioned to reach Latino families. Chances are you'll be in the right place at the right time with the right product. If you are not yet actively pursuing these buyers (even if you are already selling to them), it's time to develop and implement culturally tuned marketing strategies to attract Latinos to your communities. The question facing home builders from California to the Carolinas, Tallahassee to Topeka, Dallas to Detroit and almost everywhere in between is not *whether* to develop strategies to reach Latino buyers, but rather *how* to do it.

Measuring the Market

With contributing factors as broad as the cultural diversity found among potential Latino buyers, the effect of minority household formation in the coming decades is expected to be so dramatic that, according to The Joint Center for Housing Studies of Harvard University, it could offset the combined projected effects of increasing interest rates and declining baby boomer home sales—dubbed the "baby bust."

According the Center's *State of the Nation's Housing 2004* report, two of every five net new home owners from 1994 to 2003 were minority buyers. Immigrant buyers also made their mark during this period. Foreign-born households made up 12% of first-time home buyers in 2001, and purchased about 8% of new homes between 1998 and 2001.[4] These are significant numbers, especially when judged within the context of the challenges that face these home buyers. Although it is important to avoid generalizations, Table 2.1 presents excerpts from notable studies that describe some selected buyer traits.

These numbers will only be bolstered as hurdles to ownership are overcome with new policies and opportunities, including renewed community focus on planning and production of affordable housing, increased access to innovative financial programs targeting Latino and other minority buyers, and expansion of new pilot programs creating paths to homeownership for undocumented families. (These barriers to homeownership and innovative solutions are discussed more fully in Chapters 10 and 11.)

With public assertions from the likes of Fannie Mae to create 1.8 million new minority home owners by 2014 through its American Dream Commitment, Chase Home Finance's $500 billion pledge to its Dream Maker Commitment program, GMAC Mortgage's Settle America flexible qualification program, and new offerings from Bank of America's Neighborhood Advantage, more doors are opening that will drive growth toward home builders in these markets.

Even more innovative programs are on the way that could drive Latino homeownership rates higher. According to a 2004 study conducted by the National Association of Hispanic Real Estate Professionals (NAHREP),[5] if more traditional barriers like citizenship and standard credit rating requirements were lowered or eased in the mortgage application process, it would open the way for 216,000 currently undocumented Latino householders to become home owners, generating $44 billion in new mortgage originations. The report also states that 172,626 current undocumented renter households could potentially afford a home worth $94,500 or more.[5]

Bank of America and Mortgage Guaranty Insurance Corporation are already testing flexible financing requirements in several states. Changes include allowing Latino home seekers to use ITINs (individual tax identification numbers) in place of Social Security numbers on their mortgage applications and to demonstrate an ability to pay based on income and payment history, including money sent to home countries, in lieu of a traditional credit rating.

Table 2.1 Latino Buyers at a Glance

Average number of people per household*
foreign born: 4.5
U.S. born: 3.4
Median size of home purchased*
foreign born: 1,144 sq. ft.
U.S. born: 1,321 sq. ft.
Neighborhood composition[†]
57% live in mixed neighborhoods
43% in Latino-majority neighborhoods
Of renters surveyed in Los Angeles, Houston, and Atlanta[‡]
44% are planning to buy within 5 years
11% are actively involved in process
California Latinos hope to find homes that cost[‡]
<$80,000: 12%
$80,000–100,000: 20%
$100,000–150,000: 22%
$150,000–200,000: 13%
>$200,000: 19%
Latinos in California bought homes that cost[‡]
<$80,000: 23%
$80,000–100,000: 12%
$100,000–150,000: 25%
$150,000–200,000: 14%
>$200,000: 12%
Recent California Latino home buyers[§]
44% have owned homes for fewer than 5 years
>70% are first-time buyers
>75% financed with 30-year fixed-rate loans
64% preferred to conduct the purchase in Spanish
Latino home buyers are looking for[‡]
Low crime rate: 44%
Good schools: 39%
Friendly neighborhood: 24%
Proximity to work: 22%
Rising home values: 17%
Access to public transportation: 10%
Proximity to relatives: 9%
Latino composition: 6%

*Joint Center for Housing Studies of Harvard University. *The State of the Nation's Housing 2004.* www.jchs.harvard.edu

[†]*Hispanics, A People in Motion.* In *Trends 2005.* Washington, DC: Pew Hispanic Center, January 2005, p. 7.

[‡]Lee, Jongho, Louis Tornatzky, and Celina Torres. *El Sueño de su Casa: The Homeownership Potential of Mexican-Heritage Families.* Los Angeles, CA: The Tomás Rivera Policy Institute, May 2004.

[§]Kotkin, Joel, Thomas Tseng, and Erika Ozuna. *Rewarding Ambition: Latinos, Housing and the Future of California.* Pepperdine University, Davenport Institute, September 2002. publicpolicy.pepperdine.edu/davenportinstitute/reports/rewarding/rewarding1.html

Gateways to the Markets

The wave of Latino homeownership that started in California and spread through the Southwest to Texas is now hitting new "gateway" states with high-rate growth of Latinos. (See Chapter 1 for more on gateway states.) These new openings will increase the market opportunities in many locations. Some builders have already identified and begun working to address these opportunities.

KB Home started pursuing Latino home buyers more than 10 years ago in California, and already 50% of new home sales are to immigrant families, according to Chief Operating Officer Jeff Mezger. Courting these new home buyers has become a core part of KB Home's business. The lessons learned in developing, marketing, and selling homes in communities that attract Latino buyers are being applied at KB divisions in some of the gateway markets, such as Arizona, Colorado, New Mexico, Texas, Georgia, North Carolina, Illinois (Chicago metro area), and Florida.

Tampa-based Jim Walter Homes has been advertising on Spanish-language radio for 20 years, and in some of its Texas branch offices, half the sales are to Latinos. But even with this early success and great market positioning, the company is looking beyond the gateway cities and traditional Latino destinations of California, Florida, Texas, and Illinois. According to Roger Crabb, vice president of market research and analysis, Jim Walter Homes plans to be one of the first builders to enter new markets with a full Latino marketing plan. They engaged the University of Illinois to conduct a study on the impact and opportunity of the Latino market and go beyond the Census reports to show the growth patterns in targeted locations. The research showed that areas such as Denver and Philadelphia have enough Latinos with buying power to support such efforts.

All Sales Are Local

National demographics will give you a basis of understanding that can help guide your efforts as you target new markets, but you also need to go to the next level and learn all you can about each local market and the people who live there. For example, broad characteristics such as whether the people you are trying to reach are U.S. born or foreign born or first- or second-generation Americans and how long they've been in the U.S. will give you an idea of where they might be along the path toward homeownership.

Source: © Corbis.

In the broadest sense, the likelihood of homeownership among Latinos increases with age. Those who are U.S. born are far more likely to own homes than those who were born elsewhere. Those who were foreign born who entered the U.S. before 1990 are more than twice as likely to buy a home than those who came afterward.[6] Finally, 65% of sales to foreign-born Latinos are to families with children, reflecting a much stronger tie between family and homeownership than in other immigrant populations.[7]

These facts make sense when you consider the time it takes for new residents to settle into their surroundings, establish their sources of income, and begin to save for future purchases. Acculturation accounts for a wide difference between U.S.-born and foreign-born homeownership rates. U.S.-born Latinos are generally better educated, earn more, are more likely to speak English, and are less intimidated by the home buying process than their foreign-born compatriots.

The next step is to dig into the local market to find information about countries of origin, their immigrant status, where they currently live and work, where their kids go to school, where they shop, where they socialize, and what they want in a new home and neighborhood. These factors should guide your steps in planning the location, design, price range, and especially sales and marketing efforts for your communities. Without this local knowledge, you won't be able to reach Latinos culturally or properly address their needs when they walk into your sales office. In many ways this local research is no different from your efforts to design products for any first-time and first-time move-up buyers. But in other important ways, it is completely different.

Latino home buyers want many of the same things as any home buyer. The Tomás Rivera Policy Institute's *El Sueño de su Casa: The Homeownership Potential of Mexican-Heritage Families* report found that prospective home buyers are looking for homes in safe, friendly communities with good schools, close to public transportation and work, where home values are rising, and where they can be close to relatives and other Latinos. Sound familiar? Except for the specific reference to Latinos, this wish list probably matches lists you've developed for other first-time, and first-time move-up markets (Table 2.1).

Given so many similarities to other buyers, how can you find out what will distinguish your communities and attract Latino buyers?

Consider the advice of Eric Elder, vice president of marketing and communications for The Ryland Group: Don't make assumptions about who is in a market, and don't treat all Latinos as if they're from Mexico. Every group has special needs and different expectations.

Ryland has developed its understanding of the different cultures and levels of acculturation among Latinos through focus groups and local research. This knowledge allows the company to adjust to the buyers' needs accordingly. When it comes to guiding prospective buyers through the buying process, Ryland uses this knowledge to tune its approach to its target audiences. Ryland takes a different approach if selling to an upscale young Latino professional in Houston than for a first-generation, first-time buyer in San Antonio.

It will take a combination of traditional market research and grass-roots networking to get the full picture. Some will cost you money, the rest will cost you time. And with both, you will probably be making new contacts in each market. Jim Walter Homes' University of Illinois study used focus groups, surveyed Latino prospects who shopped but didn't buy from the company, outlined best practices, and identified underserved markets.

Although Census data can be useful, your local studies should go beyond rehashing these numbers and provide real feedback from focus groups and community leaders in each targeted location. Depending on the number of markets studied and the level of detail, you can get your analysis completed for between $5,000 and $20,000.

Because of the defined focus on their markets, smaller builders may already be more in touch with their communities and, therefore, with the local Latino home buyers' needs. But even these builders need to do their homework. Del Valle Homes in Modesto, California, is a perfect example. With a very large Latino population in the area, Del Valle president Scott Salazar Myers saw an opportunity to compete with larger builders by targeting this niche. He studied local demographic reports from The Tomás Rivera Center and Pepperdine University and put his own cultural background, Spanish fluency, and community connections to work.

Of Del Valle's first 15 homes selling for between $120,000 and $140,000, all but one sold to Latino buyers. That was in 2000. In 2005, Del Valle began developing a 178-lot community for which the company had 2,500 families on its "interested" list and two pre-qualified buyers for every unit, 80% of whom were Latino.

Grassroots research will go a long way, if properly conducted. Networking with community leaders, school principals, employers, ministers, and nonprofit organizations can help you gain the local insights to guide your planning and development, especially as it will relate to your marketing efforts. This outreach will go better with a Latino representative from your company making the contacts, preferably someone with the same cultural background as the target community you are researching.

Want to dig deeper? Contact one of the affiliates of the National Council of La Raza (NCLR), the nation's largest Hispanic organization. Through its NCLR Homeownership Network, 38 NCLR affiliates in 17 states (at this writing) conduct first-time home buyer education programs that include financial guidance and one-on-one counseling during and after the home buying process. NCLR counselors could become valuable allies as you develop your local research.

Source: © Corbis.

Supporting community organizations and local events is another great means of connecting with Latinos in your markets. From sponsoring youth soccer to funding nonprofits to joining in local fiestas, your presence in the community's special events will show your commitment on a personal level and help your branding. Getting behind efforts that mesh well with your company's values will also help your word of mouth. Del Valle supports a local organization called El Concilio, which helps immigrant families with child care, financial advice, education, and legal services, as well as an organization called PIQE that promotes parent involvement in their kids' educations.

Gary Acosta, a California mortgage banker and co-founder of NAHREP, a 14,000-member organization with 40 chapters across the United States, firmly believes that the more you know about your Latino buyers, the better. He urges builders to learn the countries of origin of the people in their markets and understand how that heritage shapes the characteristics they bring to dealings. It allows you to customize your relationship with buyers. Although you may not typically work with Realtors, establishing a creative relationship with a local Hispanic NAHREP member in your target market might help you unlock some cultural treasures and give you an edge with local buyers.

Meeting Buyers' Needs

To succeed, you and your team will have to integrate the cultural awareness you've gained into almost every aspect of your operations. By creating new layers of personalized services, you'll build a bridge to Latino buyers stronger than any targeted marketing campaign or home design you could create. Although Latino home buyers may want many of the same things anyone might want in a new home, they will look beyond location, floor plans, price, and selections. They will look above all else for a trusting relationship based on respect, patience, and promises.

Ryland's Eric Elder sees casting a net without having an infrastructure to handle Latino customers as the biggest mistake a builder can make with this market. It makes sense to put your entire system in place before soliciting, including placing bilingual people on your phones, in your sales offices, and in your mortgage departments. Even those buyers who speak English often feel more comfortable doing business in Spanish or with other Latinos. Conduct culturally specific training. You'll make deeper connections with your buyers by hiring people with similar cultural backgrounds.

Source: © Corbis.

Myers created Del Valle Homes' HELP Center (the home owner education, loan, and product "design" center) to attend to the very different needs of Latino buyers. In one central location, Del Valle's Latino buyers are guided through the company's various stages during a purchase, from contract signing and mortgage qualification to design center selections, by a 100% Latino staff.

Myers focused on placing Latinos into the staff positions that would interact directly with customers and found that it was a good move. To make buyers feel even more at home, Myers decorated the HELP Center's walls with Latino paintings and art depicting landscape and agricultural scenes from the San Joaquin Valley. Buyers reacted positively and said they felt they were understood. But Latino buyers face more hurdles than just language.

Address the Challenges

Of all the challenges facing your bid for Latino buyers—and their bid for homeownership, bridging the language gap might be the most obvious and easiest to address. After all, hiring and training bilingual staff could actually help you take care of language and cultural issues at the same time. But other culture-related obstacles are even more challenging.

Latinos are often faced with a lack of information about home buying, and therefore have misconceptions about the process. They may have trouble getting credit, sometimes because they have blemished or nonexistent credit histories, which may be because they are "unbanked" (not associated with a bank) and operate in a cash economy. They spend more on housing and send significant portions of their incomes to their families in their home countries, which makes it harder to save for a down payment. The home buying process can be unfamiliar, complex, and confusing, so simplify it in any way you can.

Discrimination is the other major hurdle. When mystery shoppers "shopped" 15 sales centers at 15 builders in Washington, DC; Chicago; and Los Angeles, 13 of the 15 transactions favored the white shoppers.[8] This occurred despite the fact that the Latino mystery shoppers had better financial profiles than the white "control" shoppers. It is critical to avoid mistakes related to fair housing. Helping Latinos reach their dreams of homeownership will require your investment into helping them get past these challenges successfully.

Source: © Corbis.

Educate Your Buyers

I have stated the case for establishing close cultural connections with your Latino buyers, including personal guidance and counseling during the purchasing process. But your first best move in this area will be helping Latinos overcome the "information gap" by providing home buying and home owner education seminars in Spanish. You might even consider going into the community with basic money management, banking, or credit seminars. Demonstrating that you want to help raise their level of financial literacy will make Latinos more comfortable with your process and build trust in the community for your company.

KB Home conducts Spanish-language home buying seminars in each of their cities. Held at one of their design studios or a local

Source: © Corbis.

hotel, they teach buyers how to save money, establish credit, qualify for a mortgage, and ultimately how to buy a new home. The company's infomercials on Spanish-language TV also present "how to buy a home" information and serve both educational and branding purposes at the same time.

Your Web site is another great place to offer education and begin branding. Adding Spanish versions of your "How to Qualify" and "How to Buy" links could get the ball rolling in your direction. Make it easy to find the *en Español* button on your home page, otherwise it will seem like an afterthought and you'll be off to a bad start. Better yet, promote the direct URL to your Spanish content in any ads, brochures, or promotional materials, as have builders using www. beazerenespanol.com, or www.pultespanish.com. The same rules apply for translation of your web content: Carefully edit and review your Spanish-version content before going "live."

With the documented growth of Internet use among Latinos, your Web site will increasingly gain importance. Ryland sees the Internet as a valuable education and trust-building tool, and generates 15% to 30% of sales via their Web site. Don't forget to include the "Find Your New Home" button.

Marketing *En Español*

The first thing to understand about expressing your advertising and marketing messages in Spanish is that you can't just take your English ad campaigns and collateral materials and translate them directly into Spanish. Chances are your snappy copy and catchy phrases won't come across the same way *en Español*.

The second thing is that you can't just hand your materials to a native speaker in your company for translation. You need to craft a campaign specifically for your market, use professional translators familiar with real estate and construction terminology to convert your materials into Spanish, and most important, create a review process that includes members of your target audience. This will assure that your message gets through clearly and appropriately without any embarrassing blunders or offensive oversights.

And there's a third consideration that will come into play in some markets now and more in the future: You may not have to advertise in Spanish at all. You may only have to adjust your message and change your images to reach a growing younger population of second- and third-generation Latinos who identify with their cultural backgrounds but primarily speak English.

Segment marketing is everywhere, and you'll be faced with the decision about how best to reach Latinos with your message or capture their imaginations and attract them to your communities. Ryland's Hispanic marketing efforts include its presence on the top-rated Spanish-language radio and television channels in Los Angeles and Phoenix, relationship marketing that includes sponsorship of the Dallas Burn MLS soccer team, and advertising on *Mi Casa*, a weekly television home show. They believe it is most efficient to use radio more than newspapers and electronic more than print media.

Del Valle Homes conveys their commitment through a strong ad presence, primarily print ads and billboards, and word-of-mouth. They also ran a high-profile new home giveaway on Univision in concert with its community involvement to attract buyers.

Avoid stereotyping your audience, and consider the difference between catering to Latinos and patronizing them. Look outside of the building industry for examples of successful targeted marketing campaigns, notably auto manufacturers, retail, food and beverages, and banks and finance services, and identify the best practices. It's also pertinent to recognize the importance that women have in the home buying decision.

As far as developing ad campaigns that resonate, there is a minor industry of Latino ad agencies cropping up in every market that can help guide your message and its delivery to your market. The Association of Hispanic Advertising Agencies can help in your efforts to develop targeted marketing. Their Web site (www.ahaa.org) lists member agencies in every state. Review the Yankelovich Monitor Multicultural Marketing Study or their Multicultural Marketing Special Report 2004. Both can help you plan where to spend your marketing dollars (www.yankelovich.com).

Finally, don't let up on building your word-of-mouth reputation. The network you created when you were doing your research will continue to be important as you develop your market. Continue to support community organizations, attend meetings, sponsor family events, and treat your Latino construction crews as part of your marketing team because they will share their feelings about your company—good and bad.

Selling to Latinos

Nowhere are your efforts to reach and serve Latinos going to be more important than in your sales offices. If you succeed in attracting these potential buyers to your community, but they leave feeling confused, rushed, offended, or alienated, they won't come back and neither will their families, friends, or neighbors. On the other hand, if you can make them feel welcome, show respect for their culture, honor the way they make decisions, and convey a sincere desire to help, you'll win their trust, loyalty, one sale, and lots of referrals.

Michael Lee, a multicultural consultant and president of EthnoConnect in California, believes that builders do the marketing but that most of them don't know how to make Latinos feel comfortable when they come into their sales offices. This is where a lot of your training efforts need to focus, Lee says, so your sales staff can become culturally sensitive.

Many Latino buyers will arrive with extended family members to check out your communities and tour your homes. It makes sense to set up your meeting rooms to accommodate the many family members who may be involved in the home buying decision. Gary Acosta says you can judge whether a builder is used to dealing with Latinos by the number of chairs in his or her sales office. With so many people in the picture, the group involvement can also require more flexibility on your part when it comes to setting appointments and scheduling meetings. This is where patience and respect play large roles.

Look for signs within the family group indicating who will make the decisions. The group will generally turn to look at the decision maker when you ask them questions. This often is an older male but increasingly women end up making the final decision, although this may occur privately.

Will there be more than one owner on the title? Who is going to be living in the home? It isn't uncommon for Latinos to pool resources to buy a home. In fact, two or more people share legal ownership of the home (indicated by mortgage title) in 70% of the homes owned by Latinos in California.[9]

Multicultural consultant Lee believes that Latinos tend to be tactile and like to see things and suggests that you walk them through your model homes early on. During the tour, demonstrate the expandability of the home. If you've merchandized a first-floor suite as a library with bathroom, have a poster showing it set up as a first-floor master suite for the grandparents.

Finally, make no assumptions. The home buying process will be a first-time experience for most Latino home buyers. Lee also strongly advises placing clear signage in your models that explains that the furnishings and decorations are not included in the price of the home.

Closing Time

Many Latinos may prefer to conduct a home purchase in Spanish. However, when it comes to the final documentation, most builders are still using their original forms in English to close, for two reasons. First, translation of these legal documents might be the trickiest of all—so they don't want to risk inaccuracies. And second, according to Ryland's Elder, in his experience, Latinos want to sign the same documents that everyone else uses. The finance and banking industry have gone further than builders, and there are a number of sources for Spanish-language documentation (Table 2.2), but this will be your choice based on your local research and your legal advisers.

The Latino market has tremendous potential, but it will take some genuine work to get into proper position to tap into it. Big builders can take advantage of their size by spreading lessons learned from work in the established Latino markets to the emerging locations. Smaller builders can use their intimate local knowledge to carve out their niche. But builders of all sizes should apply the same principles to reach and serve this rich and exciting market. This is just the beginning. As Del Valle's Scott Myers points out,

Table 2.2 Resources

Joint Center for Housing Studies of Harvard University www.jchs.harvard.edu *The State of the Nation's Housing 2004,* www.jchs.harvard.edu/media/son_release_2004.htm
Fannie Mae www.fanniemae.com *Understanding America's Homeownership Gaps,* 2003 Fannie Mae National Housing Survey, www.fanniemae.com/commentary/ *From Homeland to a Home: Immigrants and Homeownership in Urban America.* Demetrios Papademetriou and Brian Ray, March 2004, www.fanniemae.com/global/pdf/media/survey/survey2003.pdf *Reaching the Immigrant Market and Creating Homeownership Opportunities for New Americans: A Strategic Business Planning Workbook,* Andy Schoenholtz, Kristin Stanton, and Natasha Shulman, Fannie Mae Foundation and Institute for the Study of International Migration, Georgetown University, 2003, www.georgetown.edu/sfs/programs/isim/
National Association of Hispanic Real Estate Professionals www.nahrep.org *Real Voices,* the Quarterly Magazine of National Association of Hispanic Real Estate Professionals, www.nahrep.org/RealVoices/FrontPage.aspx
The Tomás Rivera Policy Institute www.trpi.org
Pepperdine University, Davenport Institute http://publicpolicy.pepperdine.edu/davenportinstitute/

learning to capture the good opportunities presented by first-time Latino home buyers will lead to even more opportunities as brand-loyal Latino home owners move up.

Endnotes

1. Lee, Jongho, Louis Tornatzky, and Celina Torres. *El Sueño de su Casa: The Homeownership Potential of Mexican-Heritage Families.* Los Angeles, CA: The Tomás Rivera Policy Institute, May 2004, p. v.

2. Lopez-Aqueres, Waldo, Joelle Skaga, and Tadeusz Kugler. *Housing California's Latino Population in the 21st Century.* Los Angeles, CA: The Tomás Rivera Policy Institute, December 2002, p. 31.

3. *Hispanics, A People in Motion.* In *Trends 2005.* Washington, DC: Pew Hispanic Center. January 2005, p. 3–4.

4. Drew, Rachel Bogardus. *New Americans, New Homeowners: The Role and Relevance of Foreign-Born First-Time Home Buyers in the U.S. Housing Market.* Cambridge, MA: The Joint Center for Housing Studies of Harvard University, August 2002.

5. Paral, Rob, and Associates. *The Potential for New Latino Homeownership Among Undocumented Latino Immigrants.* Washington, DC: National Association of Hispanic Real Estate Professionals. http://216.178.164.52/nahrep //////////includes/NAHREP_Study.pdf.

6. Lee, Jongho, Louis Tornatzky, and Celina Torres. *El Sueño de su Casa: The Homeownership Potential of Mexican-Heritage Families.* Los Angeles, CA: The Tomás Rivera Policy Institute, May 2004.

7. Drew, Rachel Bogardus. *New Americans, New Homeowners: The Role and Relevance of Foreign-Born First-Time Home Buyers in the U.S. Housing Market.* Cambridge, MA: The Joint Center for Housing Studies of Harvard University, August 2002, Fig. 7.

8. Caulfield, John. "Barriers to Entry." *Builder* 27(14):102, 2004.

9. Kotkin, Joel, Thomas Tseng, and Erika Ozuna. *Rewarding Ambition: Latinos, Housing and the Future of California.* Malibu, CA: Pepperdine University, Davenport Institute, September 2002, publicpolicy.pepperdine.edu/davenport institute/reports/rewarding/rewarding.html

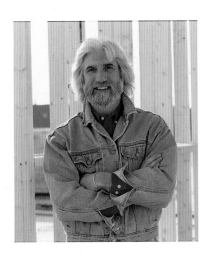

Rick Schwolsky, a former home builder and NAHB member, is an editor-in-chief at Hanley Wood Magazines and edits both *El Nuevo Constructor* and *Tools of the Trade* magazines. *El Nuevo Constructor* is the industry's only Spanish-language magazine and the official magazine of the United States Hispanic Contractors Association.

Source: Daryle Gibbs, Pier 1 Imports.

CHAPTER 3

Capturing the Latino Spirit in Interior Design

Victoria Sanchez

The influence of Latin America on the housing industry extends well beyond patios and tiles. The texture, tone, and spirit of a Latino home are often dictated by the art and the traditions of a family's homeland or by a lifestyle statement the family wants to express through furnishings and accessories.

What we know as "Spanish colonial" will typically offer many features that can trace their inspirations and styling to Spain, Mexico, Central and South America, and the Caribbean. Everyone, from traditional home builders in the Southwest to trendy designers on the East Coast to Midwestern architects, whose goal is to reach the new influx of Latinos seeks to capture the Latino aesthetic.

Sometimes a designer is lucky enough to be able to incorporate a family heirloom into a room that speaks volumes about the family's culture and lifestyle. Perhaps it is an old trunk from colonial Peru, a collection of hand-carved santos (wooden statues of Catholic saints) from Puerto Rico, oversized terra cotta pottery from Mexico (see facing page), or multicolored curtain fabric from a Guatemalan market. Latino families in my experience are sentimental about their furnishings.

The Roots of Latino Style

The Latino spirit has been present in the United States since the arrival of the first Spanish Europeans. The Latino influence on inte-

Figure 3.1 Shuttered balconies in Old San Juan, Puerto Rico.

Source: Mónica Pérez Nevárez.

riors can be traced back to early 15th century Spanish explorers. They brought to the New World design aspects that were immediately incorporated into churches, government buildings, schools, and new residences.

For example, the Alhambra in Granada, Spain, has had far-reaching influence in the interior aesthetics of Latino homes. Constructed over a span of centuries, the Alhambra is full of colorful hand-painted tiles. Many of the same intricate designs can be found in Mexico and other areas of Latin America. The carved wood ceilings and shuttered balconies in the Caribbean also evoke the Moorish architectural elements seen all over Andalusia (Figure 3.1).

Ceramics

After the Spanish conquest of Mexico in 1821, native Mexicans were trained in the art of making ceramics. Mexico soon became known worldwide for their *cerámica,* which can be seen all through the interior and exterior of Latin American houses.

The Talavera pottery seen all over Latin America is also a Spanish import. A type of majolica earthenware with a white background and multicolored, intricate drawings, it gets its name from Talavera de la Reina, Spain, where the technique originated. Spanish monks brought with them craftsmen to teach the indigenous people of Puebla, who already were accomplished potters, how to use the potter's wheel or tin-glaze the pottery. There are Talavera pots, plates (Figure 3.2), jars, and religious figures as well as "azulejos," or tiles.

Saltillo tiles are also very popular in Latin America. They are named after the Saltillo region in Northern Mexico, which has large deposits of natural clay used to make the tiles. They are handmade and come in various sizes and textures. Although inexpensive to buy, the installation can be time consuming and costly because they need to be sealed and later glazed. Glazed ceramic tiles could be a less costly alternative to the real thing. They are often used as flooring but can also add a rustic look to backsplashes and countertops.

Southwestern Style

What is commonly known as Southwestern style originated in Arizona and New Mexico. Adobe or stucco exteriors, covered porches, and exposed-beam ceilings called "vigas" reflect the influence of the local Native American Tribes, the Navajo, Hopi, Zuni, and Mimbre. Interiors tend to have rounded contours, and rooms are constructed with many arches and curved entryways. The use of desert colors like tan, brown, and orange is typical of the Santa Fe style, as it is also known, with Indian pottery, area rugs in bright geometric patterns, and colorful folk sculpture adding character to the rustic look.

Latino Art

Artwork can reflect the home owner's family roots and can be used to enliven a neutral palette. Religious iconography is often seen in many South American homes. Some examples are hanging Day of the Dead skeleton masks or intricately sewn molas that use several layers of colored fabrics. The Kuna women of Panamá are known for creating colorful hand-sewn mola blouses. Because molas are sewn in panels depicting animal and other figures, some designers recommend framing a panel for display.

Geographical Influences

In serving Latino clients, it is important to demonstrate that you respect and understand their desire to reflect the aesthetics of their culture in a home setting. Not all Latinos are alike. There are design differences between the Caribbean and Central and South America.

In the Caribbean, where the weather is hot and humid, homes typically are built high above the ground to make the most of the island breezes. There is usually a terrace that wraps around the house and flows into the living area and bedrooms, which provides the feeling of living both indoors and outdoors. Wicker and rattan are still very

Figure 3.2 Three examples of hand-painted Talavera pottery.

Source: Talavera Emporium.

Figure 3.3 Caribean-inspired furniture by Oscar de la Renta, Punta Cana collection.

Source: Century Furniture.

popular (Figure 3.3), and you see more tropical themes and palm tree motifs in the architectural details and decorative touches (Figure 3.4).

Darker, heavier design elements are more typical of the colder climates in Central and South America. Stone is widely used inside the homes. Leather furnishings and colorful striped fabrics that reflect the country's Indian roots are also common in the region.

Faux Latino Design

Frequently, consumers don't know what elements contribute to the interior of a Latino home. Limited travel to Latin America or lack of exposure to the culture's art and traditions might be at the heart of what has caused some stereotyped designs to emerge. Also, many people, including designers, have simply never been in the home of a Latino family.

The décor at Mexican eateries is sometimes mistaken for Latino interior design, but restaurants do not represent how a Mexican family might decorate their home. Although vivid yellow, green, and pink paint might find their way into some interiors, serapes (Mexican blankets or shawls) do not really hang on the walls of most Mexican homes.

The enormous purple velvet sombreros with gold trim are cheap imitations of the real thing and are usually found only in restaurants and auto shops, not residences. The cheaply fabricated souvenir merchandise that is so commonly offered at roadside stands along the Mexican border is not how Latinos decorate their homes. These items are meant as souvenirs, not lifestyle statements.

The presentation of faux design products that we see portrayed in movies, television programs, magazine photos, and pulp fiction is misleading. Sometimes the portrayal of a Latino home in a movie will show common stereotypes that home builders and designers might be tempted to emulate.

Quality Matters

Most families live on a budget. With this in mind, home builders and designers should always choose quality over quantity. A design scheme can be more successfully executed using fewer high-quality pieces of furniture.

In choosing quality items, the overall effect of a cultural statement remains intact. Use cheap products, and the point is missed. With the help of knowledgeable furniture manufacturers and interior designers, maintaining high standards of taste and integrity will become more apparent in the future.

Spending large sums of money is not the goal. A functional, inspirational interior does not necessarily have to be expensive. Here are some tips for working within a budget.

Figure 3.4 Tropical-themed dining area by Oscar de la Renta, Punta Cana collection.

Source: Century Furniture.

Figure 3.5 Ornate bar on a stand, inspired by the lifestyle of Latin media notable Christine Saralegui.

Source: Casa Cristina Collection by Pulaski Furniture Corporation.

- Choose lively paint colors.
- Elaborate faux finish techniques that mimic stucco.
- Incorporate inherited cherished furniture or accessories (Figure 3.5).
- Consult a designer's fresh pair of eyes and hands to help regroup furniture and collections.
- Add a few quality pieces to serve as focal points.

Builders can also work within the same principle of quality over quantity. A house can offer a few well thought out architectural features to enhance a space. The flavor of the Latino spirit will shine with

- arched openings
- stucco exteriors
- tiled roofs

The concept of less is more really applies here. It can keep a home from being cheapened and instead offer a wonderful reflection of a Latino spirit.

Kitchen Area

So many of my childhood memories come from my abuela's (grandmother) little kitchen. It was a modern American kitchen with the latest appliances, shiny pots, and sparkling china—anyone would have thought so. But to me, it was more than that: It was the smell of pinto beans cooking, with sopapillas in the oven and homemade beef jerky and roasted green chilies on her wooden cutting board.

Often a meal is an excuse for an impromptu party. Among most Latino families, the kitchen is the center of activity. Traditional recipes cause many Latinos to prefer gas over electricity for their cooking.

Colorful dinnerware often reflects traditional designs from a specific Latin American country or even the client's hometown. Simple wooden utensils from Latin American markets are also a way of incorporating cultural tradition in everyday surroundings.

Dining Room

Other things at abuela's house were different, too. For example, she had an amazing set of dining room furniture from Nicaragua—solid mahogany with hand-tooled leather chairs. I had never seen furniture like this at my friends' houses.

She had gathered all sorts of decorative items from her years of travel in Latin America. Every item represented a little taste of each country, whether it was an oil painting of a Costa Rican lake, a cookbook from Honduras, or hand-woven linens from various countries.

Figure 3.6 Stone-top four-poster bed reflects Cristina Saralegui's sense of family and tradition.

Source: Casa Cristina Collection by Pulaski Furniture Corporation.

I was particularly impressed with her humble accessories. They weren't massive pieces like those sold in many furniture stores. Wrought iron can be used to make beautiful light fixtures or hardware for doors and hinges, and it can also make a dramatic table base.

Bedrooms

The Latino spirit can be brought into the bedroom by mixing brightly colored patterned fabrics with neutral furnishings. Striped cushions, blankets, and area rugs can soften the heaviness of Spanish-style wooden dressers and carved armoires. Four-poster beds (Figure 3.6) and crisp, white cotton sheets trimmed with lace (Figure 3.7) also bring back the look of colonial Spain.

Bathrooms

Mosaic tile or honed stone look terrific on bathroom floors and walls as well as on top of vanities. Terra cotta or Talavera tiles can also be used to add a distinctive Spanish flavor. Mirrors framed in intricately punched tin sheets can complement the look. Personal touches can be added; for instance, in her bathroom, my abuela had a small mahogany chest with a tray that stored the antique masonry jars she collected.

Patios

Patios and courtyards also evoke a great Latino feeling. In films like "Zorro," you see the Spanish-style courtyard with bougainvillea trees

Figure 3.7 Bed by Oscar de la Renta, Punta Cana collection.

Source: Century Furniture.

growing tall over wrought-iron windows and gates and glimpses of hand-painted cerámica surrounding the stone fountain in the center. Wrought-iron chairs and tables with tiled tops are popular outdoor pieces in Spanish-speaking countries, great for fiestas and family gatherings (Figure 3.8).

Going Mainstream

Latinos, the nation's largest minority group of home buyers, are likely to spend $7 billion on furniture over the next six years, according to a survey conducted by Nielsen Media Research.

Furniture manufacturers are offering furniture that is culturally sensitive because it makes economic sense, turning to designers like Oscar de la Renta and celebrities like Cuban-born talk-show host Cristina Saralegui to meet the growing demand.

Figure 3.8 Indoor-outdoor iron furniture incorporating painted tiles.

Source: Daryle Gibbs, Pier 1 Imports.

Pulaski furniture tapped into the Latino growth potential, by launching the "Casa Cristina" collection in spring of 2005. The collection includes everything from hand-carved wooden dining room tables and chairs to colorful tablecloths and wrought-iron lamps. For inspiration, Pulaski's design team used Cristina's Miami-Mediterranean style home as a guide. For the Casa Cristina Euro-Mediterranean line, designers drew from a variety of influences, starting with her existing furniture and art collection to a selection of textures and design elements that are found throughout Latin America and the Caribbean.

They believe that Cristina will connect with these new home owners. Her furniture tags are printed in both English and Spanish in an effort to educate Latino consumers about their purchases. As additional furniture manufacturers become sensitive to this consumer group, more furniture lines will be designed with a Latino spirit.

Conclusion

The floor plan of a home can be fine-tuned to enhance the social lifestyle of the family and to reflect the family's roots. Home builders, architects, interior designers, and the furnishing industry have the power to educate the public and to maintain high standards of taste and protocol.

Victoria Sanchez has been an interior designer for more than 22 years. Her business is located in Alexandria, Virginia.

CHAPTER 4

The New Latino Home: Single Family

Jorge Velasco

Despite what some builders, think there is no need to develop the quintessential "Latino house." In choosing housing to buy, Latinos must consider the same factors as anyone:

- the size of their household
- their stage of life: small children versus an empty nest
- the desired location: suburban versus city living, proximity to workplace
- whether the home is also place of business
- what the household can afford

Although each of these factors is very important in determining where people want to live, ultimately, purchase price is the driving factor behind the home the family purchases. All other factors are negotiable.

However, there are cultural differences that are important in how the spaces in a single-family home are utilized and common cultural elements that define common Latino preferences in the style and design of houses. Specific rooms or areas in this type of house can be adapted to better fit the Latino lifestyle. I will identify design elements that Latinos tend to focus on when shopping for a house to buy and share the specific preferences Latino families have in the use of interior and exterior materials, colors, and other elements of a single-family house.

Most of my knowledge about Latino buying preferences was acquired while selling more than 2,000 houses to this market. Although working for the Latino market may seem daunting for someone just starting to sell to this group, there are patterns of behavior that determine how Latinos make decisions about buying houses or financing them. And there are ways in which home builders who wish to serve the Latino community might increase their success by appealing to Latino heritage, culture, lifestyle, and values.

Roots of Latino Preferences

First Generation

First-generation Latinos show a preference for houses that remind them of their native land. Generally, Latin American homes stress the importance of the dining room and living room, where family interaction is at its highest. Another aspect is the porch, traditionally the area where families socialize and receive visitors. In smaller cities, people spend time on their porches waiting to see their neighbors, then greet them or invite them to visit. The back yard is also vital. Many first-generation immigrants have a past linked to the agricultural industry. The back yard offers the freedom and space to plant flowers, grow vegetables, and work the lawn. When first-generation Latinos arrived in the United States, they may have moved in with two, three, or even four families into tight quarters. So in many cases, any configuration of home will do as long as it provides more space than their previous situation.

Second Generation

This group has a strong sense of heritage passed down from their immigrant parents. They like ample open spaces for the dining, living, and family rooms. They use porches less but still place a high value in socializing with neighbors and tend to spend more time at the grill in the back of the house. For this reason, a backyard where they can barbecue and socialize with neighbors and friends is important.

Third Generation

This generation carries significant heritage values from their parents, grandparents, and other ancestors. However, in terms of housing, they are less focused on porches and back yards. For them, functional spaces are critical. They value more space at an attractive price and are willing to sacrifice some of the "cultural" elements of the house, namely the porch, for more space in the master bedroom or a small extra room that could be used as an office.

Location

Location is not always an option necessarily. Latinos preferably will live close to where they work and in small cities that resemble the towns they relocated from in their native countries. However, there are certain cities, like Los Angeles, Atlanta, Chicago, Houston, and Miami, in which it is difficult for Latinos to live close to the workplace.

Large Versus Small Cities

Because of high urban housing costs, Latinos have been moving to the suburbs where they spend significant amounts of time commuting to and from work. When commuting time is less than 40 minutes in large cities or less than 25 minutes in medium-sized cities, there is a preference to live in smaller cities. Latinos associate a higher quality of life with living in these smaller cities. According to their mindset, safety in smaller cities is higher, level of interaction with neighbors and friends is stronger, and whole Latino communities are more welcoming of new members.

Suburbs

Even though we can assert that living in suburbs is preferable to living in large cities, housing price trends greatly influence this decision. Twenty years ago, when housing prices were lower in the suburbs, we saw a significant trend toward living in suburbia. Suburbia provided the best of both worlds: easy access to the city with a quieter "small town" life in welcoming surroundings. However, suburban home values have increased significantly as the suburbs became more populated and as demand for new housing has greatly exceeded the supply of new communities.

Inner Cities

In inner cities, new communities are developing to provide affordable housing to a growing blue collar workforce. In many areas across the country, this is comprised of Latinos. There have also been inner-city developments of higher-end residential products for white collar workers who conduct their business activities nearby. Generally, inner-city projects in large cities take the form of multifamily projects. However, there is a growing trend in large cities like Houston toward building single-family housing in high-density areas.

Source: © Corbis.

Single-Family Home Design

What do Latinos look for when shopping for a house? It depends. When you have not been a home owner, you do not necessarily focus on functionality. Instead, your goal is usually to maximize space. Once you have owned a home, you bring your experience into the process and spend time looking for a layout that appeals to your stage of life, family size, and budget. You consider more sophisticated issues like porches, back yards, barbecue pits/grills, and other peripheries. Here are the most relevant differentiators for Latinos when they are considering purchasing a single-family home.

Living Space

Almost half of Latino households have more than four members. This is significant. It implies that Latino families have at least two children on average. These buyers want to maximize space.

With the median age close to 26 years, these buyers are generally younger and are starting or have growing families with small children. Thus, the family may live in the house for some time, perhaps the next 10–12 years. For a majority, family size will continue to increase, which means that Latinos generally will be better served by houses of at least three bedrooms but preferably four. They want more bedrooms as opposed to larger bedrooms. They may have to convert garages to accommodate additional children, in-laws, or other family members. If the space is available, they will find a way to make it function to suit their needs.

House Layout

In terms of floor plans, Latinos would be attracted to designs that distribute the common areas in ways that facilitate daily interaction between parents and children, the family as a whole, and friends. Latinos would have a preference for two-story models where the social interactions of family with friends are independent from the privacy of bedrooms (Figure 4.1). Also, these models would provide larger living areas and provide for larger back yards as they are built in less overall square footage.

A higher number of rooms is always preferred by Latinos when shopping for a home. The emphasis on intimate or private spaces is not as high as with other ethnic groups. The preference for larger areas applies mostly to the first floor, where dining room and kitchen are the preferred spaces for this group. Why?

In Latino cultures, much social interaction revolves around food. Emphasis is given to the preparation of meals, so kitchen layout is important. Generally, preference will be given to kitchens that can accommodate more people so that several family members can participate simultaneously in meal preparation. Families also spend time together in the dining room (Figure 4.2). Latino families will gather for at least one meal each day, but frequently two, breakfast and dinner.

The family room is less important for Latinos than the kitchen and dining room. Families spend time together mostly in kitchens and dining rooms. Family rooms are used for watching TV or as a children's playroom. The room should provide a clear line of sight for parents working in the adjacent kitchen. Some house models have eliminated family rooms in favor of larger kitchens and dining rooms.

Flex-Space: The Garage

In Latino households, it is common that garages don't serve their intended purpose. For the family, the garage is a valuable space that can be used to increase the living area of the house. Latino home buyers try to maximize their amount of living area when buying, but budgetary considerations can be restrictive. One of the easiest and most cost-efficient alternatives for providing an additional 400–600 sq. ft. area is to remodel the garage area as living area (Figure 4.3). It can then accommodate in-laws or other extended family members who are adopted into the household. It can also

Figure 4.1 Two-story affordable house.

Source: Author.

Figure 4.2 Eat-in kitchen that allows a large family dining table.

Source: Author.

Figure 4.3 House with garage conversion.

Source: Author.

be used by older children who crave privacy or transformed into a playroom. These extra square feet prove especially valuable for first-time home owners.

Some builders have successfully prepared the garage to be used as a special functions room. Their house models consider the garage as a separate entity from the house. One design for this is to locate overhead doors at both the front and rear of the garage. With these two openings, the garage can be used as a special functions or party room. This configuration also creates a "corridor" that connects the front of the house with the back yard bypassing the inside of the house. For families who barbecue in the front yard, this arrangement is convenient.

Latinos are an entrepreneurial group and often conduct business from home. It is not uncommon to see at least one neighbor in a subdivision of affordable housing who has an auto repair shop based at home in the garage. The double-door garage can be a good configuration allowing for work space while providing enough privacy and noise insulation. Other service-oriented businesses, such as baking, catering, tutoring, or a beauty salon, can also benefit from having an independent space adjacent to the home that does not invade the privacy of the home.

The Yard

Latinos look for yards, especially areas behind the house, in which their children can safely play. Yards are also a focus for social activities for Latinos. The preferred location of outdoor social spaces varies according to subgroups. Although I cannot quote research statistics on this, I have informally witnessed the trends that home buyers of Puerto Rican and Dominican heritage prefer to socialize in front yards, whereas those from Mexico and Central America seem to prefer back yards. Whatever the case, architects and designers should consider the importance of incorporating areas in which to barbecue and socialize in yards (Figure 4.4).

Inside the Latino Home

Along with the garage, it will pay to carefully consider the design and details of the most important rooms in the house, the kitchen and playroom. Many builders and architects wishing to cater to Latinos have focused on arches, niches, and cathedral ceilings with positive results, and a combination of these features is especially appealing to this market.

Builders in the South Texas Valley have used this Latino preference for arches by emphasizing homes with arches in their marketing campaigns. Arches create a semiclosed space without making the house appear smaller. This element helps in the transition from the living room to the dining room or from the kitchen to the dining room (Figure 4.5). Cathedral ceilings also create the perception of large spaces in smaller rooms. Niches in walls in the family room, living room, and master bedroom provide additional integrated spaces for decorative purposes (Figure 4.6).

The Kitchen

The kitchen is where functionality meets ambiance. This room stands at the center of whether a house

Figure 4.4 Front yard as a focal point for socializing.

Source: Author.

Figure 4.5 Arches provide sight lines between rooms.

Source: Author.

Figure 4.6 Decorative wall niche.

Source: Author.

Figure 4.7 An open, well-lit kitchen.

Source: Author.

makes the final cut in the minds of Latino customers. Two critical elements are involved: the visual and the practical.

The kitchen is where mom or dad will be cooking meals. It is where the family will prepare not only the daily foods but the banquets reserved for special occasions. It will also be the place where children will interact with their parents before sharing meals. It needs to be visually attractive and inviting, with warm and tasteful colors on the walls and sufficient natural light (Figure 4.7).

In terms of the practical, a cable TV hookup is a great differentiator for Latino families. A telephone outlet and a couple of extra electrical outlets for the TV and radio are as important as space for the dishwasher and stove. Some families, especially first-generation Latinos, want to cook using natural gas, although they may be amenable to cooking with electricity.

The sink is another important practical consideration. Even though using a dishwasher is a must nowadays, the cleansing of some hardware used in food preparation must be done by hand. In such instances, it is preferable to have a double sink with bowls of equal sizes rather than a double-bowl sink where one bowl is much larger than the other.

Finally, when the quality of the cabinets satisfies an adequate benchmark, most people prefer to have as much storage space as possible. With so much home cooking going on in the Latino family, dozens of different utensils, pots, and pans are needed. Some dishes require their own specialized cookware, which in turn requires more storage space. Kitchens that offer a good number of cabinets with plenty of storage space will be ranked high by Latino customers.

Children's Playroom

There is a growing need, especially among the first-time Latino home buyers, for a dedicated area inside the home to serve as a children's play area. First-generation Latinos, even if they grew up in a very small house, always had a specific room where the children played. Some builders have simply renamed the family room the "playroom" without changing the design. Others have been more audacious, offering family rooms on the second floor instead of at the back of the house. In terms of preferences, some Latino families want the playroom on the first floor near the kitchen and under the watchful eyes of adults. Other families prefer the playroom on the second floor, which enables adults to entertain friends on the first floor without disruption.

Outside the Latino Home

Latinos will approach the outside of a prospective home by focusing on two aspects: the materials used in construction and how they wish to use the back yard, porch, and patio areas. Outside areas that are viewed as conducive to socializing are essential elements when building and selling homes that are highly desirable to Latinos.

Figure 4.8 The brick house—a symbol of strength and durability.

Source: Author.

Exterior Surface

For many Latinos, especially first-generation immigrants whose ties to their home countries are strong, a brick home is a symbol of strength and durability (Figure 4.8). Often, they remember the slow and much anticipated construction of their parents' home, witnessing the construction of each wall, which was most likely built using brick or a concrete substance.

In the U.S., builders who offer only brick have an advantage over those who provide a combination of brick and other materials. A combination of materials is perceived by Latinos as inferior and less durable. Even though offering all-brick walls will cost more, the cultural identification with the materials is critical to the success of selling the product.

Grill Pit

Among the most critical outside features are cooking areas. Grill pits use a small amount of space while promoting high social activity (Figure 4.9). The cost can be recovered through pricing. A large builder in the South Texas Valley discovered that TV and other media ads that highlighted the social interactions developed during barbecues were highly effective at capturing interest in the house and differentiating it from competitors. Therefore, builders that incorporate this

Figure 4.9 Builder's grill pit offering.

Source: Author.

Figure 4.10 A classic, inviting front porch.

Source: James Rojas.

element into the design of new houses will cater to the Latino market segment.

Porches

The front porch is important to Latinos, most of all to first-generation families. It is the place where our grandfathers and grandmothers used to entertain their guests. It was also the place where stories were told and read from a swinging chair and where parents courted and later spent time with their infant children. The porch is as nostalgic for Latinos as it is for others (Figure 4.10).

Decorating with Colors and Materials

Fashion is an important driver of what colors, materials, hues, and so forth will be in demand or be used by a family. However, even though we cannot determine with precision that certain colors will always be preferred by Latinos (or other ethnic groups), there are some common trends that can be applied to the preferences of this cultural group. For instance, brick homes are valued among Latinos. This is especially true with first-generation Latinos, who have a firm belief that brick is the most lasting material with which to build a house. In terms of interior colors, Latinos favor white or light tan, which makes a house look bigger (Figure 4.11). For a first-time home buyer, space is a primary motivator.

Wall Color

Even though neutral beige tones throughout the whole house will not likely go out of fashion, new trends have emerged. One is to create contrasts in some rooms by painting a single wall with a different and contrasting color. This is attractive to the eye and also creates several contrasting spaces within the same home. Another trend moving toward brighter colors in bedrooms is underway. Most of the time, builders stay away from these decisions and provide the standard product to customers. In my experience, Latino customers will do the paint job themselves or hire a professional painter or interior decorator to assist with this task. Although most builders do not offer custom interior painting as an option, it is important to recognize that having painted walls is gaining in popularity.

Another trend in interior design is the use of a variety of wall finishes in addition to conventional painting. These designs can use contrasting colors and different finishing techniques that improve the appearance of the interior space as well as the house profile. Even though most builders do not offer such a high degree of customization due to lack of economic feasibility in affordable and middle market housing, this option represents a good alternative marketing differentiator. It also becomes a lot more costly to perform these wall treatments once the family has moved into the house.

Figure 4.11 Larger room feeling provided by beige wall color.

Source: Author.

Exterior Color

Among Latinos, white, beige, and neutral house colors are still preferred. When purchasing all-brick homes, Latinos demonstrate a preference for the red or dark red-brown brick varieties; however, I have noticed a recent growing acceptance of lighter brick colors such as beige (Figure 4.12). When considering external colors and materials, remember to note any restrictions made by some developers to assure that the community will present a pleasant and harmonious look.

Floor Covering

The decision of whether to use wood, ceramic tile, or carpet on floors is a matter of preference. From a cultural standpoint, wood is preferred over ceramic or carpet flooring. The reason for this is that the customer perceives this material to be stronger and more damage resistant than ceramic or carpet. Even though Latino heritage may have an impact on the decision, people will generally choose carpet in all rooms and common areas when they have younger children. The "carpet factor" provides a sense of higher security for them that outweigh the inconvenience of the added effort in keeping carpet clean and dust free. For

Figure 4.12 Increasingly popular lighter brick.

Source: Author.

other families, ceramic floors make more sense because they cost less to maintain and take less time to keep clean.

Conclusion

There are cultural differences between Latinos and other ethnic groups that help shape behavior, tastes, and goals. Yet shopping for a house is, for the most part, just as challenging and exciting for Latino families as for anyone. Learning about Latino culture and social patterns will help home builders serve the needs of this emerging market more efficiently.

Jorge Velasco is president and CEO of Qualitas Homes International based in McAllen, Texas. A native of Mexico, he brings over 15 years of experience in understanding and catering to the Latino market in different industries. He is involved in the building and financing of home and business projects across the Rio Grande Valley and in Dallas, Houston, and San Antonio.

Source: Christine B. Charlip.

CHAPTER 5

The New Latino Home: Multifamily

Hipolito Roldan

Multifamily housing in America has evolved from focusing on the growing need for economically efficient housing that is accessible to public transportation and near jobs to something that now is aimed at meeting the budget constraints of young families and individuals.

Multifamily housing has provided multitudes of immigrant generations with a "home base" from which to find work, educate their children, establish cultural and social relationships, and generally grow roots in America. For many Latinos, multifamily housing in the United States has become the urban village, farming community, or small town from which they emigrated. This access to affordable multifamily housing prepares the family or their children for the next economic stage in America—homeownership.

Latinos' need for working-class multifamily housing will grow exponentially over the next two decades. During this period, Latino households in the U.S. will double, with annual purchasing power growing to over $1 trillion. Community resistance to dense multifamily developments can be mitigated with purposeful community planning, sensitivity to cultural and neighborhood context, and thoughtful exterior architecture and apartment designs. Also beneficial is the recruitment of marketing and property management consultants and staff who reflect the values, needs, and desires of Latinos. They must also work to connect the proposed development to the community successfully.

Multifamily development in Santa Ana, California. *Source:* Transportation and Land Use Collaborative of Southern California, Los Angeles.

Multifamily Housing and Immigration

History of Multifamily Housing in America

For builders to work successfully in today's Latino markets with regard to multifamily housing, it is necessary to understand the connection between this type of housing and immigrant groups.

As America entered the Industrial Revolution in the mid-1800s, cities increasingly became centers of burgeoning manufacturing enterprises. The demand for labor to run factories effected enormous population shifts from rural areas to cities. This growth of employment opportunities, especially for unskilled workers, fueled migration to American cities from numerous European countries as well.

Low wages and the need for proximity to workplaces narrowed housing options, especially for families with children. Highly concentrated and densely built, multifamily housing was the logical and economical solution to the growing demand in factory-centered city neighborhoods.[1]

In New York City, an architectural design competition produced the notorious "dumbbell" tenement, whose footprint covered 100% of its city lot and which provided residents light and air via internal shafts. This design was actually an improvement over earlier tenement designs. Life was difficult at best in this poorly designed and built housing. The few occupancy regulations that existed went unenforced, and massive overcrowding prevailed.

Jacob Riis, a social reformer, who lived on the Lower East Side of Manhattan, wrote several books that depicted the harsh daily realities of tenement living and the abuses that landlords imposed on their impoverished tenants. In his book *How the Other Half Lives*, Riis described how one apartment could house three separate families who worked and slept in different shifts, by placing their bedding on fire escapes while they were "out."[2]

By the end of the 19th century, massive and notorious tenement slums existed in New York, Chicago, Philadelphia, and Baltimore. Worsening conditions gave rise to a potent social reform movement that helped create new housing laws and building standards and eventually led to public policies that cleared slums and planned and rebuilt entire neighborhoods. In the 1860s, New York's super wealthy had traditionally chosen to live in residential brownstones and mansions clustered on the southern tip of Manhattan and the Upper East Side, fashionably close to Central Park, but a new era was approaching that slowly changed conventional attitudes.

Increasingly prominent and wealthy families left their homes and moved into elaborate custom-built apartments. By the 1920s, apartment living was all the rage. One of the last hold-outs, Mrs. E.F. Hutton was lured from her mansion by the promise that her home would be entirely recreated as a penthouse. The result was a 54-room, three-story apartment, complete with private elevator—the largest and most elaborate apartment ever built in New York City.[3]

The Latino Experience

For the past 60 years, many generations of Latino immigrants have made multifamily housing occupancy their first stop on the road to growth, financial stability, and prosperity in America. Affordable apartments that meet a myriad of family needs become the operational base from which to explore, grow, and prosper for household members. Proximity to employment centers and access to good public transportation is essential to wage earners within the family.

Good local schools are perhaps the most important criteria for selecting a place to live for families with children. Other important neighborhood amenities include good, large, and close supermarkets; places of worship; and playgrounds, parks, or even public plazas within walking distance. Ethnic and language familiarity is vital for enhancing social and psychological comfort within the community. Banks, hospitals, day care centers, and other neighborhood institutions that are bilingual send powerful messages of inclusion and make family assimilation less difficult.

Latino Demographic Imperative

Latino population in the U.S. today is estimated to be 40 million, representing approximately 14% of the total population. There are more Latinos in the U.S. today than the total population of Canada. The Latino population grew at the explosive rate of 57.9% during the 1990s, compared with the country's overall population increase of 13.2%.

Today's Latino growth rate is three times faster than the general population. Demographers agree that Latino population growth will

Table 5.1 Latino Growth and Purchasing Power Projections

	1990	1997	2000	2010	2020
Average Income (in 1997 dollars)	$34,350	$35,883	$36,561	$38,914	$41,418
Number of Households	6,222,000	8,590,000	9,864,613	15,644,791	24,811,867
Purchasing Power (in billions)	$213.7	$308.2	$360.7	$608.8	$1,027.7

Source: Hispania Capital Partners. *The U.S. Hispanic Market: An Investment Opportunity* (research report), 2001, www.hispaniapartners.com.

Table 5.2 Home Purchasing Capacity of the Average Latino Family

	1990	2000	2010	2020
Average Family Income	$34,350	$36,561	$38,914	$41,418
Income-Based Sales Price (5% down payment)	$131,800	$136,400	$141,700	$147,700
Actual Median Sales Price	$122,900	$169,000	$267,176*	$395,485*

*Projected at 4% annual increase from 2004 median sales price of $219,600.
Source: Annual New Home Sales, 1963–2004. Washington, DC: National Association of Home Builders.

Table 5.3 Mix of Multifamily* and Single-Family Housing (2000)

	Total Housing Units	Multifamily Housing Units	Percent Multifamily
New York	3,200,912	1,945,829	60.8
Miami	148,554	65,919	44.4
Los Angeles	1,337,668	586,956	43.9
Dallas	484,053	207,215	42.8
Chicago	1,152,871	456,700	39.6
Denver	251,435	94,533	37.6
Phoenix	495,793	132,292	26.7
San Antonio	433,108	98,841	22.8

*Multifamily is defined as ≥5 units.
Source: Living Cities: The National Community Development Initiative. Washington, DC: The Brookings Institution Center on Urban and Metropolitan Policy, 2003.

actually accelerate over the next 15 years, creating the most profound demand/supply housing gap America has ever experienced (Table 5.1).

Affordability

The growing gap between rapidly rising housing costs and the average family wages, exacerbated by increasing property values, "NIMBYism," and restrictive zoning, threatens the normal assimilation of future Latino growth into America's housing sector.

Although the collective purchasing power of Latinos is estimated to be over $1 trillion by 2020, the average family income will only be $41,400. Table 5.2 shows how the financial capacity for the average working-class Latino family to purchase a median priced home is dramatically eroding over time.

As future affordability of homes drops for prospective Latino purchasers, there will develop an increasing demand for quality, well-designed multifamily housing. This scenario is already manifesting itself in cities with large Latino populations (Table 5.3).

Multifamily Design and Development

Multifamily Building Types

Multifamily housing services a substantial portion of the population and also tracks the growth and financial evolution of families over time. Families with children who choose rental housing can live in a variety of development types that can service their space, financial, and other family requirements.

Town homes or multilevel structures that appear to be town homes that provide multiple units on site can usually achieve the density that establishes affordability. These types of developments are also more acceptable to communities because of their visual appeal.

Garden apartment developments provide larger family-sized apartments and are of sufficient scale to provide amenities such as swimming pools, clubhouses, health facilities, and assigned parking.

Elderly empty nesters and single individuals are usually accommodated within midrise and high-rise structures that primarily contain one- and two-bedroom apartments in four- to twenty-story dense elevator buildings. This housing type normally provides numerous amenities to meet tenant needs. Elderly-oriented projects may provide dining room meals served daily for an additional fee or regular on-site medical services. More active adults could be provided state-of-the-art health facilities, club houses for private social events, or advanced Internet wiring features.

Sensitivity to Neighborhood Context

A smart developer and his or her architectural team will naturally give thoughtful consideration to the location, building placement, and site context of a proposed development within a community. The experience of developers of multifamily housing in working-class communities has been that the traditional definition of architectural context needs to be expanded by exploring additional community dynamics that relate to the site.

Information should be gathered not only from local elected officials and regulatory agencies but from all major neighborhood institutions, including churches, hospitals, block clubs, homeowner associations, day care centers, and schools. Small private meetings with neighborhood citizens are also recommended. This sometimes excruciatingly slow democratic process serves to identify and clarify community needs, concerns, and desires regarding the site and the project and how it will function within the community up front and helps avoid being blindsided by community resistance later in the development process. Perhaps most important, this approach also creates ownership by the community and adds power and authority to the development approval process.

An excellent example of this community planning process is Bernal Gateway, a 55-unit affordable multifamily development built in San Francisco (Figure 5.1). It is located on an irregularly shaped sloping parcel in the dense multicultural neighborhood of the Mission District.

Figure 5.1 Bernal Gateway multifamily development, San Francisco.

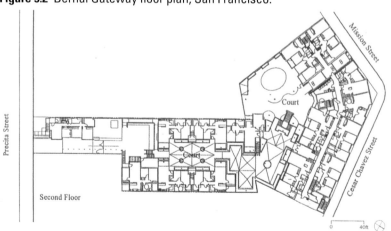

Source: Pyatok Architects, Inc.

Figure 5.2 Bernal Gateway floor plan, San Francisco.

Source: Pyatok Architects, Inc.

Pyatok Architects worked closely with neighborhood groups to shape a design that accommodated the new family housing, open play areas, and extensive community facilities while respecting the scale and character of the surrounding neighborhood. The ground floor, facing Mission and Cesar Chavez Streets, houses a child care center and the Family School, a neighborhood-based adult education center (Figure 5.2). At the interior of the site, town homes face a series of stepped courtyards linked by a private through-block passage. The development's design is the result of an extensive participating design process using building kits and involving about 75 residents of the Bernal Heights neighborhood in five design teams to explore options.[4]

Hispanic Housing Development Corporation in Chicago completed a 120-unit development in 2003 that evolved through a three-year community planning process. Gateway Centre Apartments, a newly constructed 10-story, transit-oriented apartment building for the near-elderly (55 and over) is located two blocks from Lake Michigan in the Rogers Park neighborhood of Chicago (Figure 5.3). The project, part of a larger mixed-use development on a 12-acre tax increment financing–designated site, had numerous false starts with various developers over a 10-year period. Finally in 2001, a massive community organizing effort, formidable political will, and an improving community economy helped attract a retail anchor for the commercial site of the development. Valuable community input for the design and building operations included a requirement for an articulated façade (not a rectangular box), large and numerous windows for improved community and lake views, and brick exterior walls versus painted concrete. Five layers of rents, ranging from $350 to $800 per month, were created to service a broad range of tenant incomes. The completed development proved extremely popular and leased quickly and continues to operate with virtually zero vacancy.

Figure 5.3 Gateway Centre Apartments, Rogers Park, Chicago.

Source: Hispanic Housing Development Corporation.

Latino Preferences

In my professional experience, design preferences that have been traditionally requested by Latino families in multifamily developments include

- family-sized apartments (2–4 bedrooms)
- hard-surfaced flooring, e.g., wood, tile, sheet goods, in nonbedroom areas
- three-quarter bathroom, which includes a shower, for the second bathroom instead of the traditional half bath, to relieve morning rush for workforce family members

- nine-foot ceilings, which make small rooms feel larger and make regular-sized rooms seem gracious
- satin or eggshell finish paint on walls instead of flat, which can be cleaned easier
- use of additional wall insulation between living areas and bedrooms for noise attenuation
- use of 5/8" drywall on wall surfaces because children can accidentally kick through 1/2" drywall
- wonderboard over greenboard on walls for tub surrounds
- eat-in kitchens
- gas ranges
- outdoor patios or balconies
- commercial-grade door hardware
- communal gardens
- "child-proof" windows
- socially interactive spaces, e.g., outdoor play areas, community rooms
- on-site child day care facilities

In addition, elderly residents have advocated for

- outdoor balconies (despite depression liability on developer's part)
- communal dining facilities
- visual ID intercom systems
- windows that are easily operated
- in-apartment emergency warning devices
- pull-out kitchen faucets

Exterior Design Considerations

Climate, local design trends, and neighborhood expectations have enormous influence over the exterior design of multifamily developments. In cities, the urban and historical contexts are also important considerations. Harsh or extreme climate areas have wreaked havoc with otherwise serviceable building materials.

For example, exterior insulated finished surface (EIFS) construction has not fared well in cold-weather states. Powerful community preferences can occasionally surface during the design planning process. In Chicago, where numerous downtown high-end high-rise condos are painted concrete structures, many working-class neighborhoods insist on brick facades to compliment surrounding blocks of small apartment buildings.

Fenestration and the orientation of the structure in relation to the daily and seasonal path of the sun are crucial design issues. The use of balconies, not only as an exterior amenity but also as an attractive design element on the façade of the structure, is important (Figure 5.4). The design of the simple and less expensive rectangle or box has virtually disappeared even in affordable developments. Creative use of design elements to establish visual attraction and elicit interest is now paramount in the process. Window placement, columns, building articulation, gracious building entrances, and materials and colors are now being creatively used to design unique products that make strong architectural statements that are targeted to their specific markets and are climate appropriate.

Unit Composition Evolves from Market Needs

Traditional market research studies are useful in arriving at the appropriate unit mix in multifamily developments, but in Latino markets, a deeper understanding of the culture's social and economic stage within the larger society as well as ethnocentric tendencies is also necessary.

Latino urban professionals tend to live close to, or within, the neighborhoods in which they grew up. Often, this is where their families still live. The compelling connection to family, friends, culture, food, and social entertainment dictates proximity in choice of residence, especially for renters.

Latinos continue to be the primordial extended family culture. Not only do the elderly very often become part of the growing household, but many first- and second-generation immigrant families graciously offer their homes as "temporary" quarters for newly arrived relatives or close friends emigrating from their former towns or villages.

As a teenager in Brooklyn, New York, I was dumbfounded that my parents,

Figure 5.4 The Teresa Roldan Apartments on Paseo Boricua, Chicago.

Source: Hispanic Housing Development Corporation.

Figure 5.5 Open floor plan, the Teresa Roldan Apartments, Chicago.

Source: Hispanic Housing Development Corporation.

Figure 5.6 Balcony provides natural light at the Teresa Roldan Apartments, Chicago.

Source: Hispanic Housing Development Corporation.

who emigrated at different times from the same small Puerto Rican town of Aguadilla coincidentally met in a city as large as New York. What were the odds? Surely it was the result of divine providence so that I could be born. I remained bewildered until in a moment of lucid revelation I understood that immigrants arrive with a lifeline to relatives, close friends, former neighbors, and others who have established themselves in the "new world." Very often these familial connections are the reason the risk of exploration was taken in the first place.

It is no surprise that Latino immigrants tend to live in the same apartment, building, block, and neighborhood as their family, friends, and former village neighbors. They attend the same churches, schools, social gatherings, and funerals in their new communities and move ahead with the confidence that others before them, just like them, have "made it." Therefore, it is important that property owners and managers recognize that the behaviors associated with housing Latinos—cultural graciousness, generosity, and a willingness to lend a helping hand—are important family values.

Apartment Design

The state-of-the-art in multifamily apartment design is not very different from the design of working class homes except for fundamental cost constraints. Open floor plans, including kitchens with pass-throughs or integrated breakfast counters that are connected visually and adjacent to dining areas, are preferred (Figure 5.5). Large windows providing plenty of natural light and nine-foot ceilings, which are only incrementally costlier but create the illusion of larger square footage, are also desired (Figure 5.6). Three-quarter baths with a shower are preferred over half baths, and ample closet space, along with additional storage elsewhere in the building, is a must for families with children. Wood kitchen cabinets are preferred over laminate surfaces as are washer/dryers (usually stacked) within apartments.

Specific Latino preferences in apartment design include:

- colorful carpeting, tile, and paint
- visual ID entry intercom systems

- open kitchens that permit social interaction between the cook and the guests in the living areas
- wood decks, usually located off a kitchen door

Culturally Inclusive Management

The effective operation of multifamily housing is vital to its long-term appreciation as an asset. Property management is a delicate balance between generating additional income and controlling expenses, each within the context of providing a quality residential experience to tenants.

For Latinos, the human side of this business endeavor is of great importance. Having management employees, especially those living on-site, who not only speak their language but also understand their cultural heritage and family values and who respect them as individuals makes the difference between simply renting and psychological ownership of their apartment communities. It makes the place become theirs. In Chicago, Hispanic Housing Development Corporation organizes its tenants to elect "floor leaders" to act as representatives and to function as advocates in regular meetings with management to discuss development operations and issues of concern to residents. This process opens a very direct and clear communication system between management and residents. It is also company policy at Hispanic Housing Development Corporation to recruit and train residents in the property management field and ultimately employ them in developments where they live. This adds enormous credibility and value, because they already are an integral part of the social fabric of the community.

Conclusion

Over the next decade, approximately half of the rapidly growing Latino population will continue to rent. These families, singles, and elderly will constitute a huge portion of the rental market in America and represent an enormous opportunity for developers who attempt to address their housing needs. This market sector desperately requires builders to devise mechanisms that provide affordable housing. Those in the housing industry who understand the Latino community will succeed on a grand scale.

Endnotes

1. Schmitz, Adrienne, et al. *Multifamily Housing Development Handbook*. Washington, DC: Urban Land Institute, 2000, p. 6.

2. Riis, Jacob A. *How the Other Half Lives: Studies Among the Tenements of New York*. New York: Charles Scribner's Sons, 1890, p. 162 (hypertext edition at www.yale.edu/amstud/inforev/riis/title.html.).

3. Hawes, Elizabeth. *New York, New York: How the Apartment House Transformed the Life of the City (1869–1930)*. New York: Alfred A. Knopf, 1993, p. 237.

4. Crosbie, Michael J. *Multi-Family Housing: The Art of Sharing*. Victoria, Australia: Images Publishing Group, 2003, p. 86.

Hipolito Roldan is CEO of Hispanic
Housing Development Corporation in
Chicago. He has developed over 2,800
affordable apartments and townhouses
in 35 developments for families and
elderly residents of several Hispanic
communities in Chicago.

Desirable gathering spaces are framed by buildings and uses that shape and define the public life of a community. *Source:* © Michael B. Morrissey, MRAIC.

CHAPTER 6

Creating the New American Community

Thomas Gallas and Roberto Moranchel

Latinos coming to the United States are often drawn to or supported by other Latino families who have immigrated previously. This repeating social cycle, along with the inherent cultural preference to live in places that have characteristics similar to the country of origin, has a notable influence on the living patterns and choices of Latinos in this country.

Today, the "new American community" that will attract Latinos and other immigrant groups is in essence fashioned after the traditional towns, communities, and neighborhoods that were developed by our immigrant forefathers prior to World War II. These communities, developed over time, provide a strong sense of identity and diversity that have spawned the spirit of homeownership in this country known as the American dream. These idealized places to live are characterized by offering an interwoven balance that enables individuals to have their own sense of identity and at the same time fulfills the need for people to be physically, socially, and psychologically connected to their neighbors as part of a diverse and vibrant community.

As the Latino population coming to this country pursues and attains the promise of the American dream, they will aggressively seek the best housing and communities that the United States has to offer. At the same time, they will demand living environments that satisfy their ongoing desire to contribute their strong sense of culture to their new communities. The new American community must therefore offer a vibrant fusion of diversity and social connection to satisfy this demand.

What Latinos Seek in a Neighborhood

The Latino culture brings with it an interesting contrast associated with the concurrent need for balance of the private and public lives of families. The focused needs of the family represent the foundation of Latino life. Equally critical is the degree of sociability of the Latino lifestyle both inside and outside the home. The most attractive communities to satisfy the need for balanced public and private lives are those where homes and public spaces are designed to be leveraged, each to the other, to create the interactive social fabric of community life.

Community interaction is a vital element of the Latino lifestyle. The physical plan and opportunities for connectivity of the community have a lot to do with the appeal of living areas for Latinos. Active and animated community gathering spaces encourage residents to interact and engage in safe and healthful outdoor activity. These dedicated parks, plazas, and play areas must be carefully placed so that they can be owned and controlled by the community through a "defensible space" strategy. Their placement must also consider convenience for all ages, located within walkable distances from homes, and leveraged against nearby services, shopping, transportation, and other life amenities to encourage and enable their use (Figure 6.1). Green corridors that provide linkages between these public spaces are also effective ways of enhancing the livability appeal for Latino families.

Balancing the needs of cars and pedestrians is a failure of most recent suburban developments. These single-use residential developments that represent the modern model of the American dream are typically located in areas that are cut off from services, retail, and

The "new American community" for Latino families offers a diverse range of housing choices for home buyers and renters at all income levels. *Source:* Torti Gallas and Partners.

Figure 6.1 Pedestrian-friendly mixed-use communities such as Santana Row in San Jose, California, seamlessly blend retail, commercial, and residential uses to create a vibrant street scene.

Source: Torti Gallas and Partners.

other life amenities. This automobile-dominated model requires that Latino families have access to a car. The more appealing model for Latinos locates housing near public transit or in walkable, mixed-use communities with access to employment, shopping, and other resources. Opportunities for live-work spaces within the home or garage for "cottage businesses" are also desirable. Other design measures that encourage a pedestrian-friendly community incorporate an interconnected network of streets and sidewalks and homes that are carefully placed on streets with porches and setbacks to encourage neighborly interaction.

The private zones within the home and backyard represent the areas where family activities are centered (Figure 6.2). These levels of living provide appropriate spaces for comfort, quiet enjoyment, and entertaining invited guests. As one moves from the entry foyer deeper into the home, there is a hierarchical transition from semi-private areas (i.e., living room, dining room) to private areas (i.e., kitchen, family room, bedrooms). The deeper one moves or is invited into the private areas within the home, the more closely one is intimately

Figure 6.2 The home offers both public and private zones.

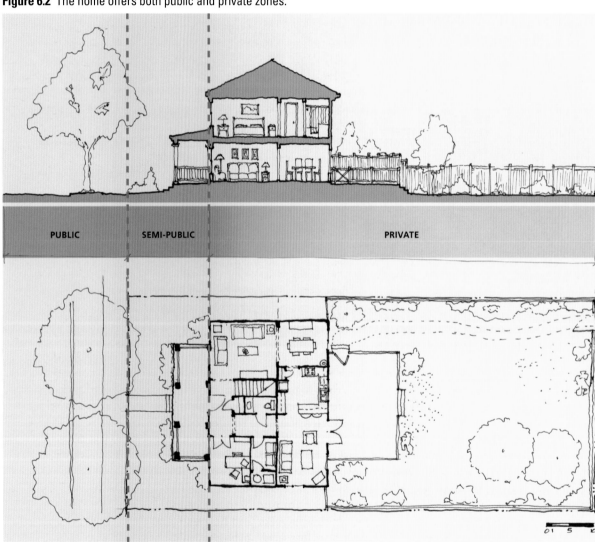

PUBLIC   SEMI-PUBLIC   PRIVATE

Source: Torti Gallas and Partners.

attached to the home or its residents. Lifestyle characteristics of Latino families establish the need for large and flexible spaces for entertaining and for large family gatherings. Large, expandable kitchens and patios are heavily used spaces for congregating. Other innovative home features include easily movable walls that enable the economical adaptation of interior spaces as the lifestyle of the family changes from empty nest to full nest to empty nest again. Private backyards are highly desirable for allowing entertaining to flow seamlessly from inside to outside the house.

Well-defined public and private zones bring order to a community by providing formal and informal guidance on the levels of physical participation for residents and visitors. The public realm is made up of the shops and civic buildings, streets, sidewalks and alleys, and public places, parks, and open spaces that are for the use of everyone in the community. In contrast, the private realm is "owned" by the family or individual, and is made up of the front yard and porch, the home, and the backyard. These relative community layers form a continuum of physical engagement and privacy that successfully connects people to their community and each other.

Community Adaptation to Region

The new American community is not a "one size fits all" solution. Although many elements of traditional towns in the U.S. are consistent throughout the country, their look and feel are different in each region. These traditional towns were heavily influenced by the people that settled there and built them, as well as by other significant factors such as climate and locally available materials.

The idea of developing communities that have Latino appeal throughout the nation is based on a concept that requires adaptation relative to the community's surroundings and context. The goal of most Latino immigrants or their descendants is to succeed in this country through assimilation into the physical fabric of their surroundings—not to bring their house with them across the border. However, the principles of community and home design, pedestrian friendliness, and mix of use must be adapted to each specific development in each location to ensure a win-win for the residents, the community, and the developer. The front porch is an excellent example of how a house design element has been adapted through regional and cultural assimilation (Figure 6.3).

Figure 6.3 The front porch as a design element shows cultural and regional assimilation.

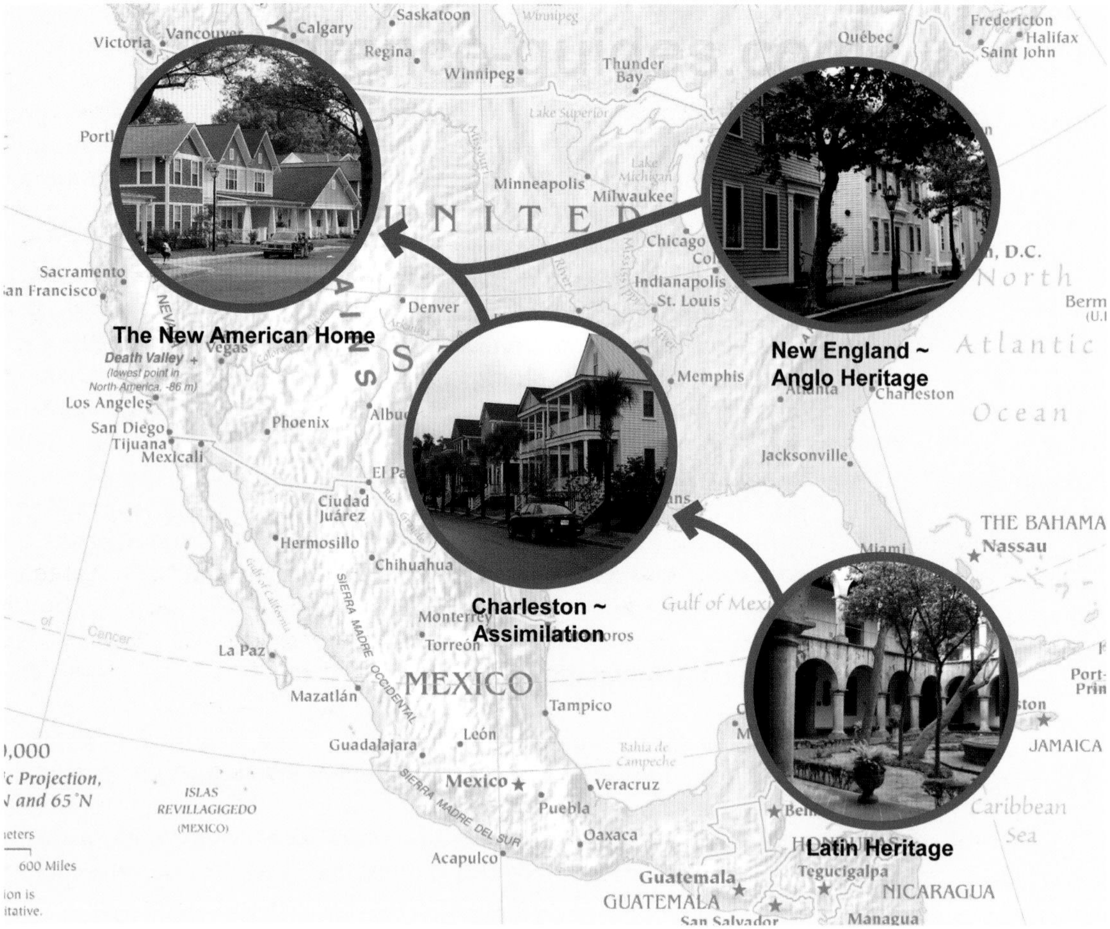

The New American Home

New England ~ Anglo Heritage

Charleston ~ Assimilation

Latin Heritage

Source: Torti Gallas and Partners.

The architectural styles, materials, and overall character of the region must be appropriate to embrace the history, tradition, culture, and environment of the new development. To be truly successful, the development must be compatible in scale, density, color, and housing form with the character and traditions of the existing housing market in each locale.

The "Multi" Effect

Communities that appeal to Latinos offer a wide variety of options and choices that support a vibrant and active lifestyle. This "multi" effect reflects the diverse range of needs and desires of the Latino community. It is recognized that there are no absolutes or perfect solutions. The premise is that not all communities can necessarily provide all of these choices and characteristics, but the more dynamic the diversity offered, the more appealing the community will be to the Latino population (Figure 6.4).

- *Multi*cultural: A community that offers appeal to a mixture of cultures and backgrounds.
- *Multi*social: A community that seamlessly integrates social activity between family, friends, and the broader neighborhood.
- *Multi*generational: A community that supports the continuum of lifestyles of the young, middle aged, and senior (including the extended family) through housing choices and community activities.
- *Multi*income: A community that offers housing choices for a range of household incomes and where the quality and character of the housing for various income levels is indistinguishable throughout the community.
- *Multi*tenure: A community that offers both homeownership and rental housing options.
- *Multi*use: A community that offers multilingual places to live, shop, work, play, entertain, learn, and worship.
- *Multi*house types: A community that offers a wide variety of housing types that supports the lifestyle needs of residents.
- *Multi*density: A community that offers an urban gradient ranging from a dense center to agrarian edge.
- *Multi*architectural styles: A community that offers a variety of architectural styles to provide residents with individuality and their own sense of pride and identity.
- *Multi*technological: A community that offers "smart home" technology for voice/data and mechanical systems.

Appropriate Scale of Development

Addressing the variety of community needs of Latinos is dependent on understanding the relative size, scale, and location of the development and its proximity to surrounding amenities. The documented human comfort level for walking is 1/4 mile, which equates to a five-minute walk for the average pedestrian. Strategically planned amenities and public spaces located within this walking distance will encourage convenient use by residents of all ages. The extent to which existing amenities are in close proximity to the new

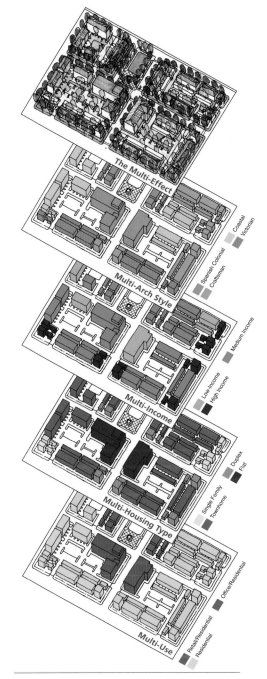

Figure 6.4 A community that exhibits the "multi" effect offers the highest appeal.

Source: Torti Gallas and Partners.

Figure 6.5 Large greenfield parcels must create their own amenities.

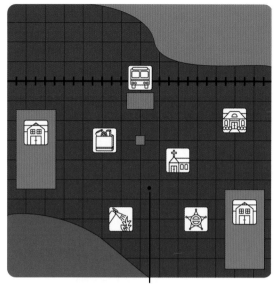

Large new development

Source: Torti Gallas and Partners.

Figure 6.6 Small infill parcels can share existing amenities.

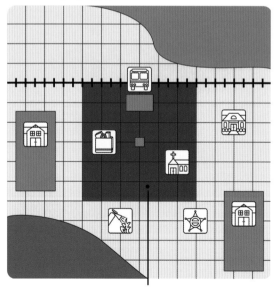

Small new development

Source: Torti Gallas and Partners.

development will have a large impact on the strategy for attracting Latino buyers. Highly desirable schools, churches, plazas, parks, shopping, or transit can add tremendous market appeal and value to a development.

The development area can be structured within an understandable community hierarchy that is measured at the home, block, and neighborhood/village levels. Depending on the size and scale of the development, the amenities must be sized and located to support the hierarchy of the community structure. Three models demonstrate the scales of development.

Large Greenfield Parcel or New Town

Because of their size and outer edge location, these developments must often create all or most of their own amenities (Figure 6.5). Unlike most current suburban developments, the developer of these large new communities must think beyond merely building the house and the road infrastructure to get you there and back, but must also create "a place" for residents to gather and interact. In essence, the value and appeal of these communities increase as the amenity package is utilized to enhance the livability factor for its future residents.

Small Infill Parcel

In contrast, these small parcels tend to be the sites that were passed over because they did not offer quick and easy development opportunities during the rush to develop the city and suburbs. Whether due to site, entitlement, environmental, or other difficulties, small parcels are available for development but inherit the existing context and surrounding amenities that are available (Figure 6.6). To the extent that these parcels are in or near valuable locations, they can leverage the stronger existing community assets into the overall value and marketability of the new community. New amenities may be added as part of the new development to augment existing elements in the surrounding area.

Refill Site

The redevelopment of a small parcel is usually because the current land value exceeds the value of its current use. Most often, this site has the opportunity to be better integrated with its surrounding amenities and infrastructure than it was in its previous use (Figure 6.7). To the extent that these parcels are in or near valuable locations, they too inherit and leverage the existing community assets into the overall value and marketability of the community.

Community Social Patterns

Many American towns and cities have been historically formed around "mononeighborhoods," where immigrants with a common culture are drawn to one another (Figure 6.8). Many cities have a "Chinatown," "Little Italy," or "Little Havana." In the early socio-economic stages of the immigrant life cycle, first-generation immigrants are typically clustered in higher-density patterns around areas where jobs, transportation, education, and services are available. As socioeconomic status matures and improves with each new generation, the living patterns have tended to dissipate from these clusters into the outer rings and suburbs. This suggests a "move up and out" mentality to achieve social assimilation.

In contrast, the new American community embodies the multi-effect, where people of mixed cultures, incomes, generations, and tenures

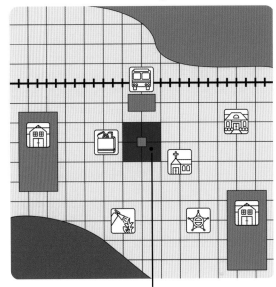

Figure 6.7 Refill sites take advantage of high land value.

Tiny new development

Source: Torti Gallas and Partners.

Figure 6.8 Historical social patterns are clusters of cultures.

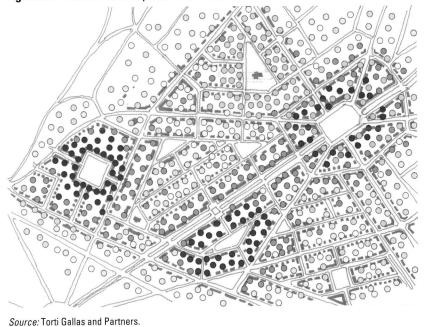

Source: Torti Gallas and Partners.

SOCIAL PATTERNS DIAGRAM KEY

First Generation

■ Culture #1
■ Culture #2
■ Culture #3

Second Generation

■ Culture #1
■ Culture #2
■ Culture #3

Future Generations

■ Culture #1
▦ Culture #2
□ Culture #3

(owner versus renter) are drawn together because of the variety of opportunities offered by these places to set down roots (Figure 6.9). A mixture of cultures will be drawn to these new communities because of their physical layout, amenities, and employment options. By offering expanded opportunities in terms of diverse house types and sizes, as the socioeconomic status of residents matures and improves with each new generation, the assimilation of Latinos and other immigrants into the new American community will become a "move up and stay" social pattern.

Affordability

To serve the first-time Latino home buyer, the reality is that a large portion of the market must be delivered at affordable prices. In practical terms, this means that developers will have to realistically assess the potential incomes of the target market and determine how to best deliver value to its potential buyers. Once the community is established and roots are planted, immigrants may find the appeal of "moving up and staying" rather than the "up and out" mentality of the past. Revenues earned from the sale of the higher-end homes

Figure 6.9 The new American community demonstrates a mixture of cultures.

SOCIAL PATTERNS DIAGRAM KEY

First Generation
- Culture #1
- Culture #2
- Culture #3

Second Generation
- Culture #1
- Culture #2
- Culture #3

Future Generations
- Culture #1
- Culture #2
- Culture #3

Source: Torti Gallas and Partners.

can contribute to the construction cost of the physical and social infrastructure of the broader mixed-income community in a fashion that supports a higher quality community overall.

Where feasible, use energy-efficient and sustainable designs, e.g., solar orientation of homes, solar-shading devices, Energy Star appliances, and low-impact development to "make running water walk," i.e., slowing storm water runoff so that most is retained on the site through natural absorption. Each of these valuable steps can improve the overall life cycle affordability of operating the home.

Conclusion

Developers and builders interested in creating serious demand from the burgeoning Latino population must recognize that in the end, Latino families are seeking not just a house—but a home. Homes—not buildings—make a community. The concept of the new American community that Latinos are seeking must integrate not just houses, but homes, into vibrant "multieverything" communities that enable them to turn their American dream into American reality.

Thomas Gallas, of Torti Gallas and Partners, is an award-winning architect based in Silver Spring, Maryland.

Roberto Moranchel, a native of Mexico, is the Senior Urban Designer for the Virginia Department of Community Planning, Housing, and Urban Development of Arlington County.

CHAPTER 7

Latino New Urbanism

Michael Anthony Mendez

In many regions of the United States, the emerging Latino demographic will change the urban landscape, and their characteristics and lifestyle choices will have a direct effect on planning and land use patterns. How and where Latinos live will shape neighborhoods, cities, and suburbs for generations to come. As the composition of residents change, housing policies and models should also change. The challenge for policymakers and the building industry is to create the right market, land use, and other regulatory climates to accommodate population growth in a more sustainable manner. This implies that policy makers and the building industry should look beyond their perceived notions of Latino characteristics and think of the desirable and beneficial outcomes of incorporating them into development projects.

New urbanism is the leading alternative model to suburban sprawl that accommodates population growth. However, advocates of this land use reform have largely overlooked new urbanism's connection to urban forms found throughout Latin America. Design elements from this region have migrated north to the United States.

Although much of the Latino population is currently engaging in a lifestyle compatible to the principles of new urbanism, builders and planners ignore the cultural preferences of Latino home buyers. Preferences by Latinos for compact neighborhoods, large public places, and a strong sense of community can provide the home building industry an opportunity to profit from the large projected housing

The transformation of an historic church into a community center and new affordable housing above market arcades are incremental changes envisioned for San Ysidro, California. *Source:* Teddy Cruz for Casa Familiar.

demand and assist states in reining suburban sprawl. States throughout the country but particularly California (where Latinos will outnumber whites by 2020), Nevada, and Arizona will need to find innovative solutions to manage the projected development boom while facing limitations on land and natural resources.

Latino Architecture and Design

Latinos are transforming homes and communities to meet their criteria of what the built environment should encompass. This synthesis generates an environment that is familiar and hospitable to Latino families.

Accordingly, we need to develop a new model that acknowledges Latino architecture and designs that maximize social interaction and uses. At the community level, this approach incorporates rich mixtures of land uses, not just within the same district or block, but also within the same building or dwelling. The integration of land uses can also facilitate the formation of small businesses and family enterprises.

The courtyard house in Latin America internalizes the synthesis needed to accommodate mixed uses and mixed-income residents within a single neighborhood. In the courtyard home, different uses are often unseen behind its walls. The patio or courtyard can be used as live/work space, which allows it to coexist in close proximity to similar buildings. The courtyard home adapts to the evolving environment in a way that the conventional suburban home placed in the center of a lot cannot do without visibly appropriating the front yard.

Housing designs in the U.S. need to follow similar form and be highly flexible and adaptable to address the unique needs of its residents. Because Latino household income is not keeping pace with inflation and home prices continue to soar in many regions of the country, housing designers should recognize that many families must earn additional income from home-based businesses or accessory dwelling units ("granny flats") or by subleasing their residential space for other uses. For instance, it is estimated that the addition of a granny flat can yield a rental income of $600–700 a month, earning home owners roughly double the cost that the unit adds to their mortgages.[1] New housing design, therefore, should facilitate home and apartment designs that include income-generating opportunities.

Additionally, architectural designs should integrate themes familiar to Latinos, such as the California mission style, Southwestern adobe, and tropical-Caribbean motifs, with courtyards or patios in the center of the home or verandas situated at the front of the residence (Figure 7.1). Incorporating these designs would be consistent with the charter developed by the Congress of the New Urbanism.[2] The charter states that urban places should be framed by architecture and landscape design that celebrate local history, climate, ecology, and building practice. Correspondingly, in regions such as the Southwest, the landscape has historically incorporated Latino motifs, and they remain popular façade options in newly built communities. Communities should also be developed to enable social interactions among residents by dedicating space for community plazas and parks.

Through the dynamics of what can be termed *Latino new urbanism*, an environment can be formed to be compatible with Latino preferences and customs. Latino new urbanism is an urban design philosophy that incorporates diverse types of land uses and housing designs within a neighborhood, promotes compactness, and accommodates unit types and site planning for extended family living arrangements and income-generating opportunities. Latino new urbanism is an alternative model that captures and promotes the environmental, social, and economic benefits of the Latino lifestyle. Hence, this new synthesis provides the home building industry with a development model that is more appealing and satisfying for Latinos and also serves the non-Latino middle class.

Figure 7.1 Casitas de las Florecitas, a first-time homeownership project in San Ysidro, California, developed by Casa Familiar, Inc.

Source: Harry Connolly and Casa Familiar, Inc. developers

Source: Poster Frost Associates.

New Urbanism and Latino Lifestyle

New urbanism is an attempt to reform the sprawling pattern of suburban growth. Through a wide-ranging approach of architectural planning and design, new urbanism seeks to reconstruct community settings normally observed in cities like Charleston, South Carolina, and Old Town Alexandria, Virginia. New urbanism favors a notion of residential development that includes small lots, short housing setbacks, alleys, front porches, and compact walkable neighborhoods with abundant public spaces and parks. Through the mix of diverse housing styles, land uses, and green space, new urbanist developments construct a place that promotes social interaction and a sense of community.

Latino families for generations have been combining traditional values with more modern ones. The present-day American Latino family is a fusion between the social and cultural heritages of North and Latin America. The combined old and new ways are continually being redefined, creating something different from either the traditional or Anglo forms of action. The fusion of Anglo and Latin cultures creates manifestations compatible not only to compact cities (in terms of high-density housing and compact commuting) but also to new urbanist communities.

The Latino lifestyle, accordingly, represents an untapped resource that can enable the development of more sustainable communities throughout the country. Latinos' cultural inclinations for social interaction and their adaptive energies have in many regions created a de facto environment that currently supports compact city and new urbanist lifestyles.

Adaptive Reuse

Such new urbanist principles are already present in many established Latino communities throughout the country. Latinos have continually used adaptive methods to transform their communities to suit their needs. This is most apparent though their adaptive reuse of homes, parks, and public spaces. The nature of Latinos' strong inclinations for close social interactions and their subsequent adaptive reuses has conceivably created a spicier Latino new urbanism.

Latino Housescapes

Examples of the adaptive reuse of homes by Latinos are found throughout the country. In East Los Angeles, for example, a distinct spatial form represents the cultural, economic, and regional solutions residents have developed to meet the Latinos' set criteria of what the built environment should encompass. The urban landscape in East Los Angeles is a fusion of several architectural and cultural styles, none of which are entirely Mexican, Spanish, or Anglo. The transformation of homes, according to urban planner James Rojas,[3] typically follows three stages:

- Minimal changes, in which the house is characterized by the use of the residents
- Minor changes, such as the addition of fences, painting, or stuccoing
- Major structural changes showing investment, such as the addition or enlargement of the front porch (including changes in architectural styles), baroque style wrought iron fences, fountains, ethnic icons, and other amenities (Figures 7.2A and 7.2B)

The adaptive reuses in East Los Angeles parallel earlier work completed by Professor of Geography Daniel Arreola, in which he examines elements of the Latino "housescape," i.e., a landscape that is comprised of a detached single-family dwelling and its immediate surroundings in urban Latino communities.[4] The Latino housescape is a complex of elements that includes the front yard up to the property enclosure. Arreola contends that the use of color on exterior facades, a practice used by the Spanish during the colonial era, can identify a Latino housescape, as can the placement of ethnic icons and other amenities in the front of the house.

Figure 7.2 Latino new urbanism transformation in southern California: before (A) and after (B).

Source: James Rojas.

The introverted American-style homes in essence have evolved into extroverted Latinized homes. Distinct from the typical middle-class suburban home, which draws itself in from the outside environment, the Latino house expands itself to all four corners of the lot, thereby allowing for a more efficient and maximized use of space than the traditional suburban home. The evolution of the homes in Latino communities, particularly in the Southwest, presumably derives from attempts to emulate the traditional Latin American courtyard-

Markets and housing edge a community garden corridor planned for San Ysidro, California. *Source:* Estudio Teddy Cruz for Casa Familiar.

style home, which is built up to the street line and designed with a patio or courtyard in the center or at the front of the house. Unlike the American-style home, the Latino home as explained by sociologist Ellen Pader's research,[5] is not designed to induce privacy but rather to maximize social interaction among household members.

Privacy as incorporated into housing design is used primarily for security purposes. The courtyard or patio style home achieves security through architectural definition rather than by acquiring a larger lot size. In the U.S., housing designs achieve security mainly by consuming more land, which inhibits the development of compact settlement patterns. Andrés Duany, a Cuban American who established the founding principles of the new urbanism movement, suggests that the courtyard-style home is a superior housing design to its U.S. counterpart because it is aesthetically pleasing and maintains densities and sociability required to facilitate compact city lifestyles. He states,

> It's also relatively economical to build (courtyard style home) because instead of having to detail multiple elevations, you can finish just one exceptionally well, the street façade, concentrating resources. Often a beautiful window and entrance door are all you need for the initial architectural expression. Second, security is established at the perimeter of the dwelling, rather than at the level of the community. Compare this with the more vulnerable North American freestanding house, which has to resort to gated access and blocked roads, for security which erodes the open network of circulation that is synonymous with urbanism . . . The patio house achieves impressive densities while maintaining outdoor privacy. With this building type, Latin American towns may well achieve the New Urbanist ideals of compact, walkable, diverse communities far more effectively than their U.S. counterparts. Here's another instance in which Latin American New Urbanism may have much to teach to us in the north. As New Urbanism moves south and stimulates design innovation, I'm sure it will generate a corresponding wave of influence washing back north in return.[6]

Duany's contention is that new urbanist design innovations in Latin America will journey north to the U.S. and influence how communities are shaped. In part, this has already materialized. In the absence of the courtyard-style home in the United States, the front yard in many Latino communities has emerged as a heavily used social space, resulting in a housescape that is defined by the property line rather than the floor plan and wall of the house. In contrast, in the American-style home, spaces for social interaction migrate inside the home toward the backyard.

Driveways and porches are also an important element in the housescape in Latino communities. In Latin America, courtyard-style homes and patios are used for social functions. Consequently, in the U.S., the driveway is used as a substitute to accommodate parties, barbecues, and other social festivities. Porches in the Latino housescape are often enlarged and expanded. The use of porches facilitates the reinforcement of the front yard as an integral spatial location for family social interaction.

Porches are modified architecturally to suit the needs and preferences of residents. For example, most porches in East Los Angeles were originally constructed in a Victorian or California Bungalow style (Figure 7.3). However, residents have transformed their

Source: James Rojas.

Figure 7.3 Adaptation of a home to include Latino elements such as porches and a balcony to facilitate social interaction.

Source: James Rojas.

wooden banister and column fixtures to Latinized versions, entailing baroque-style wrought iron railings, Spanish arches, and stuccoing. The evolution of the front porch assists in creating sociability within the home and surrounding neighborhood. Similar to the objectives of new urbanist developments, the front porch in the Latino housescape invites neighbors to gather, enhancing social interaction and a sense of place.

On the East Coast, particularly in New York City, Latino cultural inclinations for close social interaction and a sense of place are also evident but in different ways. The history and built environment of the East Coast differs significantly from that of other Latino population centers in the Southwest. The housing stock of New York City is dominated by multiple-unit structures (not houses) developed by Anglo-European settlers, and Latino immigrants were latecomers into an already-built environment. In contrast, Spanish and Mexican settlers developed the initial landscape of the Southwest. The housescapes, plazas, and other cultural identifiers of Latino landscapes cannot be applied directly to Latino neighborhoods in New York City or other tightly spaced areas.

Latino Streetscapes

Residents in New York have little control over residential façades. However, similar to the elements of the Latino housescape, the use of color and other public symbols such as religious icons can be found in the streetscape. Colors and cultural artifacts from national flags, national shields, emblems, and icons are commonly included in façades and on the awnings of businesses throughout commercial corridors.

Geographer Ines Miyares argues that immigrants make their presence known in a community through what she terms the *Latino streetscape*.[7] Businesses use signs and a variety of visual clues to identify and establish a sense of place and, more important, to attract potential ethnic customers. Miyares defines the Latino streetscape as the transformation and evolution of urban streets that typically follow three stages:

- Enclave streetscape: Landscapes dominated by a single national group. Historically the prevalent streetscape, this type is found in very few areas of the city today. Although goods and services are offered to all residents in the immediate neighborhood, they reflect principally the preferences of the dominant group.

- Multiethnic streetscape: Landscapes influenced by demographic changes among the entrepreneurs and the communities being served. In this stage, the retail landscape is fashioned to mirror the ethnic diversity of the area. The entrepreneurs who establish firms on such a street tend to be adaptive to their clientele as they expand their businesses out of the initial ethnic main street.
- Streetscape of incorporation: Landscapes where new immigrants take advantage of a site and situation to establish an economic banner street. In this process, neighborhood succession occurs and new groups typically transform landscapes as they establish businesses on ethnic main streets.

Generally, throughout the Latino streetscapes, public artwork such as murals, display pride in the community and culture (Figures 7.4 and 7.5). Themes of murals are reflective of the population and advocate pride in the transnational character of the community.

Hence, the Latino housescape and streetscape exemplify the fact that Latinos are continually adapting the built environment to suit their needs, specifically to promote social and economic interaction. The adaptive energies of Latinos are expanding homes where all space within the housing lot serves a specific purpose (particularly for social exchanges) and are used on a daily basis, similar to the goals sought in new urbanism. Such expression and adaptations afford a more efficient use of space than the conventional middle-class suburban home, and the fact that this is occurring implies that current housing development patterns are not satisfying the needs of the emerging and fast-growing Latino population.

Figure 7.4 Latino streetscapes establish a sense of place and identity.

Source: James Rojas.

Figure 7.5 Mural depicting Cesar Chavez.

Source: James Rojas.

Latinization of Parks and Public Spaces

Physical environments supporting social interaction among family members and friends are an important element of Latino culture. The appropriation of space in parks for social activities provides another example of Latinos' adaptive energies to transform the built environment to meet their physical and social needs.

There is an obvious carryover of preferences from Latin America to the U.S. for parks and plazas to serve as the core social setting of a community or city (Figure 7.6). Several bodies of work have acknowledged the importance of plazas and parks (public spaces) for Latinos. Social historian Charles Flaundrau, awed by the significance of Mexican plazas, wrote,

Figure 7.6 The commercial center of the city of Santa Ana, California, features a plaza with Mexican motifs.

Source: Transportation and Land Use Collaborative of Southern California, Los Angeles.

There are city parks and squares in other countries, but in none do they play the same intimate and important part in the national domestic life that they do in Mexico . . . The plaza is in constant use from morning until late at night . . . By eleven o'clock the whole town will, at various hours, have passed through it, strolled in it, played, sat, rested or thought in it.[8]

For Latinos, the park in the U.S. serves as their primary social space outside of the home. Similar to the evolution of the Latino housescape, the neighborhood park's supportive nature for social interaction affords a surrogate for the misplaced plaza as the nucleus of the built environment in Latin America. Consequently, Latino cultural values influencing the built environment coincide with the objectives of many new urbanist developments. New urbanism attempts to create a greater sense of community by rethinking the "public realm," especially public spaces and recreational facilities. The Congress of the New Urbanism, the leading organization for the movement, believes cities and towns should be shaped by physically defined and universally accessible public spaces and community institutions.[9]

Urban planning Professor Anastasia Loukaitou-Sideris' extensive survey of park usage among different ethnic and racial groups in metropolitan Los Angeles shows that Latinos are the most active and frequent users of parks.[10] Loukaitou-Sideris' work revealed that Latinos place a high importance on public space, which leads to a very intensive use of neighborhood parks. Furthermore, Latinos were observed in more social activities that involved large groups. Most Latinos at parks consisted of immediate and extended family members, because Latin American culture places the family at the center of both private and public spheres.

The survey results observed Latinos at parks to be more involved in social uses, including parties, picnics, and celebration of birthdays, baptisms, and communions. Their group behavior involved talking while sitting or standing, eating, breaking piñatas, playing sports, and keeping an eye on their children. Maintaining the traditional uses of parks in Latin America, young Latino couples were found on dates strolling through the park, dancing or drinking beverages under the park's gazebo (similar to the kiosko that is centrally located in plazas in Latin America), and brewing coffee in portable pots.

Consequently, park usage by Latinos is in great contrast to that of Anglos, who primarily participate in mobile solitary activities such as jogging, walking, bicycling, or dog walking. Loukaitou-Sideris concluded that Anglos valued the park more for its aesthetic qualities and natural elements than Latinos, for whom its importance is social interaction.

Latinos were also more likely than other ethnic groups to develop adaptive methods to actively appropriate the neighborhood parks to suit the activities in which they were engaged. For instance, if no soccer fields were present in the park, players normally would modify the space to their needs, bringing their own goal posts and portable goods with them. According to lawyer Robert Garcia of the Center for Law in the Public Interest, the discrimination against soccer as an "immigrant sport" resulted in fewer soccer fields compared to fields for baseball or other sports.[11]

Both park usage and soccer remain vital social elements for Latinos throughout the country. Geographer Patricia Price contends that

Source: FogStock, LLC, Index Open.

through soccer leagues, Latino immigrants in metropolitan Washington, DC, have created cultural spaces for themselves.[12] Her survey work shows thousands of individuals from El Salvador, Bolivia, Honduras, and Peru gathering on weekends at local parks for social interaction and physical activity.

In Washington, DC, due to a tight housing market and late arrival of immigrants from diverse countries, Latinos are not concentrated in specific neighborhoods and are spread sporadically across the region. This dispersed pattern of residential settlement is not conducive to the formation of ethnic enclaves. As a result, Price contends that homegrown immigrant soccer leagues in Washington developed from the need for a flexible social space.

Immigrant-run soccer leagues link immigrants with their communities of origin and create a cultural space that is familiar, entertaining, and inexpensive. They enable the establishment of multigenerational social centers that supply participants with information about employment, news from home, opportunities to enjoy cuisine from native countries, and spend time with co-ethnics. Given the limited resources and space available to recent immigrants in Washington, the soccer field has become an important social network for many Latinos. In cities all over the U.S., soccer fields may likewise serve as a vital node of immigrant social networks and place-making activities.

In areas like New York City that were not developed as plaza towns, neighborhoods are dotted with small parks and playgrounds that assume the role of the plaza in Latino communities. Additionally, where Latino neighborhoods have wide sidewalks, these may serve as social spaces outside of the home. This is primarily achieved through the placement of permanent furniture, such as benches, or temporary furniture, such as lawn chairs and card tables, that support social activities such as domino games. Microenterprises common to Latin American plazas, such as churro, tamale, and fruit drink vendors, have also materialized on these sidewalks. Emulating customs and activities in Latin American plazas, music, lively conversation, and playing children also fill these public spaces.

Correspondingly, in the few places where there is no need for a surrogate for the misplaced plaza, the plaza remains a symbol of Latino cultural identity and a focal point of the community. For example, Latinos in Las Vegas, Nevada, have created a strong connection to the plaza.[13] Unlike in other southwestern towns that have transformed their plazas into places that appeal only to tourists, in Las Vegas the plaza continues to function as a social gathering place and has evolved to accommodate chiefly community-based activities (Figure 7.7).

Similar to Latin American custom, the plaza in Las Vegas is used on a daily basis by residents. Not only are people attracted to the surrounding shops, but residents also use the open space for highly personal uses. Individuals were documented sitting on benches and conversing and walking dogs, children were playing, and young adults were looking for opportunities to socialize in the plaza. In warmer months, political groups call for action and young couples marry on the steps of the kiosko. The plaza in Las Vegas serves its traditional function as a community gathering place, and as a result, the plaza remains a significant social space where people congregate to participate in activities that express their membership within the community. In summary, whether it is a park, street, or an actual plaza, Latinos are continually transforming their built environment to suit their sociocultural needs.

Latino Assimilation

In the Latino culture and lifestyle, housing, public spaces, and parks are much more than buildings and open spaces that function as refuge from the elements or are valued for their aesthetic qualities. Parks and housing are a vital component of an individual's social and ethnic identity. As the Latino house, streetscape, and park usage demonstrates, the fusion of Anglo and Latin cultures produces manifestations compatible not only with compact cities (in terms of high-density housing and compact commuting) but also with new urbanist communities.

Figure 7.7 The Las Vegas Plaza, Nevada, is a gathering place for music as part of a community event.

Source: Jeffrey S. Smith, PhD, Department of Geography, Kansas State University, Manhattan.

Latinos' cultural preferences for social interaction and their adaptive reuses and lifestyle choices have conceivably created a de facto Latinized version of new urbanism. The persistent notion that immigrants must adopt the suburban living model that dominates U.S. culture to fully integrate into mainstream society mitigates the opportunity to utilize and build on Latinos' cultural propensity for compact and new urbanist lifestyles. Hence, the traditional path of assimilation may intensify environmental impact and housing shortages in communities across the country.

Latino Sprawl

Literature on immigrant adaptation and assimilation is based primarily on the assumption that there is a natural process by which diverse ethnic groups develop a common culture and achieve equal access to all the opportunities society offers. This process consists of slowly abandoning old cultural and behavioral patterns in favor of modern ones. Once it has begun, it is argued, this process moves inevitably and permanently toward assimilation.

Source: FogStock, LLC, Index Open.

Assimilation literature further suggests that immersion into dominant society is a voluntary, effortless action.[14] However, for many Latino immigrants in communities across the country, it is often a forced process. Cities have adopted measures that are direct disincentives to sustaining Latino lifestyle and cultural behaviors. These measures are designed to provide limited housing choices and force Latinos to abandon their compact city lifestyle behaviors and emulate the conventional model of suburban middle-class living. In essence, as the Latino community continues to grow substantially nationwide, conventional growth patterns and policies are encouraging a higher dispersion of Latinos into conventional auto-oriented, low-density suburban housing units. This movement is sometimes called *Latino sprawl*.

As a result, compact city behavior, principally mass transit usage, is not a permanent characteristic of immigrants. As recent arrivals conform and assimilate to American society, they improve their economic status and begin to commute like their native-born counterparts. From the standpoint of immigrant upward mobility, this is an ideal result, but in terms of sustaining regional transportation networks and decreasing traffic congestion and air pollution, it poses major obstacles for policymakers.

Fighting Sprawl with Planning

In the next several decades, particularly in the Southwest, newly arrived immigrants will comprise a smaller portion of the total population. Upward mobility will greatly decrease the current client base for compact cities. These changes will require policymakers and builders to expand the consumer base for compact cities through reverse assimilation of the middle-class and native-born Latinos. Reverse assimilation describes the conversion of the middle class and non-Latinos from established environmentally harmful lifestyles to those more compatible with compact cities.

The middle class and native born need a variety of residential options other than low-density housing. Most new housing production is low density because of political opposition and zoning practices that attempt to curb overcrowding. The durability of both housing and zoning regulations will limit the residential choices of future residents. These consumers likely will be forced to live in the housing that was developed to meet the preferences of past population groups.

Latino new urbanism development in Santa Ana, California, with community courtyard.
Source: Transportation and Land Use Collaborative of Southern California, Los Angeles.

According to the Brookings Institution, by 2030, almost half of the buildings in which Americans live, work, and shop will have been built after the year 2000.[15] The nation will need nearly 427 billion square feet of built space to accommodate 2030 growth projections. The largest component of space built between 2000 and 2030 will be for homes. Over 100 billion square feet of new residential space will be needed by the end of 2030. These projections demonstrate that nearly half of what will be the built environment in 2030 doesn't even exist yet, giving builders and policymakers an opportunity to reshape future development and lifestyle choices. Recent trends, particularly among Latinos, indicate that demand is increasing for more compact, walkable, high-quality living environments.

Accordingly, builders should take notice of cultural preferences in housing, because many cities throughout the country will be multicultural in the future. The household preferences of Latinos could become an attractive model to help address the irrational growth patterns in communities. However, as Urban Planning Professor Dowell Myers suggests, for the planning of compact cities to be successful, other population groups must convert to lifestyles consistent with the model.[16]

For the planning of compact cities to be broadly acceptable, participation needs to include non-Latinos. In forging a new lifestyle built from multiple cultures, the middle class and non-Latinos will need to adopt aspects of the compact lifestyle. What is required in essence is a redefining of what constitutes the desired middle-class lifestyle in the U.S., so that when immigrants assimilate they have models other than suburban sprawl.

Likewise, the development of compact communities for the middle class and non-Latinos must first overcome governmental regulations and the perception that dense residential communities are associated with lower incomes, noise, and crime. This can be partly achieved through more fashionable and innovative designs. A visible supply of high-quality, diverse, compact city housing is required for consumers to explore appealing alternatives to the conventional low-density, single-family home.

Latino Drivers for Housing Market Growth

The stimulus for an increase in the visible supply of high-quality housing models requires the home building industry to recognize that Latino home buyers present the greatest driver of market growth of any demographic group in the country. In California for instance, Latinos represented 15% of total purchasers of resale homes in the state in 2001. By 2020, Latinos will demand over 1 million housing units, and by 2030, they will represent the largest share of all prospective home buyers.

These projections may convince the home building industry to understand the unique characteristics of this burgeoning client base. Financial, insurance, and real estate professionals are already changing product advertising and promotions by using the Spanish language to cater to this growing housing market.[17] However, more than Spanish language translation of documents and services is required. Builders interested in capitalizing on this potentially lucrative market must recognize the housing preferences and needs of Latinos and develop housing models accordingly.

When developing housing models and marketing approaches for Latinos, the building industry must understand the degree to which families play a dominant role in Latino society and how they influence individual behavior. For Latinos, what is in the best interest of the family dominates any decision, including home selection, school proximity, neighborhood safety, and projected monetary appreciation of a particular home.

Source: James Rojas.

Such dominance is supported by survey research from the Davenport Institute of Public Policy at Pepperdine University, which found that nearly 30% of all Latino home owners indicated that "more room for a growing family" was the main reason for purchasing a home.[18] This greatly overshadowed the second strongest reason, homeownership as a form of financial investment, identified by only 22% of survey respondents.

Latino family dominance in consumer spending can best be explained by marketing analyst M. Isabel Valdes' "ecosystemic" model, which approaches consumers from the perspective of the individual and his or her relationship with society.[19] This model evaluates how individuals from different cultures interact between and within the various layers of society.

The ecosystemic model reveals several aspects of the Latino decision-making process. The Latino individual attempts to make his or her decisions consistent with the needs of the family, whereas the Anglo individual tends to make decisions unilaterally. Latinos are more likely to focus on relationships, whereas Anglos are inclined to be task oriented. For Anglos, individual achievement dominates, whereas for Latinos, family interdependence takes priority.[20]

The ecosystemic model demonstrates the need for the home building industry to acknowledge that interactions within the Latino family are different than those of Anglos. Family interdependency may explain why more Latinos have multiple-generation households or adult children who remain living at home longer than non-Latinos or why Latinos adapt their homes and the built environment to facilitate social interaction.

Correspondingly, because Latinos tend to form strong bonds within the family and are supportive of their communities, housing developments should be produced to reflect these cultural values and preferences. As discussed with housing, parks, and streetscapes, Latinos are already adapting the built environment to maximize social interaction and activities consistent with compact city lifestyles. However, housing developments should also acknowledge the external variables influencing Latino households, specifically housing affordability, and develop methods to effectively address those variables.

Source: James Rojas.

Latino Economic Constraints

Various reports and publications cite the enormous purchasing power of Latinos. *Hispanic Business* magazine reported that the purchasing power of U.S. Latinos reached $540 billion in 2002.[21] In California, buying power has been estimated around $171 billion, with a projected increase of up to $260 billion by 2007.[22] Although the estimates of Latino purchasing power are impressive, they overlook the realities and constraints Latinos encounter in high-cost housing markets.

The high home prices and rents throughout the country make it difficult for many, including Latino families and first-time home buyers, to achieve the American dream of homeownership. Housing affordability does not affect just low-wage Latino workers, but also those who command annual salaries of $50,000 a year. In 2002, fewer than 15% of Latino families could afford the median-priced home in the state of California. In contrast, 43% of Anglo families were able to afford that same home.

Rising home prices have the greatest impact on those with the lowest purchasing power. Based on 1999 data by the Tomás Rivera Institute, even a 5% increase in the median price of a detached single-family home can force as many as 222,446 households (including 44,833 Latino households) out of the market in California alone.[23] Historically, homeownership has made the greatest contribution to wealth accumulation for millions of working and middle-class families. However, the reality is that many families, a large proportion of those Latino, may not be able to further accumulate wealth through homeownership. Because Latino household income has not kept pace with inflation and home values are steadily increasing, the ability of many Latino families to purchase the conventional single-family home will continue to decline in the next several years.

Latino Lifestyle, Affordability, and New Urbanism

A development model that can address Latinos' cultural values and economic constraints is new urbanism. New urbanist communities provide affordable housing by developing single-family detached and attached housing on smaller lots. The compactness increases affordability because less land is purchased and basic services can be provided with less infrastructure. Economic studies by legal analyst Andrew Dietderich show cost savings of 24% with higher-density construction of compact subdivisions and a 50% cost savings from compact development of condominiums.[24]

The Brookings Institution also estimates that providing public infrastructure and delivering services in compact development patterns can reduce costs and save taxpayers money. Their studies show that increased use of more compact development patterns from 2000 to 2025 promise the following savings for governments nationwide: 11% or $110 billion from 25-year water and sewer costs and roughly 3% or $4 billion for annual operations and service delivery.[25]

Consistent with Latino housescapes and cultural values, new urbanism also encourages strong social interactions. A study by social psychologist Barbara Brown showed that new urbanist designs are

Casitas de las Florecitas of San Ysidro, California. *Source:* Poster Frost Associates.

in accordance with the behavioral and social goals they are intended to support.[26] Brown tested the behavioral and social interactions of residents in a new urbanist subdivision (NUS) and a standard suburban subdivision (SSS). The results of the study validated most new urbanist design goals. The NUS had gridded streets, smaller lots, homes with front porches, and back alleys with accessory apartments; the SSS lacked these characteristics and had cul-de-sacs and 47% larger lots. After controlling for income, price, and age of homes, the NUS residents reported more neighborly activities, outdoor use, and positive reactions to alleys and apartments than SSS residents.

New urbanist designs are also consistent with Latino compact commuting characteristics through the incorporation of mixed-use and transit-oriented development. These development types encourage walkable communities by reducing car impact with more accessible and pedestrian-friendly street forms. Hence, new urbanist communities provide the production of affordable homes that are consistent with Latino propensity for compact city lifestyles. Moreover, new urbanism affords the home building industry the prospect of capitalizing on the enormous projected Latino housing demand that would not be possible under conventional suburban development patterns.

However, new urbanism in its current manifestation is primarily presented as a revival of New England and Victorian town living portraying idyllic and sedate design elements.[27] Unless it is marketed and presented to Latinos as addressing their housing needs and preferences, the potential of new urbanism to address Latino housing demands may not be realized.

Transforming Cities with Latino New Urbanism

The building industry and some local governments are already realizing the profitability of multiculturalism and are developing innovative initiatives similar to Latino new urbanism to capitalize on this growing client base. Communities that have traditionally used zoning practices to prevent ethnic touches in development are now working to promote the building of more compact and Latino new urbanist–type communities. The link between economic self-interest and cultural dynamics is transforming the basis of business and city development practices throughout the country.

The city of San Diego, California, approved five "pilot villages" in 2004. One of them, Mi Pueblo in San Ysidro near the Mexican border, incorporates Latino new urbanism principles. Façades of new homes are inspired by Mexican architecture with bright colors, linear designs, and displays of public art. Mi Pueblo will eventually have 1,143 residential units, about 25% of them moderately priced, and will include new parks, plazas, and other public spaces.

In the nearby Barrio Logan community, the Mercado Apartments were developed in the 1990s and designed with elements that reflect the cultural identity of the neighborhood.[28] The building facades wear bright colors, and the architectural style of the complex was chosen to emulate the simple and clean "pueblo-adobe" look found in small Mexican villages. The Mercado apartment complex consists of 144 compact units with patios and balconies facing the street.

The city of San Fernando, a small suburban city outside of Los Angeles with a population that is 90% Latino, is working to attract housing, retail, and services so residents and upwardly mobile Latinos don't have to go to wealthier communities for shopping and entertainment. The city plans to develop parks, apartments, homes, and condos in the downtown area. About 15% of new housing will sell below the city's single-family home median price. The city's first major Latino new urbanist project opened in 2002. Library Plaza is a redevelopment project on the main downtown thoroughfare that expanded and modernized the county library and provided an additional venue for new businesses to locate within the city (Figure 7.8). Keeping with the city's history and Latino

Figure 7.8 Latino new urbanism transforms the city of San Fernando's downtown into a vibrant and walkable destination.

Source: City of San Fernando, California.

Figure 7.9 City of San Fernando's Cesar Chavez Transit Memorial promotes transit use.

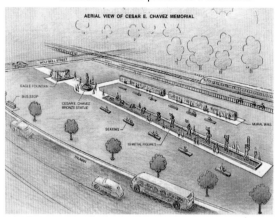

Source: City of San Fernando, California.

new urbanism principles, the design of Library Plaza incorporated mission motifs in the architecture of the building and dedicated a large plaza and water fountain at the center of the complex. The plaza is the focal point of the complex and facilitates an atmosphere where consumers and residents can shop and interact socially. On nights and weekends, the Latino-themed coffee house holds musical and cultural events in the plaza.

The City of San Fernando also recently completed the Cesar Chavez Memorial Transit Plaza (Figure 7.9). The transit plaza includes a memorial for the farm worker hero, a public rest area for MetroLink commuters and bus riders, and a bikeway connecting the transit-oriented housing development of Village Green to the MetroLink commuter rail station. The city is also scheduled to complete Heritage Park, which is intended to provide needed park space that acknowledges the contributions and histories of the indigenous people in the region (Figure 7.10).

These projects reveal that cities can develop environments that allow residents to express their cultural preferences and needs in a well-functioning community that is compatible with notions of achieving a high quality of life in America. The visibility of such developments may convince more local governments and developers to assess the profitability of integrating Latino preferences in housing developments.

Figure 7.10 Heritage Park in the city of San Fernando is an integral part of the community.

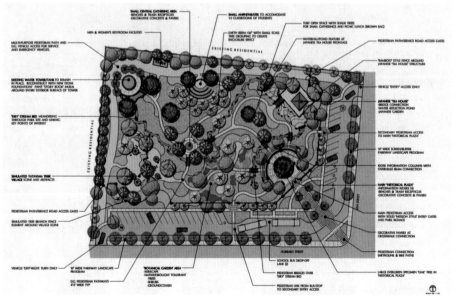

Source: City of San Fernando, California.

How Latino New Urbanism Will Influence Future Housing Development

In the next several decades, ethnic diversity will dramatically alter the physical and cultural landscapes in communities throughout the country. The Latino population boom will place dramatic demands on services, particularly those associated with housing. This large projected population growth will pressure local governments and builders to modify the methods by which they develop cities and suburbs. The ability of local governments and the housing industry to create innovative models to support sustainable regions will principally be determined by how they choose to configure people into communities and housing units.

Like any other American demographic group, Latinos are diverse in terms of economic status, lifestyles, and values. Many are new immigrants who can easily adapt to the notion of Latino new urbanism. However, other Latino families have been here for generations and have assimilated the conventional auto-oriented suburban housing lifestyle. This indicates that the same forces that have driven other middle-class families to move to the suburbs are working on Latinos.

Therefore, we must examine the outcomes of assimilation that may take place in the next several decades as new immigrants move into suburban homes and adopt the auto-oriented lifestyle. This Latino sprawl will have a great impact on the environment, land consumption, economics, and air quality. For example, automobile usage is the leading source of pollution in most U.S. cities, including those where the majority of Latinos live and work. Nearly 92% of Latinos live in urban areas, where air pollution may increase the risk of illnesses, including asthma and cancer.[29] Latino sprawl will only exacerbate these conditions throughout the country.

As the composition of residents changes, housing policies and models should also change. Despite the multicultural nature of America, many individuals who favor compact lifestyles may not be allowed to pursue them. Most new development is low density. This practice undermines the Latinos' cultural propensity for compact, new urbanist lifestyles, hindering any prospects of leveraging those attitudes into the development of more sustainable communities. Forcing Latinos toward dispersed housing rather than encouraging the middle-class and non-Latinos to place greater value on compact cities could produce detrimental consequences not only for Latinos, but for the future of the general population in many cities across the U.S.

Latino new urbanism permits individuals to pursue their preferences for compact cities in a way that is compatible with achieving middle-class status in America. Latino new urbanism, moreover, offers the middle-class and non-Latinos an opportunity to live in an alternative environment with various residential types and amenities that satisfy their needs and incomes. Latino new urbanism forges together new urbanist principles with the American dream of homeownership.

The population increase and the new development needed to meet this projected growth are inevitable. Policymakers and builders have the option of providing diverse housing models that provide the American dream of homeownership to all. Latino new urbanism represents a strategic opportunity to accommodate population growth, reduce environmental impact, and offer developers a viable model to profit from the enormous housing demand projected over the next several decades.

Endnotes

1. Sperber, Bob. "Taking Granny (Flats) to Market." *Housing Zone*, January 1, 2005.

2. Fulton, William. *The New Urbanism: Hope or Hype for American Communities?* Cambridge, MA: Lincoln Institute of Land Policy, 1996.

3. Rojas, James. "The Enacted Environment: The Creation of Place by Mexicans and Mexican-Americans in East Los Angeles." Master's Thesis, Massachusetts Institute of Technology, 1991.

4. Arreola, Daniel. Mexican-American housescapes. *Geographical Review* 78(3):299–315, 1988.

5. Pader, Ellen. Spatial relations and housing policy: Regulations that discriminate against Mexican origin households. *Journal of Planning Education and Research* 13(2):119–135, 1994.

6. Castillo, G.A. New urbanism's Latin connection: Interview with Andres Duany. *Aula: Architecture & Urbanism in Las Americas* 3:81–95, 2002.

7. Miyares, Ines M. Changing Latinization of New York City. In *Hispanic Spaces, Latino Places: Community and Cultural Diversity in Contemporary America*. Arreola, Daniel, Ed. Austin: University of Texas Press, 2004.

8. Flaundrau, Charles. *Viva Mexico*. Champaign: University of Illinois Press, 1964.

9. Fulton, William. *The New Urbanism: Hope or Hype for American Communities?* Cambridge, MA: Lincoln Institute of Land Policy, 1996.

10. Loukaitou-Sideris, Anastasia. Urban form and social context: Cultural differentiation in uses of urban parks. *Journal of Planning Education and Research* 14:89–102, 1995.

11. Garcia, Robert. *Dreams of Fields: Soccer, Community, and Equal Justice. Report on Sports in Urban Parks to the California Department of Parks and Recreation*. Los Angeles, CA: Center for Law in the Public Interest, 2002.

12. Price, Marie and Courtney Whitworth. Soccer and Latino Cultural Space: Metropolitan Washington Futbol Leagues. In *Hispanic Spaces, Latino Places: Community and Cultural Diversity in Contemporary America*. Arreola, Daniel, Ed. Austin: University of Texas Press, 2004.

13. Smith, Jeffrey S. The Plaza in Las Vegas, New Mexico: A Community Gathering Place. In *Hispanic Spaces, Latino Places: Community and Cultural Diversity in Contemporary America*. Arreola, Daniel, Ed. Austin: University of Texas Press, 2004.

14. Hirschman, C., P. Kasinitz, and J. DeWind. *Immigrant Adaptation, Assimilation, and Incorporation. The Handbook of International Migration*. New York: Russell Sage Foundation, 1999.

15. Nelson, Arthur C. *Toward a New Metropolis: The Opportunity to Rebuild America*. Washington, DC: Brookings Institution, December 2004. http://www.brookings.edu/metro/pubs/20041213_rebuildamerica.htm

16. Myers, Dowell. Demographic Futures as a Guide to Planning: California's Latinos and the Compact City. *Journal of the American Planning Association* 67(4):383–397, 2001.

17. National Association of Hispanic Real Estate Professionals. Targeting Hispanic or Mexican Heritage to Expand Your Business. *Real Voices* 9 (March–April), 2001.

18. Kotkin, Joel, and Thomas Tseng. *Rewarding Ambition: Latinos, Housing, and the Future of California*. Malibu, CA: Pepperdine University, Davenport Institute, 2002. http://publicpolicy.pepperdine.edu/davenportinstitute/reports/rewarding/rewarding.pdf

19. Valdes, M. Isabel. *Marketing to American Latinos: A Guide to the In-Culture Approach*. Ithaca, NY: Paramount Market Publishing, 2000.

20. Valdes, M. Isabel. *Marketing to American Latinos: A Guide to the In-Culture Approach*. Ithaca, NY: Paramount Market Publishing, 2000.

21. Paden, Ramona. Online Rivals' Market Plays. Hispanic Business. Jan–Feb 2003. http://www.hispanicbusiness.com

22. Kotkin, Joel, and Thomas Tseng. *Rewarding Ambition: Latinos, Housing, and the Future of California*. Malibu, CA: Pepperdine University, Davenport Institute, 2002. http://publicpolicy.pepperdine.edu/davenportinstitute/reports/rewarding/rewarding.pdf

23. Lopez-Aqueres, Waldo, Joelle Skaga, and Tadeusz Kugler. *Housing California's Latino Population in the 21st Century: The Challenge Ahead*. Claremont, CA: Tomás Rivera Policy Institute, 2003. http://www.trpi.org/update/economics.html

24. Dietderich, Andrew. An egalitarian's market: The economics of inclusionary zoning reclaimed. *Fordham Urban Law Journal* 24:41, 1996.

25. Muro, Mark and Robert Puentes. *Investing in a Better Future: A Review of the Fiscal and Competitive Advantages of Smarter Growth Development*

Patterns. Washington, DC: Brookings Institution, March 2004. http://www. brookings.edu/metro/publications/200403_smartgrowth.htm

26. Brown, Barbara B. New urban and standard suburban subdivisions: Evaluating psychological and social goals. *American Planning Association Journal* 67(4):402–419, 2001.

27. Hall, Kenneth B. Jr., and Gerald A. Porterfield. *Community by Design: New Urbanism for Suburbs and Small Communities*. New York: McGraw-Hill, 2001.

28. Herzog, Lawrence A. Globalization of the Barrio: Transformation of the Latino Cultural Landscapes of San Diego, California. In *Hispanic Spaces, Latino Places: Community and Cultural Diversity in Contemporary America*. Arreola, Daniel, Ed. Austin: University of Texas Press, 2004.

29. Natural Resources Defense Council. *Hidden Danger: Environmental Health Threats in the Latino Community.* Washington, DC: NRDC, October 2004. http://www.nrdc.org/health/effects/latino/english/contents.asp

Michael Anthony Mendez is a fourth-generation Californian and the child of an immigrant. His background includes the Latino Issues Forum, a public policy and advocacy institute in San Francisco; the Los Angeles County Metropolitan Transportation Authority; and the City of Los Angeles Department of Neighborhood Empowerment. Michael holds a master's in city planning from the Massachusetts Institute of Technology, specializing in environmental policy and housing, community, and economic development. He has spoken and written extensively on the intersections between Latino demographics, housing needs, environmental impact, and development patterns. Michael serves as a consultant to the California State Legislature, with expertise in environmental policy and urban development.

Source: Greater Minnesota Housing Fund.

CHAPTER 8

Building Sustainable Affordable Housing

Warren Hanson

Affordable housing is vastly more myth than reality in the United States today. In a time of skyrocketing housing prices in most major American cities as well as in small towns, the American dream of homeownership is elusive for many families. The demand for affordable housing will continue to grow as the Latino population explodes. Because many Latinos are employed in low- to moderate-income jobs, the need for rental and for-sale affordable housing is critical.

A crisis exists in the stock of affordable housing for a variety of reasons. Many developers are avoiding the affordable housing market because they perceive that their ability to earn a profit is diminished by low housing prices. In addition to this, many federal funding and housing tax incentives have ended. Exclusionary zoning policies, such as minimum lot size requirements, have also created developmental barriers that restrict the development of affordable housing in many communities.

Despite these apparent barriers to affordable housing, there is good news. Many communities are working with nonprofit organizations, religious groups, and government agencies to provide affordable housing. They have employed a variety of design principles to lower construction costs and create single-family homes and multifamily units with flexible floor plans and features commonly found in lower-cost market-rate homes. This new model of affordable housing looks very different from the high-rise apartments of the 1960s. Today's affordable housing communities are comprised of townhouses and mid-rise, high-rise, mixed-use, and mixed-income buildings in a number of American cities.

What Is Affordable Housing?

Affordable housing is not an easy term to comprehend. Generally, the government views 30% of a household's gross income for housing as the standard for affordability. The assumption is that if families spend more than 30% of their income on housing, they will not be able to afford transportation, food, health insurance, and other needs. In the Twin Cities, for example, a single-family home is considered affordable if a family earning 80% of the median income spends no more than 30% of their income on housing costs. The standard for rental housing is 50% of the median income.

To qualify for affordable housing, families must be "income eligible," a figure that is adjusted for the median income in an area and for the size of a family. "Extremely low income" describes a family with an income at or below 30% of the median income of a region, "low" income represents families at or below 80% and "moderate" falls at or below 120% of an area's median income.

Confused? Even the experts find it confounding. It will help to look at an actual region, the Twin Cities of St. Paul and Minneapolis, home to approximately 2.7 million people and, according to the U.S. Census, one of the nation's wealthiest metropolitan areas. Using 2005 statistics from the state and federal government, 30% of the median income for a family of four is $23,550; 50% is $39,250 and at 80% is $62,800.

Translating this further, a family at the 30% mark lives in affordable housing if their home rents for less than $589 per month or costs $52,500 to purchase.* At 50% of the median income, the figures jump to $981 for rent and $114,000 to purchase; at 80%, the figures are $1,570 for rent and $207,500 to purchase. As you might have

---

*This simplified purchase price calculation assumes a 30-year conventional fixed-rate mortgage at an interest rate of 6.5%, with the home buyer putting $1,000 down and paying no more than $2,000 in annual taxes and property insurance. This simple calculation excludes private mortgage insurance, which is a requirement for many low-income home buyers that further reduces their purchasing power.

guessed, such figures have resulted in an affordable housing crisis in the Twin Cities, where even homes in once disadvantaged neighborhoods can cost $175,000. The average home in the Twin Cities is now more than $225,000, and the region's affordable housing stock has dwindled significantly.

The guidelines used to determine income eligibility in the Minneapolis–St. Paul region are not much different than those used throughout the country. They help developers, government planners, and nonprofits understand the size of the affordable housing market to make plans based on the population.

Housing Markets and Products

For decades, government-funded and -operated housing was considered among the few widely available housing options for low-income Americans. But over the past 20 years, the affordable housing market has been largely built by the private sector. With the need so great for all levels of affordable housing, good opportunities exist for businesses to contribute to the common good of a community.

Although the National Association of Home Builders (NAHB) recognizes the nation's record-high homeownership rate, it acknowledges two pertinent facts:[1]

- one in four households still spends more than 30% of its income on housing
- less than half of Latino families own homes

When President George W. Bush issued the America's Homeownership Challenge in 2002, NAHB responded to the president's request for help from the private sector to establish at least 5.5 million new minority home owners by the end of the decade. NAHB's ambitious plan focused largely on tax incentive programs to help finance affordable housing rather than cost-reduction strategies. In this chapter, I will present design modifications in both residential architecture and in neighborhood layout that can reduce costs and help the nation reach its affordable housing goals (Figure 8.1).

The Latino Need for Affordable Housing

Latinos in the United States today are 40 million strong, representing approximately 14% of the total population. As a result, there has

Figure 8.1 The Heritage Greens neighborhood in Cambridge, Minnesota, features afford-able craftsman-styled homes in a mixed-income neighborhood designed using cost-saving strategies. Developed by Metro Plains Development, LLC.

Source: Greater Minnesota Housing Fund.

been an increase in Latino participa-tion and influence in the mainstream U.S. economy. Latinos represent bil-lions of dollars in purchasing power, and they boasted a homeownership growth rate of 16.7% between 1994 and 2001, outpacing the rate of 6.6% for non-Hispanic whites.[2] In com-parison, during the 1990s, the home-ownership rates among African Americans only increased by 2.9% and by only 1% for Asian Americans.[3]

With an emerging middle class, the mortgage bankers and realtors have begun aggressively courting the Latino community. In the process, they are removing barriers to home-ownership by hiring more Spanish speakers, translating documents into Spanish, offering seminars on home buying, and helping a culture tradi-tionally unaccustomed to paying with credit establish the credit history necessary for securing mortgages.

Yet, for new immigrants or first-generation American-born Latinos, safe and decent housing will remain unattainable without affordable housing options. Latinos living well below the median income represent a burgeoning population with a demonstrated need for affordable rental and owner-occupied housing. The following issues must be con-sidered when developing affordable housing for Latinos:

- **Age.** With a median age of 26 (compared with 35 years for all U.S. residents), the boom in the Latino population is being experienced in a generation just entering the workforce and approaching their peak home-buying age.[4,5]

- **Workers per household.** Latino households are 35% larger than the average American household (see Chapter 1, The Rise of the Latino Home Buyer). With extended family traditionally living together or children living at home well into adulthood, larger households often mean more working family members contributing to the household income. Former HUD Secretary Henry Cisneros has pointed out that even though Latinos still earn lower wages, they have two, three, or four workers per household. In Southern California, 52% have at least three workers in the home. Family members may work as gardeners, but together, the household functions as a middle-class unit.[6]

- **Latinos new to market.** With Latinos accounting for 17.5% of the overall rise in nationwide homeownership levels between 1998 and 2000, the population is establishing itself in the housing market, especially as purchasers of starter homes.[7] In a 2002 homeownership survey, the Davenport Institute at Pepperdine University found that 44% of Latino homeowners in California had owned their home for less than 5 years. More than 70% told researchers they were living in their first home.[8]

Source: FogStock, LLC, Index Open.

- **Desire for affordable housing.** California's Latino population buys at the lower end of the housing market, with 60% of their homes purchased for less than $150,000. Eighty-three percent of California renters surveyed said they wanted a home for less than $150,000,[9] with a down payment of less than $10,000. Surveys found 69% are confident they will be able to buy a home within the next 5 years.[10]

- **Income.** More than half of Latinos in the labor force work at low- to moderate-income jobs with nearly half (46.4%) concentrated in three of the lowest paying occupations (service occupations; operators, fabricators, and laborers; and farming, forestry, and fishing occupations).[11] A small but growing middle class has blossomed, although the Latino middle class does not represent as significant a portion of its population as other groups.

- **Cost burden.** Latinos also share a high housing cost burden, with 41.8% paying more than 30% of their income for housing, compared with 29.7% nationwide (see Chapter 1, The Rise of the Latino Home Buyer).

- **Motivated home owners.** Traditionally, Latinos have a strong work ethic combined with strong family and community bonds. With the need for more room for their families and the belief that owning a home is better for raising a family, they are highly motivated prospective home buyers.

Strategies for Building Affordable Housing

Every community needs affordable housing. Businesses are attracted to areas with adequate workforce housing where their employees can comfortably rent or buy homes. Communities suffer when a significant portion of their workers—especially public employees such as teachers, firefighters, and police officers—cannot afford to live in the communities where they work. With rising land and labor costs, builders are finding it increasingly difficult to build quality, affordable housing to meet the needs of families seeking to achieve homeownership.

However, there are many excellent programs to help low-income families obtain affordable housing, such as Habitat for Humanity, which relies on volunteer labor and donated materials and appliances, and state and local community development efforts that provide financing and tax incentives for first-time or low-income home buyers. Another approach utilizes cost-reduction techniques through better home designs and thoughtful land use planning to help lower the development costs associated with home building.

Home owners realize the benefits of ownership long after the purchase of the home through its increasing value; the livability of the neighborhood; and lower maintenance, utility, and tax costs. Architect Gary Everton of Everton Oglesby Architects, Nashville, Tennessee, has commented on the constant battle needed to spend money on design in affordable housing. Yet, Elena Marcheso Moreno has found that curb appeal and well-executed street edge can almost guarantee the success of a project.[12]

Building structures that employ a combination of design and sustainability reduce long-term costs and increase the likelihood that home owners can afford to stay in their homes. Attention to aesthetics and design add value to the development, if the balance of cost-reduction and value-added techniques are carefully weighed relative to the builder's budget. Many of the same techniques can be incorporated into both affordable starter-home neighborhoods and market-rate developments. The integration of cost-effective design becomes important as mixed-income developments become more common.

Although many starter homes are actually single-family structures, the strategies outlined in this chapter are not exclusively geared toward this segment of the affordable housing market. Most of the cost-reduction strategies and design principles will yield even more savings when applied to attached or multifamily housing because more open space can be preserved, resources can be pooled to add or upgrade amenities, and the higher density saves on land and infrastructure costs as well as ongoing operating costs.

Compact developments that are linked by interconnecting sidewalks and biking trails allow nonmotorized traffic to commute easily between home, work, school, shopping, or recreation. Land conserved through compact development becomes valued open space for recreation. A full range of housing choices is also one of the hallmarks of new urbanism, a movement that uses traditional design principles to create mixed-income and mixed-use communities (Figure 8.2).

Michael Mendez, who coined the term *Latino new urbanism*, believes that Latino-American culture, a fusion of Anglo and Latin American social and cultural heritage, welcomes this type of community design (see Chapter 7, Latino New Urbanism). In general, Latinos prefer compact neighborhoods with large public places that help create a sense of community. According to Mendez, builders who utilize new urbanist principles can keep starter residences affordable and address the needs of the Latino home buying market.

Particular strategies have helped developers save thousands while producing livable communities. The architects and developers of the following projects paid special attention to site selection, street and lot design, and the engineering of each home.

Figure 8.2 A mixture of family-friendly market-rate homes, affordable single-family homes, and multifamily townhomes provide choices for residents of the Harvest Ridge neighborhood, Plainview, Minnesota. Developed by Three Rivers Community Action, Inc.

Source: Greater Minnesota Housing Fund.

Site Selection

Seattle-based architect Michael Pyatok ascribes to the idea that proper neighborhood planning, rather than reduced construction cost, is the key to making housing more affordable. Larger lots and the costs of scaled-up utility and street extensions in developing areas adds dramatically to a project's total development cost.[13] This financial burden is ultimately shifted to the buyer as part of the home price. In contrast, development sites that are more compact or within built-up areas will make the most efficient use of costly infrastructure.

Amenities and nearby services, such as schools, commercial districts, and civic institutions, make a neighborhood more desirable. Sidewalks and bike trails allow children, seniors, and others to stroll within and between neighborhoods.

Latino households are typically younger and have more children and working adults than the average U.S. household. This poses challenges when selecting a site for residential development, as access to public transportation is more critical to these home owners. Choosing a site close to high-traffic community areas and public transit helps both affordability and quality of life. Siting the development on well-connected transit routes can reduce the number of vehicles a family needs. This reduces household expenses related to automobile ownership, a depreciating asset, allowing income to be used in other ways, such as toward the purchase of a home, which is an appreciating asset. Life in Latin American countries is highly connected to the community, whether through important church and school functions, the ability to walk to a nearby market, or through socializing in the neighborhood (see Chapter 7, Latino New Urbanism). Good site selection can encourage strong social connections and foster more social interaction in the United States as well.

Site Planning

In Minnesota, planning modest-sized lots is the most significant cost-reduction strategy for new home construction.* A typical rural Minnesota subdivision is required by municipal zoning to have lots no less than 80 feet wide. By reducing the lots through a zoning mod-

---

*Savings based on a cost estimate of $140 per linear frontage foot for land and $200 per linear frontage foot for infrastructure, including water, sewer, and storm water pipes, curb and gutter, and paving for streets.

ification or planned unit development (PUD) plan to a more modest 50 feet, home owners save thousands of dollars before the house is even built. Such savings allow a family to upgrade the home plans to provide more finished family space, more bedrooms, or perhaps an in-home office or workshop space for a home-based business (Figure 8.3).

Smaller lots create a more compact neighborhood, which puts residents in closer proximity to amenities and services. In addition, with less land needed for houses, the remaining open space can be designed as an asset with greater utility and more opportunities for community connections for the entire neighborhood. Accessibility to parks and other open spaces is especially important in the Latino community (see Chapter 7, Latino New Urbanism). Rather than purchase a larger, more expensive home with a big backyard to host gatherings, Latinos are more likely to use shared public spaces for large events and their backyards for family activities. By reducing the lot sizes in a neighborhood, green space can be preserved to benefit the entire community (Figure 8.4).

Building townhomes or multifamily housing is a much more efficient use of land and yields an even higher cost savings per unit when compared to single-family neighborhoods. Incorporating well-landscaped parks, public open spaces, and other gathering places

Figure 8.3 Modest-sized lots in compact neighborhoods preserve valuable open space and help reduce land and infrastructure costs for renter and home buyer.

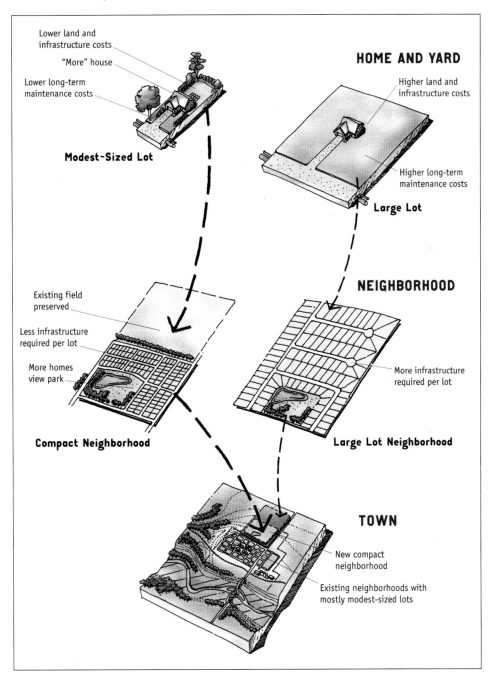

Lower land and infrastructure costs
"More" house
Lower long-term maintenance costs
Modest-Sized Lot

HOME AND YARD
Higher land and infrastructure costs
Higher long-term maintenance costs
Large Lot

Existing field preserved
Less infrastructure required per lot
More homes view park
Compact Neighborhood

NEIGHBORHOOD
More infrastructure required per lot
Large Lot Neighborhood

TOWN
New compact neighborhood
Existing neighborhoods with mostly modest-sized lots

Source: Greater Minnesota Housing Fund: *Building Better Neighborhoods*, 2001, p. 18. www.gmhf.com.

Figure 8.4 Large private lots can be a burden for home owners to maintain. Oversized lots also reduce the amount of space available in a neighborhood for public parks and open space.

Source: Greater Minnesota Housing Fund: *Building Better Neighborhoods*, 2001, p. 20. www.gmhf.com.

in a development provides residents with more access to recreational amenities, while limiting the hard costs associated with expensive infrastructure.

Streets

If no infill or redevelopment site is suitable for the proposed housing development, providing infrastructure for undeveloped land can add 15–20% to the cost of a single-family home.[15] Reducing street width and linear footage and siting buildings efficiently on the lot can bring costs down substantially. Neighborhood street width requirements for new subdivisions have grown in many communities. For neighborhood streets with very light traffic and posted speed limits of 25 mph, the additional width is unnecessary, costly, and encourages faster driving speeds, all of which detract from perceived home value and overall neighborhood livability. Because streets are one of the most expensive components of subdivision infrastructure, narrowing their widths can reduce costs associated with construction and future maintenance.[16] Developers can also realize savings when street patterns are engineered to reduce the total length of streets by avoiding cul-de-sacs and inefficient curvilinear roads (Figure 8.5).

The savings on better community designs are real. In a 38-acre subdivision in Marshall, Minnesota, the developer saved money by narrowing street widths from the original design, which reduced the amount of paving and associated infrastructure costs. The improved design resulted in a price reduction of over $1,600 per house.

Home Location

Consideration must be given to the siting of the home on the lot. Infrastructure costs can be lowered through efficient location of the housing unit. The closer the house or multifamily building is to the street, the shorter the distance to sewer, water, and utilities. In moving homes toward the street, residents are given a valuable amenity—a larger backyard.

It is common to design attached garages closer to the street because less paving is required for the driveway, helping reduce construction

Figure 8.5 (A) Wider neighborhood streets have proven to increase traffic speeds. (B) Narrower, more pedestrian-friendly streets reduce development costs and slow traffic speeds, creating safer communities.

Source: Greater Minnesota Housing Fund: *Building Better Neighborhoods*, 2001, p. 29. www.gmhf.com.

costs. Designing front-attached garages, however, can result in increased costs because this design tends to push the house back and lengthen the distance between street-based utilities and home utility connections. What the builder gains in savings due to less paving can be more than lost in the expense of a longer connection between street utility lines and the home. Garages that are more flush with the front of the home work better for cost reduction and create a more attractive streetscape[17] (Figure 8.6).

Expandable and Flexible Spaces

Latino families have more children and live in more multigenerational environments than the average U.S. family. This poses challenges for residential designers who want to create flexible, adaptable housing that can serve an expanding family for multiple generations (see Chapter 1, The Rise of the Latino Home Buyer).

Large eating areas are necessary to accommodate dining for the extended family, a Latino tradition. Open interior spaces are also popular, as they allow Latino women, who tend to be stay-at-home moms, to do household chores while watching their children. The home should also include spaces for privacy and quiet. Latino families often have members that work second and third shifts and need to sleep when babies and children are home. The home design

Figure 8.6 Houses in the Nicollet Meadows neighborhood, St. Peter, Minnesota, are sited close to the street, helping reduce infrastructure costs by shortening the distance to sewer, water, and utility hookups.

Source: Greater Minnesota Housing Fund.

should also be adaptable so as to allow elderly family members to live comfortably.

Developers can employ other strategies in the interior and exterior of homes to bring down the cost of housing. For example, houses built with unfinished space lowers the cost of the home, yet offers residents the opportunity to build sweat equity by adapting different rooms to a variety of household needs. Homeowners can decide to add extra bedrooms, put in an extra bathroom, or home office or create additional living space in the home's unfinished attic, lower level, or walkout basement.

Although garages are a big selling point, especially in cold climates, developers need not offer them when building affordable housing. A parking slab can be built allowing the home owner to build a garage at a later date.

Basements are also expected in northern climates but are not as common in warmer areas. Even an unfinished basement should be built with proper natural lighting, egress, moisture protection, insulation, and ventilation so that residents have the option of converting it into living space without compromising the health of the occupants.[18] Although these design standards make a unit less affordable than if it were built without a basement, the extra raw space offers expansion room. An alternative to basements are split-level structures or structures with garden-level basements, which save money due to less excavation.[19]

Flexibility in homes is an attractive quality to Latinos, many of whom are self-employed in occupations where storage for work tools or even production space may be needed. Designing homes with expandable and flexible spaces can meet those needs and bring additional income to the family. Garages, especially ones built on alleys, can become expandable space because an unfinished (or finished) accessory dwelling unit can be built above it for use as a home office or a small apartment. (See Box, page 141.)

Builders should also examine methods to enhance the connections between the house and outdoor spaces. Larger windows make interior spaces feel roomier, an important feature when rooms have been built small to help keep costs down. Unobstructed views of

Figure 8.7 Santa Cruz's Accessory Dwelling Unit (ADU) Program

The city of Santa Cruz, California, recognized that ADUs could increase density and provide affordable housing without affecting the neighborhood's character or burdening city budgets. In 2003, the city began the Accessory Dwelling Unit Program to help alleviate the housing crunch, and in 2005, it won the American Planning Association's Outstanding Planning Award. Santa Cruz's program amended the city's zoning to allow for the units, and the city now provides community outreach and technical and financial assistance for home owners considering building ADUs. The associated fees, which were lowered significantly as part of the program, were waived completely for home owners who rent their ADU to low-income tenants.

Source: Peter McLaughlin.

both the front and back yard allow residents to monitor young children at play. A kitchen built off a patio creates greater ease for cooking indoors and eating outdoors and while ensuring easy flow between the two. With good planning, making these changes adds no extra cost and allows families to easily use both indoor and outdoor spaces while retaining visual connections.

Green and Sustainable Building

Employing green and sustainable building practices benefits residents through lower utility bills, a healthier living environment and less frequent repairs and replacements. A home with quality construction that is built to last should contain fewer costly surprises for low- and moderate-income buyers. Smaller, more efficient units also require fewer materials to buy and less resources to build.

Downsizing allows the builder to focus on quality, not quantity, while applying the savings to materials that make the house more energy efficient. Although the argument can be made that the buyer gets "less house" or less square footage for their money, the savings in the long run may be worth it to a family looking not only for an affordably priced home, but also for a home that they can afford to maintain through the years they live there.

Figure 8.8 Homes in Kunte Development's Clover Field neighborhood, Chaska, Minnesota, feature a variety of architectural details, small yards, and welcoming front porches to enhance the street appeal.

Source: Greater Minnesota Housing Fund.

Figure 8.9 Multifamily housing can have privacy and character.

Source: Pyatok Architects, Inc.

Using green building techniques—such as orienting the house to take advantage of passive solar access and using shade trees and airflow to help naturally cool the building—only increases the energy efficiency and long-term sustainability of the home. Installing energy-efficient windows, power combustion furnaces, and digital programmable thermostats all work to maximize energy efficiency while reducing the owner's monthly energy bills.

Curb Appeal

Enhancing the appearance of the housing unit and surrounding property increases the value of the home. Options to consider include garage location, front porches, and the type of landscaping in individual yards and in public spaces (Figure 8.8).

Latino home design encourages building to the street line. This maximizes usable space on the site and typically translates into more attention to exterior enhancements to the home such as color, landscaping, or culturally meaningful design and ornamentation. Developers should include such design elements as they seek to satisfy Latino buyers' specific needs.

The design for the Bay Bridge development in Oakland, California, by Pyatok Architects, Inc., is a good example of creative landscaping in an urban, multifamily setting. The design incorporates trellises, climbing vines, and birdhouses in order to make the obligatory security screens less obtrusive (Figure 8.9).

Where appropriate, alleys can add value to the property, but they will also increase costs unless lot sizes and street widths are reduced. Alleys allow residents to store their cars and trash cans out of sight. More important, alleys allow developers to create a more aesthetically pleasing streetscape with gardens and porches that promote social interaction at the house front rather than a streetscape dominated by garages and driveways (Figure 8.10).

Landscape Systems

Although storm water management is a regulation imposed on developers, employing the principles of low impact development (LID) can help developers simultaneously meet their requirements, protect the environment, create a community amenity, and reduce

Figure 8.10 A streetscape that features landscaping, front porches, windows, and other architectural details is more attractive than a conventional garage-dominated streetscape.

Source: Greater Minnesota Housing Fund.

infrastructure costs and future cost burdens on municipalities and residents.[20] The goal of LID is to combine land use planning, best design practices, and "low-tech" technologies to protect natural resources in a cost-effective manner.

Conventional storm water conveyance and collection systems are costly because of the need for curbs, gutters, storm water pipes, and on-site retention ponds.[21] They also impact the environment, due to wider roads, larger surface parking lots, and other impervious surfaces such as roof tops. The more impervious the system, the more it will cost developers and the environment. The conventional system reroutes and deposits storm runoff, carrying oils, heavy metals, phosphorus, sand, and trash that ends up being funneled into local streams, rivers, and lakes.

Developers can reduce the need for underground storm water management systems by designing landscaped drainage swales in the boulevards along roadways and by constructing gardens in yards and open space that thrive in saturated areas. Filled with native plants, the swales and rain gardens capture runoff from nonporous surfaces and allow it to slowly filter into the ground rather runoff into storm sewers. The vegetation in swales and rain gardens provides a natural landscaped amenity and adds value to the neighborhood while storm water run off is naturally filtered of impurities before reaching local streams and lakes (Figure 8.11).

Figure 8.11 Rain gardens featuring native vegetation are a low-maintenance, cost-effective storm water management option that adds value to a neighborhood.

Source: Greater Minnesota Housing Fund.

Developers who participated in a pilot program utilizing these natural storm water management techniques saved 25% in site development and maintenance costs by reducing the need for expensive grading, pipes, curbs, and paving.[22] Where retention ponds are required, the land can double as usable public space by simply landscaping the pond with native vegetation and providing trails, bikeways, and play areas (Figure 8.12).

Sucessful Sustainable, Affordable Housing

Cameron Park Colonia

The developers of Cameron Park Colonia, a project in Brownsville, Texas, took advantage of PATH's many resources (see Sidebar, page 148). Working in conjunction with the Community Development Corporation of Brownsville (CDCB), a low-income housing provider, PATH provided technical assistance in employing advanced building technologies to reduce costs while increasing quality and energy efficiency in one the country's poorest communities. Before Cameron Park Colonia, lower-income Latino immigrants lived in deplorable conditions. Builders employed advanced framing to reduce lumber use, installed preplanned roof sheathing to cut waste, and improved insulation materials and sealants to increase the energy efficiency of the homes. The design also incorporated economical plastic manifold plumbing systems and air conditioning that complies with stricter energy codes to help reduce monthly utility costs.

Los Jardines

Los Jardines in South Austin, Texas, is the result of a collaboration between CityView, founded by former HUD Secretary Henry Cisneros, and Bruce Karatz, Chairman and CEO of KB Home. CityView works with builders to develop single-family communities in urban settings, frequently in areas with high concentrations of Latinos. Through the application of special financing techniques and cost-reduction services, CityView is able to create homeownership opportunities for middle-income and workforce families, such as local police officers, fire fighters, and school teachers. In some CityView communities, Latinos are the majority of home buyers. Affordability is also attained by gaining the benefits of economics of scale, focusing on communities of more

Figure 8.12 Cost-effective landscaping transforms a storm water requirement (A) into a community asset with native plantings, paths, and recreational trails (B).

Source: Greater Minnesota Housing Fund: *Building Better Neighborhoods,* 2001. p. 60, www.gmhf.com.

than 100 homes. Families can also qualify for various financing programs designed to reduce the down payment and closing costs.

Jingletown Homes

Jingletown in East Oakland, California, is a working-class, predominantly Latino neighborhood squeezed by sharp increases in both demand and the price of housing in the San Francisco Bay Area. New infill housing named Jingletown Homes features smaller homes with expandable attics for additional bedrooms and bathrooms, and 20 homes have space for garages, if a tenant chooses to build one (Figure 8.13). Homes have second-floor living rooms and first-floor bedrooms to provide space for home offices that are accessible on the front level (Figure 8.13B). Child care and community meeting space was also integrated within the neighborhood. By offering a variety of floor plans and well-designed outdoor community space, Pyatok Architects offered families living in Jingletown a beautiful place to work, live, and play (Figure 8.13C).

Figure 8.13 Jingletown homes in East Oakland, California, is infill housing (A) that features flexible floor plans and attractive elevations (B) and inviting community common areas (C).

Source: Pyatok Architects, Inc.

Humboldt Park

Humboldt Park is a historic Puerto Rican enclave near Lake Michigan in the heart of downtown Chicago. In recent years, the rebirth of urban living has threatened the affordability of the neighborhood, especially around Paseo Boricua, an area that stretches along Division Street from Western Avenue to Mozart. Under a city-sponsored plan called The Humboldt Park Redevelopment Area, residents joined with the Near Northwest Neighborhood Network and the Hispanic Housing Development Corporation to preserve affordability, increase community, and improve business opportunities. In 2003, with help from the city, the group developed a 59-unit senior housing complex near a health clinic and hospital for residents within 60% of the median income for the city (Figure 8.14).

Local Policy Tools

Many of the affordable housing options presented in this chapter are the results of conscientious developers effectively utilizing public policy programs to meet the needs of the community. Local policies are often outdated or were developed with an objective other than affordable housing or sustainable development, and cost reduction. For instance, higher occupancy and density assist in making housing affordable, but local restrictions may not allow this type of construction for fear of traffic congestion, overcrowded schools, and decreased access to public services. Developers and architects who are interested in creating more affordable housing should be knowledgeable about local policies in the communities where they wish to practice.

Regulatory Relief and Incentives

A variety of programs are available for developers to use at the local level, from density bonuses to waivers on costs charged in relation to housing. Check with your local housing development authorities for details. The HUD budget continues to provide funds for affordable housing through grants, faith-based initiatives, and other programs.

Maximum Densities

Zoning that imposes maximum densities per acre limit the ability of developers and builders to house more people while reducing costs.

The only recourse is to apply for a variance or push to have the ordinances changed. Many communities have inclusionary zoning, which requires developments over a certain number of units to set aside some units as affordable housing. Density bonuses are usually granted in these developments to help developers offset the cost of selling or renting below market rates. Planning departments may also help by waiving impact fees, expediting the permit process, or being flexible with design requirements.

Minimum Lot Sizes and Dwelling Footage

Minimum lot sizes and, to a lesser extent, minimum dwelling square footage are other tools a municipality uses to indirectly restrict affordable housing options because larger houses on bigger lots cost more. A growing number of communities are looking at instituting a maximum lot size in an effort to help attain affordability. As with maximum densities, a variance or zoning change for minimum lot sizes is the only recourse.

Occupancy Limits

Latino households generally contain more working members in order to offset expenses, especially those related to housing. Restrictions on the number of residents within a dwelling and their relationships can mean that these households are in violation of the occupancy code. These codes were originally developed to address the detrimental effects of overcrowding on residents' physical and mental health. When first established, the primary measurement was households per housing unit. But most occupancy limits today are measured by density of persons per room, which can impact differently on different ethnicities, nationalities, and income levels. Essentially, what is considered to be overcrowded for one population may not be for another.

Figure 8.14 The 59-unit Teresa Roldan Apartments provide affordable housing for seniors below 60% medicare income in the Humboldt Park neighborhood of Chicago. Developed by Hispanic Housing Development Corporation.

Source: Andrew Schlack.

Live/Work Space Provisions

Artists first drew attention to the live/work model when they started to occupy old warehouses and light industrial space in search of affordable housing and appropriate work space for their trade. But live/work space should not be limited to the artist's gallery below the loft or the accountant's home office. The model, when modified to accommodate lower- and middle-income entrepreneurs, offers households space to supplement the income of household members who hold jobs outside the home. Architect Michael Pyatok sees Latino households benefiting significantly:

> But not so obvious to us white-collar developers, professionals, government planners, and housing policy makers are those who earn their additional incomes not by word processing or by speculating on the stock market via the web but by repairing appliances, making clothing, running catering businesses, manufacturing and assembling toys, dolls, or plaster figurines or providing all manner of services from hair and nail cosmetics to body building and personal training—all undertaken in the confines of the homestead.

The idea of live/work spaces are gaining popularity, but zoning changes are still needed in most communities to make live/work spaces legal.

Transit-Oriented Development

The expansion of light rail and bus rapid transit in cities and surrounding suburbs combined with renewed interest by city officials in redeveloping vacant or underutilized land present opportunities for developers to build affordable transit-oriented developments (TOD).

TODs are more affordable to live in than conventional neighborhood developments because residents are given the opportunity to spend less of their income on transportation expenses. TODs offer compact housing within a five- to ten-minute walk of a transit stop and/or mixed use retail center. They provide the critical mass of residents needed to support transit stations and merchants that would be located within walking distance of housing, such as dry cleaners, child care centers, newsstands, cafes, post offices, and convenience stores.

Additional Affordable Strategies

Self-Help Housing

Self-help housing takes many forms, but the most recognized programs are the Habitat for Humanity model and the U.S. Department of Agriculture Rural Housing Service's mutual self-help program (Section 502). These models incorporate a win-win scenario. The future home owner helps build the home, thereby gaining skills that can be used to maintain the finished home. The developer benefits from lower construction costs. Both of these models offer mortgage packages with interest rates of 0–1%.

In the Section 502 program, several families are brought together to work on all of the houses for the group, thereby pooling their talents and increasing their commitment to the project. Each home owner must complete at least 65% of the construction labor for their home. Latinos are the largest group of self-help borrowers under this program.

Cohousing

Although the ownership and financing are the same as for condominiums, in that they offer individual ownership of the dwelling unit and individual mortgages, cohousing differs from condominiums in its emphasis on community. Many cohousing developments are designed with smaller dwelling units in order to maximize community space for residents. Cohousing developments generally contain a community center or community house for use by all residents. Green space is united for communal use, thereby increasing usable green space rather than parceling it off for individuals. Although cohousing can be low density and market rate, most are not, and increasing density can help lower costs and provide more shared amenities.

Mutual Housing Associations

A mutual housing association (MHA) is a nonprofit partnership of residents and civic leaders that develops, owns, and manages housing. It is governed by a volunteer board of directors. Professional staff operate MHAs with regular input and direction from residents through board participation, focus groups, surveys, and resident councils. Residents pay an affordable monthly housing charge that covers operating costs. Revenue from the operation of the housing units is used for resident programs, services, property enhancements,

Figure 8.15 The Heritage Greens neighborhood in Cambridge, Minnesota, has a 30-unit land trust component to help reduce the costs of homeownership and ensure long-term affordability.

Source: Greater Minnesota Housing Fund.

and the development of more housing opportunities. MHAs can work in both new and renovated housing.

Resident-Controlled Housing Cooperatives

In a resident-controlled housing cooperative residents own shares of stock in a corporation that owns and controls the buildings and/or property in which they live. Residents do not, however, own their own units. Members pay a monthly fee to cover property taxes, mortgage payments, utilities, insurance, and other costs. In return, they receive tax deductions and lower housing costs. Members of the co-op have a long-term lease on their space and a vote in the association's corporate governance. Residents can move and sell their shares, but not their units. The co-op model allows homeownership to be accessible to a wider market for a purchase price that is much less than a down payment.

Community Land Trusts

In a community land trust the cost of land in the housing equation is minimized because the land is held in a community trust, which limits the cost of homeownership for a potential home buyer. A CLT, usually formed by a nonprofit organization, either rents or sells the homes sited on lots that are controlled by the land trust. By doing so, the community land trust model provides homeownership opportunities to people who might otherwise be left out of the market (Figure 8.15).

Lease/Purchase Housing

Lease/purchase housing is a unique way to provide affordable housing in which a sponsor leases a home to a household that is unable to secure traditional funding. Over the time of the lease, the future home owner can build a credit history through regular payments on the lease and can also save for the down payment for the home because most lease/purchase properties are priced lower than comparable units. This model also allows future home owners to meet requirements of other mortgage entities, such as credit counseling or home buyer training while providing stability for their family.

By using the principles described in this chapter and by understanding the variety of different funding mechanisms available to help create affordable housing, most for-profit developers can find ways to make a positive difference in their communities while still turning a profit. Nonprofit developers can employ ideas related to smart growth and new urbanism to help stretch their tight budgets. Although challenging to build, affordable housing makes communities stronger, safer, and more viable, while offering greater housing choices to a larger number of community residents.

Endnotes

1. National Association of Home Builders. *Decent, Affordable Housing: It's the American Dream*. Washington, DC: National Association of Home Builders. July 2002, p. 2.

2. Bergsman, Steve. The Hispanic housing boom. *Mortgage Banking*. January 1, 2005.

3. Simmons, Patrick A. Changes in minority homeownership during the 1990s. *Census Note 07*. Washington, DC: Fannie Mae Foundation. September 2001. Retrieved April 23, 2006: http://www.fanniemaefoundation.org/programs/census_notes_7. shtml

4. Kotkin, Joel, and Thomas Tseng. *Rewarding Ambition: Latinos, Housing and the Future of California*. Malibu, California: Pepperdine University: School of Public Policy, Davenport Institute. September 2002, p. 10.

5. Fleishman, Sandra. "Homing in on Hispanic buyers." *Washington Post*. December 4, 2004, p. F1.

6. Palmeri, Christopher. Here come the Latino homebuyers. *Business Week*. March 15, 2004.

7. Friedrich, Amy, and Eric Rodriquez. Financial insecurity among growing wealth: Why healthier savings are essential to Latino prosperity. *National Council of La Raza Issue Brief*. Washington, DC: National Council of La Raza. August 2001.

8. Kotkin, Joel, and Thomas Tseng. *Rewarding Ambition: Latinos, Housing and the Future of California*. Malibu, California: Pepperdine University: School of Public Policy, Davenport Institute. September 2002, p.14.

9. *Ibid.*, p. 17.

10. *Ibid.*, p. 21.

11. Thomas-Breitfeld, Sean. The Latino workforce. *National Council of La Raza Statistical Brief.* Washington, DC: National Council of La Raza. July 2003, p. 11.

12. Moreno, Elena Marcheso. The changing face of affordability. *Multifamily Trends.* Summer 2004, p. 44–49, 68–69.

13. National Association of Home Builders Research Center. *The Practice of Low-Impact Development.* Upper Marlboro, MD: National Association of Home Builders Research Center. July 2003, p. 81–82.

14. Greater Minnesota Housing Fund. *Building Better Neighborhoods.* St. Paul, MN: Greater Minnesota Housing Fund. 2001, p. 15–22.

15. *Ibid.,* p. 27.

16. *Ibid.,* p. 28.

17. *Ibid.,* p. 35.

18. Center for Sustainable Building Research, University of Minnesota: *Minnesota Green Affordable Housing Guide, Basement.* Retrieved April 24, 2006: http://www.develop.csbr.umn.edu/freenaffordable2/factsheets/house_basement.pdf.

19. *Ibid.*

20. National Association of Home Builders Research Center. *The Practice of Low-Impact Development.* Upper Marlboro, MD: National Association of Home Builders Research Center. July, 2003, p. 29.

21. *Ibid.,* p. 30.

22. Greater Minnesota Housing Fund. *Building Better Neighborhoods.* St. Paul, MN: Greater Minnesota Housing Fund. 2001, p. 59.

Warren Hanson is president of the Greater Minnesota Housing Fund, a non-profit organization committed to increasing the supply of affordable housing for working families throughout Minnesota.

CHAPTER 9

The Path to Homeownership Among Latinos of Mexican Origin

Jongho Lee, PhD, and Harry P. Pachon, PhD

The desire to find and own a place called *home* is pervasive and has been a beacon for millions of people coming to the United States regardless of their ethnic or racial identity. Latinos are no different from other Americans in the desire to own a house. Unlike many of their fellow Americans, however, Latinos have found it more difficult to own their piece of the American dream. Although improved over the past few decades, Latino* homeownership rates are among the lowest of any ethnic group.[1] In particular, the gap between Anglo (non-Hispanic white) and Latino homeownership rates—79% and 50%, respectively, according to the March 2002 Current Population Survey—remains very large.

Importance of Homeownership to the Latino Community

Homeownership constitutes the basis of quality housing along with other elements, such as degree of overcrowding, location, completeness, and relative costs.[2] Being "ill-housed" may lead to deprivation along several dimensions such as safety, transportation,

---

*We use the terms *Latino* and *Hispanic* interchangeably to refer to individuals who trace their ancestry or origin to the Spanish speaking parts of Latin America or the Caribbean throughout the chapter. We also use the terms *Anglo* and *non-Hispanic white* interchangeably.

employment, educational opportunities, and economic stability.[3] The fact that housing is an important source of individual well-being has been extensively documented. Among other benefits, health (both physical and psychological) and financial security (both short and long term) are highly related to access to quality housing.[4] It is thus not surprising to see that home owners are found to be more likely than renters to report higher levels of self-esteem and life satisfaction and take part in public affairs.[5]

Owning a home, although costly and involving a great deal of financial responsibility, comes with a number of economic benefits in addition to the social benefits alluded to above. Not only are home owners free from increasing rents and unreasonable and insensitive rules set by landlords, but they are also more likely than renters to enjoy tax benefits and, most important, create long-term wealth and financial security.[6] Building home equity, particularly in housing markets with rapidly increasing home prices, is the primary way for Latino families to increase personal wealth. The downside, of course, is that such markets (e.g., southern California) are the most difficult ones in which to gain a foothold.

The Aggregate Demographic Picture

The nation has witnessed an unprecedented surge in the Latino population over the past decade. The popular media called it a demographic earthquake. In 1990, there were 22.4 million Latinos accounting for 9% of the nation's population. Since then, the nation has added 13 million Latinos—an increase of 58% largely due to relatively high birth rates and immigration. According to the 2000 Census, there were 35.3 million Latinos residing in the nation, representing 12.5% of the total population. According to the March 2002 Current Population Survey (CPS)—excluding over 3.8 million Latinos living on the island of Puerto Rico—this had grown to 37.4 million Latinos, making up 13.3% of the total population in 2002.

The phenomenal growth in the size of the Latino population coincides with the emergence of a substantial Latino middle class. The number of Latino middle-class households, defined as those with annual incomes over $40,000 in 1998 dollars, increased by 80% over a 20-year period from under 1.5 million in 1979 to 2.7 million in 1998 and now encompasses 35% of all Latino households.[7] Growth in middle-class households, however, was largely confined to native-born Latinos. Due mainly to increases in immigration, the percentage of Latino households defined as middle class in fact decreased over the two decades. Bean and colleagues[7] thus observed that impressive gains in education and income among native-born Latinos tend to be counterbalanced by substantial growth in poor foreign-born Latino households.

Mexican-Origin Latinos: Trends and Issues

The 2000 U.S. Census revealed that Latinos of Mexican origin account for 67% of the more than 35 million Latinos in the nation. The 2002 CPS confirmed that percentage (Figure 9.1). Although they are the driving force of the recent surges in the Latino population, Latinos of Mexican origin are among the most disadvantaged within the Latino community.[8] For example, the level of education among individuals of Mexican heritage lags behind that of all other Latino national origin groups (Figure 9.2). The proportion of Mexicans living in poverty, although smaller than that of Puerto Ricans, is greater than that of members of most other Latino national origin groups (Figure 9.3). Provided such income differences, it is not surprising that the homeownership rate of individuals of Mexican heritage trails that of many other ethnic and national origin groups (Figure 9.4).

These facts should not be taken as an excuse to discount the potential for significant future gains in education and income among Mexican-origin Latinos. With each passing generation and year of living in the U.S., as average levels of education rise and they achieve older age, their prospects for achieving middle-class status also grow.[9,10] Such anticipated progress will no doubt go hand in hand with rising homeownership rates of Mexican-origin Latinos.

Because they are the largest contributor to the immigrant population in recent decades and relatively younger, Latinos of Mexican origin constitute the largest untapped pool of first-time home buyers among all national origin groups. Despite their great potential, however, they remain rather marginalized in the housing market.

Figure 9.1 Latinos by national origin.

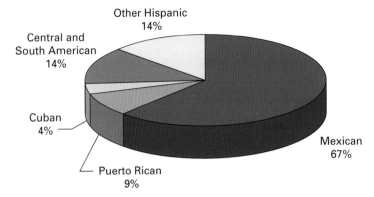

Source: March 2002 Current Population Survey.

Figure 9.2 Proportion of high school graduates (age 25+) by ethnicity and national origin.

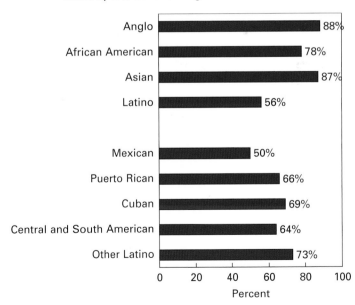

Source: March 2002 Current Population Survey.

Figure 9.3 Proportion of people living in poverty by ethnicity and national origin.

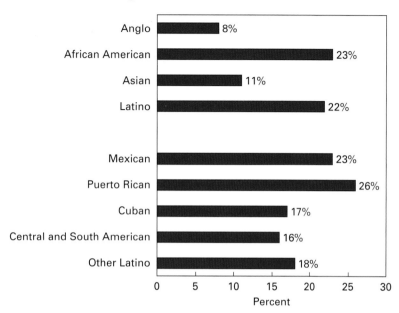

Source: March 2002 Current Population Survey.

Figure 9.4 Homeownership rates by ethnicity and national origin.

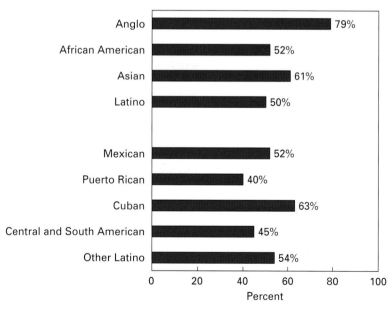

Source: March 2002 Current Population Survey.

Conceptualizing the Home Buying Process

Why do Latinos, in particular Latinos of Mexican origin, find it difficult to achieve the goal of home-ownership? This core question underlies our research. Our work extended previous research on the issue of housing[11–14] by attempting to more fully and systematically ascertain the demographic and attitudinal characteristics of those who have not attained their goal of homeownership.

We began by conceptualizing home buying as something much more time intensive and complex than a simple two-step process of deciding to purchase and then signing the final deed and mortgage documents.

Rather, it involves a process with stages, or milestones, in which people must negotiate a complex host of individuals and institutions. At any stage, or regarding any milestone, the issues confronting the home buyer are qualitatively distinct. People face different kinds of barriers to home-ownership depending on who they are and where they stand in the home buying process.

Our conceptual model proposes that prospective home buyers of Mexican origin encounter different kinds of barriers to homeownership depending on their unique mix of demographic, economic, and attitudinal characteristics. The particular barriers encountered are determined by

- what information they bring to the home buying experience
- where they are in the process
- what milestone is being surmounted

For example, immigrant status–related barriers are not applicable to native-born prospective home buyers. Likewise, those who are not yet qualified for or who have been denied a mortgage would have a greater number of barriers than are those pre-approved for a mortgage.

We posit that first-time prospective home buyers, regardless of their ethnicity or national origin, go through three distinct stages in the home buying process—dreaming, planning, and doing (Figure 9.5). People first visualize and think about having their own piece of the American dream. At the dreaming stage, their activities would be largely confined to seeking information about home buying with activities such as talking with relatives, friends, and co-workers; reading about home buying; conferring with parishioners at their church; and searching the Internet. They might start saving for a down payment but are likely to have only vague ideas of exactly what is required to move from dreaming to realizing the dream of owning a home.

When prospective home buyers come to a relatively firm decision to buy a house within the next few years, their thinking changes and they have moved to the planning stage. Activities at this stage may include a more intensified search for information on home buying (e.g., reading newspaper ads) and saving for a down payment. They will start to think of themselves as prospective home buyers, i.e., "we are looking." The planning stage might also involve fairly informal or unsystematic exploring of housing markets and opportunities.

When prospective home buyers start to formalize and intensify their activities to find and secure a house, they enter the doing stage of the process. At this point, they will be contacting and working with mortgage lenders or brokers to get a mortgage, intensively working with real estate agents to find the property to buy, making formal purchase offers, and engaging in negotiations about price and financing.

With this process in mind, we categorize renters of Mexican origin into one of the following segments of renters.

- **Visitors:** Renters who do not wish to own a home in the U.S.
- **Dreamers:** Renters who wish to own a home some day but do not plan (or consider it unlikely) to buy a home within the next five years.
- **Planners:** Renters who plan to buy a home within the next five years but haven't started to formally or intensively look for a home to buy.
- **Doers:** Renters who have started to look for a home to buy or have contacted lenders or brokers to get a mortgage.

Figure 9.5 Key milestones in the home buying process.

Renter ——— Stage 1 ——— Stage 2 ——— Stage 3 ———→ Home owner

Dreaming   Planning   Doing

Source: James Rojas.

In segmenting these groups, we assumed that a period of five years is a reasonable timetable for those who plan to buy a house within a foreseeable future. We used these groups and an additional group of recent home owners, termed *achievers*, who bought their first home during the past two years, when investigating specific barriers to homeownership faced by Latinos of Mexican origin.

Research Approach

Our research incorporated a two-tier approach consisting of

- a telephone survey of 1,400 renters and first-time recent home buyers who were Latinos of Mexican origin residing in three metropolitan areas with a substantial Latino population
- detailed case studies with 60 Latino prospective and recent home buyers of Mexican origin who were identified through the telephone survey

The former yields quantitative data that enable us to profile the characteristics of prospective and recent home buyers of Mexican heritage and ascertain specific barriers among prospective and recent home buyers at different stages of the home buying process. The latter produces context-rich qualitative information used to corroborate and strengthen results from the quantitative data. This report draws mainly on data from the telephone survey.

Our study population was Latinos of Mexican heritage who either currently rent their residence and have not ever owned a home in the United States or purchased their first home during the past two years. To account for regional variation, we selected three metropolitan areas with a sizable Mexican-origin population—more than 20,000 residents of Mexican origin—as the study sites:

- Los Angeles consolidated metropolitan statistical area (CMSA; Table 9.1)
- Houston CMSA (Table 9.2)
- Atlanta metropolitan statistical area (MSA; Table 9.3)

All five counties in the Los Angeles CMSA were studied. There, Latinos of Mexican origin constitute 30% of the total residents and 75% of Latino residents of the greater Los Angeles area. In Houston CMSA, three counties were excluded from the study sites, but 99% of Latinos from Mexico living in Houston CMSA reside in the five selected counties. Atlanta MSA consists of 20 counties, of which 4 counties were selected as the study sites. Seventy-eight percent of Latinos of Mexican origin residing in Atlanta MSA are reported to live in the four selected counties. The difficulty and cost associated with conducting case study interviews across all counties in each of these three metropolitan areas was prohibitive.

We selected these study sites because they contain Latino communities that are largely representative of others elsewhere in the country or their region. The population of Latino residents is dynamic and growing. Los Angeles CMSA includes the largest Mexican-origin enclave (East Los Angeles) and is home to one in five Latinos of Mexican origin in the nation. Houston CMSA also is known to have a large Mexican-origin enclave and is one of the most prominent gateway cities to immigrants from Mexico. Atlanta has witnessed major growth rates in Latino arrivals in recent years. Although the greater Los Angeles area is experiencing major shortfalls in the availability of affordable housing, Houston and Atlanta have a stock of affordable, entry-level properties, although limited.

Samples for the telephone survey were drawn from directory-listed households with Latino surnames within the selected counties. The sample was weighted to match data from the March 2002 CPS in regard to nativity (native born vs. foreign born) and tenure (home owner vs. renter) of Latinos of Mexican origin residing in the three metropolitan areas. The survey contained about 100 questions on the expectations, experience, and knowledge of the respondents concerning homeownership, among others. The telephone survey was conducted in the language of respondent's choice—either English or Spanish—over about three weeks from May 6 to 29,

Table 9.1 Selected Counties in Los Angeles CMSA

	Total Residents	Non-Latino Residents	Latino Residents	Residents of Mexican Heritage
Los Angeles County	9,519,338	5,277,125	4,242,213	3,041,974
Orange County	2,846,289	1,970,710	875,579	712,496
San Bernardino County	1,709,434	1,040,047	669,387	532,186
Riverside County	1,545,387	985,812	559,575	463,465
Ventura County	753,197	501,463	251,734	211,925
Total	16,373,645	9,775,157	6,598,488	4,962,046

CMSA, consolidated metropolitan statistical area. *Source:* Census 2000 Summary File.

Table 9.2 Selected Counties in Houston CMSA

	Total Residents	Non-Latino Residents	Latino Residents	Residents of Mexican Heritage
Harris County	3,400,578	2,280,827	1,119,751	814,693
Fort Bend County	354,452	279,581	74,871	51,447
Brazoria County	241,767	186,704	55,063	42,422
Galveston County	250,158	205,219	44,939	34,670
Montgomery County	293,768	256,618	37,150	27,845
Total	4,540,723	3,208,949	1,331,774	971,077

CMSA, consolidated metropolitan statistical area. *Source:* Census 2000 Summary File.

Table 9.3 Selected Counties in Atlanta CMSA

	Total Residents	Non-Latino Residents	Latino Residents	Residents of Mexican Heritage
Gwinnett County	588,448	524,311	64,137	36,016
Fulton County	816,006	767,950	48,056	32,476
DeKalb County	665,865	613,323	52,542	30,741
Cobb County	607,751	560,787	46,964	29,833
Total	2,678,070	2,466,371	211,699	129,066

CMSA, consolidated metropolitan statistical area. *Source:* Census 2000 Summary File.

Figure 9.6 Segments of renters.

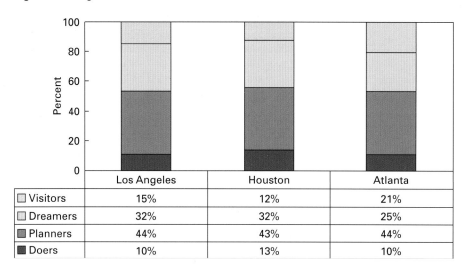

	Los Angeles	Houston	Atlanta
☐ Visitors	15%	12%	21%
☐ Dreamers	32%	32%	25%
▨ Planners	44%	43%	44%
■ Doers	10%	13%	10%

2003. Interviews were conducted with adults who were responsible for the decision to buy or rent the residence or who make important financial decisions in the household.

The Mexican-Origin Latino Home Buying Market

Our survey sample of renters was composed of 16% visitors, 29% dreamers, 44% planners, and 11% doers. There are minor variations in this composition by location (Figure 9.6). There are more visitors in Atlanta compared to Los Angeles and Houston, which is related to the fact that Atlanta has only recently become one of the primary destinations for new immigrants. New immigrants seem to be simply too busy adjusting their life to a new environment and making ends meet to think seriously about owning a home in the United States in the foreseeable future.

Figure 9.6 also reveals that the largest segment of renters are planners—those who plan to buy a home within the next five years—and less than a third are dreamers. About 10% of renters across the three metropolitan areas are doers, the group who have either started to look for a home to buy or contacted lenders or brokers to get a mortgage. When combined with planners, this indicates that more than half of Latinos of Mexican origin who currently rent will attempt to purchase a home within the next five years. This segment is a huge potential market for the entire housing industry.

Visitors

In our study, visitors constituted a small segment of renters. During the survey, those who reported having no interest in homeownership were thus asked a limited number of questions, e.g., age, country of birth, income. The visitors' average age was 41. They were predominantly foreign born, with 82% born outside the U.S. The average length of stay in the U.S. was 11 years, and they earned the lowest income. Forty-nine percent reported an annual household income less than $35,000, and 38% responded by saying "don't know" or refused to provide their household income.

When asked why they were not interested in homeownership, 42% of visitors responded that they planned to return to Mexico and buy a house there (Figure 9.7). Twelve percent of visitors indicated that they did not believe they could afford to buy a house, and 11% believed their financial situation was not secure enough to support the purchase. Only 8% of visitors reported that they simply prefer to rent. These results indicate that the visitor segment is comprised of a number of migrant workers who may not be in the U.S. permanently and who constantly move following jobs as well as those who are completely priced out of the housing market and part of an urban underclass.

Renters and Buyers

The remainder of our study group was composed of prospective home buyers and new home owners. Our data revealed that all four groups generally look similar in terms of their demographic and attitudinal characteristics but that there are notable differences between dreamers and planners on one hand and doers and achievers on the other. Specifically, dreamers and planners were relatively inactive in the homeownership market and doers and achievers were active in the homeownership market. To ascertain what factors are directly responsible for the transition to homeownership, we performed a multivariate analysis of the survey data using logistic regression, with the binary measure of inactivity or activity in the homeownership market as the dependent variable.

Four types of factors are considered to account for the path to homeownership: demographic, financial, informational, and cultural factors.[15–19]

- Demographic factors include age, marital status, number of children in the household, area of residence.

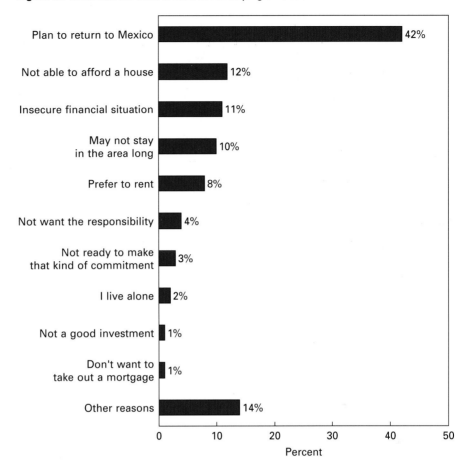

Figure 9.7 Reasons for lack of interest in buying a house.

Note: Percentages add up to more than 100% due to multiple responses.

- Financial factors include household income, job security, perceptions of financial well-being, and difficulty saving for the down payment.
- Information factors include familiarity with how to qualify for a mortgage, difficulty finding an advisor, and information on home buying.
- Cultural (immigration) factors include place of birth, length of stay in the U.S., immigration status, English proficiency, formal relationship with U.S. financial institutions, homeownership in Mexico, remittance to Mexico, and being discriminated against in the housing market.

Our logistic regression analysis showed that 10 of these factors had a statistically significant impact on the transition from being inactive to being active in the homeownership market (α <0.05, two-tailed). The factors directly responsible for the transition into homeownership are:

Demographic factors:
- Age
- Marital status
- Number of children in the household
- Area of residence

Financial factors
- Household income
- Difficulty saving for the down paymnent

Information factors
- Familiarity with how to qualify for a mortgage
- Difficulty finding an advisor

Cultural (immigration) factors
- Immigration status
- Formal relationship with U.S. financial institutions

The Path to Homeownership

Our analysis shows that those who are active in the homeownership market—doers and achievers—are different from those who are comparatively inactive—dreamers and planners—in terms of age, marital status, number of children living with them in the same household, and area of residence. Surprisingly, level of education is not a significant factor in the transition to homeownership.

Those actively seeking homeownership are on average 4 years older than those still in the dreaming and planning stages (Figure 9.8). More doers and achievers are married (79%) than dreamers and planners (63%; Figure 9.9). The third most important demographic feature is number of children in the family; doers and achievers average 2 children under age 18 per family, whereas dreamers and planners average 1.7 children per family (Figure 9.10).

Although strong housing markets help sustain the economy, many parts of the nation (e.g., southern California) have been experiencing housing crises. These are caused by the intersection of the unprecedented demand of the larger population size and rapidly increasing prices. Soaring housing prices have simply priced middle- and moderate-income families out of the housing market in many regions. For example, the California Association of Realtors reports that a median-priced house was no longer within the reach of two-thirds of California families in April of 1999,[20] where the supply of moderately priced housing—multifamily housing such as townhomes and condominiums—is particularly lacking. Adding to low housing supply and escalating housing prices are excessive governmental regulations concerning growth control coinciding with the "not in my back yard" phenomenon, which have slowed or stopped housing production and made housing construction more costly.[21–23]

In our study, 44% of home buyers in Houston and 39% in Atlanta were able to achieve homeownership, i.e., were doers or achievers, compared with 35% of home buyers in Los Angeles (Figure 9.11). This suggests the impact of this housing crisis on prospective home buyers of Mexican origin living in the Los Angeles area. In the end, the scarcity of affordable housing erects barriers to homeownership among many moderate-income families, including Latino families of Mexican origin.

Financial Barriers

Previous studies have established that the relative lack of resources due to low income level is largely

Figure 9.8 Age by segment.

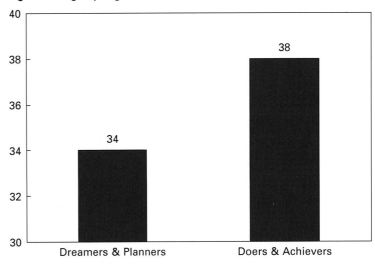

Figure 9.9 Marital status by segment.

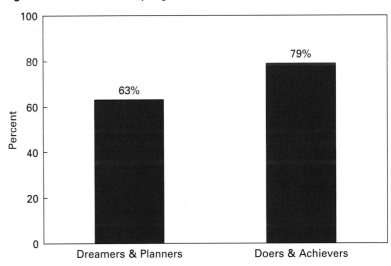

Figure 9.10 Number of children in the household by segment.

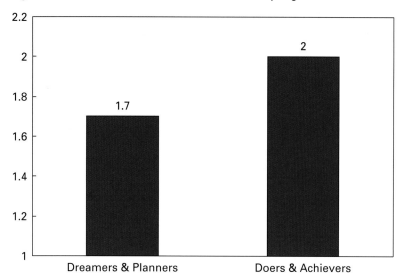

responsible for the predicament of Latinos of Mexican origin in the home buying market.[24-28] With insufficient incomes, Latinos of Mexican origin are more likely than members of other ethnic/national origin groups to face difficulty obtaining the down payment and getting a mortgage. They are also less likely to have confidence in their long-term finances in an era of economic uncertainty. Because the gap in homeownership rates that separates Latinos of Mexican origin from members of other ethnic or national origin groups, in particular Anglos, can be explained through differences in income, the disparity in homeownership may be viewed as essentially a class issue.

Our multivariate analysis confirmed that financial barriers are at work. Those who are active in the homeownership market—doers and achievers—tend to be more financially endowed than dreamers and planners (Figure 9.12). Seventy-two percent of dreamers and planners have incomes less than $35,000, whereas 53% of doers and achievers belong to this low income category. This clearly shows that household income determines where home buyers of Mexican origin are in the home buying process.

Saving for the down payment is an immediate barrier to homeownership among home buyers of Mexican origin (Figure 9.13). For example, 62% of dreamers and planners find it very or somewhat difficult to save enough needed for the down payment. Forty-four percent of doers and achievers also report that it is difficult to save for the down payment. Interestingly, other financial factors, such as perceptions of job security and personal financial conditions, were not significant in determining the transition to homeownership. Any effect they may have on the transition to homeownership appeared to be overshadowed by the powerful influences of household income and difficulty in saving for the down payment.

Figure 9.11 Proportion of doers and achievers by area of residence.

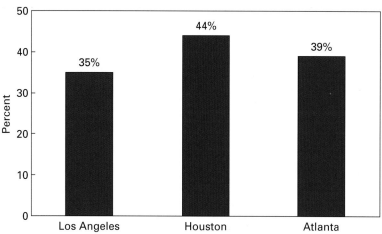

Information Barriers

For immigrants who speak little English, it is a daunting task to acquire information on and understand the complexity of the home buying process. Help from others is almost certainly required. This situation would be exacerbated among recent migrants who are not yet well placed in established community networks. As a result, they would be uninformed or misinformed about the various aspects of the home buying process, such as:

- How to get started
- Getting a mortgage (e.g., uninformed or misinformed of eligibility)
- Finding a real estate agent or broker
- Finding a house
- Making offers and negotiating

In fact, 71% of dreamers and planners reported that they are either somewhat or totally unfamiliar with how to qualify for a mortgage (Figure 9.14). In contrast, over half of the doers and achievers reported familiarity with how to qualify for a mortgage. Note, then, that almost half of doers and achievers were actively engaged in homeownership despite not being totally familiar with the mortgage qualification process. Therefore, familiarity with how to qualify for a mortgage determines the transition to homeownership but only in part.

Unfamiliarity with how to qualify for a mortgage goes hand in hand with misinformation about mortgage lending. The majority of Latino home buyers of Mexican origin did not know that banks and other lenders in the U.S. will make mortgage loans to legal permanent residents who are non-U.S. citizens (Figure 9.15). Fifty-five percent of dreamers and planners did not believe, or were not sure, of this. Even 51% of doers and achievers were uninformed about this. Although data do not provide evidence of a direct relationship between such misinformation and the transition to home-ownership, such a high level of misinformation among Latino home buyers of Mexican origin signifies an information barrier to homeownership.

Significantly, 61% of dreamers and planners consider it difficult to find someone whom they can

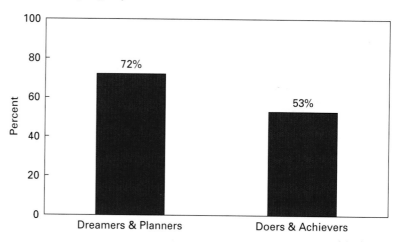

Figure 9.12 Proportion of home buyers with incomes below $35K by segment.

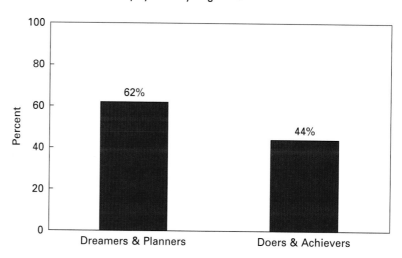

Figure 9.13 Proportion of home buyers who find it difficult to save for the down payment by segment.

Figure 9.14 Proportion of home buyers who are unfamiliar with how to qualify for a mortgage by segment.

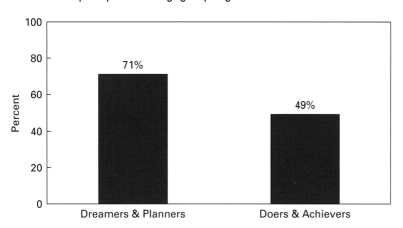

trust to advise them about the home buying process (Figure 9.16). This implies either a low level of knowledge or a high level of misinformation about mortgage loans. Fewer doers and achievers (39%) report that it has been very or somewhat difficult for them to find an advisor they can trust. This suggests that having difficulty finding a trusted advisor in the home buying process is an immediate obstacle to homeownership among Latinos of Mexican origin. Difficulty finding a trusted advisor would in turn be responsible for low levels of knowledge about various aspects of the home buying process, which would work together to prevent homeownership.

Prospective home buyers—dreamers, planners, and doers—and recent home owners—achievers—were questioned about how they would obtain or did obtain information about home buying. Real estate professionals are the most common source of that information (Figures 9.17 and 9.18). The second most frequently used sources of information about home buying were friends or co-workers and family members or relatives. Home buying seminars or classes and financial institutions, such as banks, are not among the most popular sources of information.

Latino home buyers of Mexican origin reported that they prefer to work with a Latino real estate agent. In our survey, three-quarters of both prospective home buyers and recent home owners expressed a preference to work with a Latino real estate professional. This seems to have much to do with the language preference of Latino home buyers of Mexican origin but may also reflect the additional comfort level offered by working with a co-ethnic real estate professional to achieve homeownership.

Figure 9.15 Proportion of home buyers who are uninformed of mortgage lending by segment.

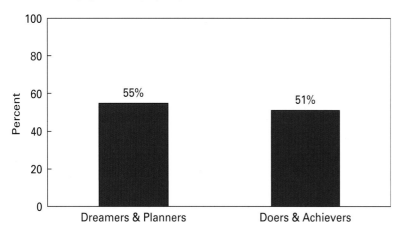

Barriers Related to Immigration

Many potential Latino home buyers are either immigrants or children of immigrants who are not yet fully acculturated to the social and cultural milieu of American society. They often do not possess a good understanding of the functioning of various institutions—including financial institutions—in the U.S. and the norms and practices of the society that are different from what they were used to in Mexico. They may distrust the banking system and shun its use, which results in not having established formal relations with financial institutions in the U.S. Furthermore, they could have unverifiable incomes and little (or no) credit and/or be unable to gather all the documents, due largely to their immigration status, needed to acquire a mortgage. As a result, Latinos of Mexican origin face various immigration-related barriers to homeownership and may be even more disadvantaged when trying to enter the homeownership market than members of other ethnic groups despite a similar level of resources.

Among various cultural and immigration-related factors we studied, immigration status and having a bank account were the significant barriers to homeownership. Nativity, length of stay in the U.S., English proficiency, current or future expected homeownership in Mexico, remittance of funds to Mexico, and being discriminated against in the housing market were not directly responsible for the transition to homeownership.

U.S. citizens and legal permanent residents are more likely than those who have not yet established legal permanent residency or are undocumented to make the transition to homeownership (Figure 9.19). Seventy-four percent of doers and achievers, versus 58% of dreamers and planners, are either U.S. citizens or legal permanent residents. Forty-two percent of dreamers and planners report that they are neither U.S. citizens nor legal permanent residents of the United States but "something else." Although it is not illegal for an undocumented immigrant to buy property in the United States, they are legally banned from acquiring certain types of loans, such as those that are federally insured.

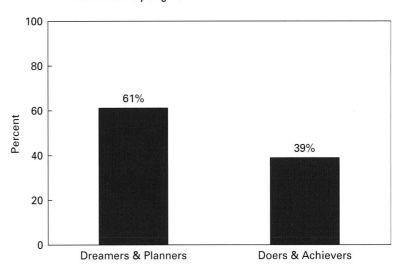

Figure 9.16 Proportion of home buyers who consider it difficult to find an advisor by segment.

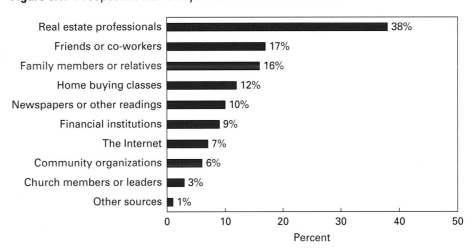

Figure 9.17 Prospective home buyers' sources of information.

Note: Percentages add up to more than 100% due to multiple responses.

Figure 9.18 Recent home owners' sources of information.

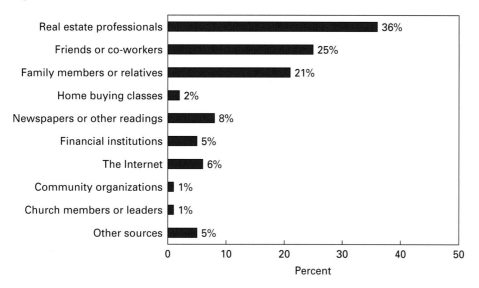

Real estate professionals 36%
Friends or co-workers 25%
Family members or relatives 21%
Home buying classes 2%
Newspapers or other readings 8%
Financial institutions 5%
The Internet 6%
Community organizations 1%
Church members or leaders 1%
Other sources 5%

Percent

Note: Percentages add up to more than 100% due to multiple responses.

Figure 9.19 Immigration status by segment.

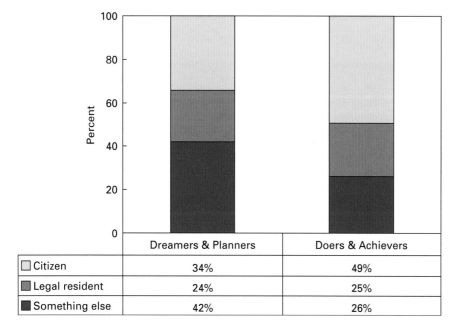

	Dreamers & Planners	Doers & Achievers
☐ Citizen	34%	49%
◼ Legal resident	24%	25%
■ Something else	42%	26%

Therefore, undocumented immigrants may rely on their family members, relatives, or friends who are legally present in the U.S. to act as proxy buyers to obtain a mortgage and buy a house.

Our data confirmed that those who are "unbanked" do not progress as far in the home buying process as those who have established a bank account. Fewer than half of prospective Latino home buyers of Mexican origin have a formal relationship with a U.S. financial institution (Figure 9.20). Yet 23% of doers and achievers report not having a bank account. How achievers managed to buy a house without having established a formal relationship with U.S. financial institutions poses an interesting question; perhaps they used proxy buyers for the purchase.

In addition, a significant portion of prospective Latino home buyers of Mexican origin does not have a credit card. Having a credit card or having financial obligations to their relatives and friends living in Mexico, however, has little direct impact on the transition to homeownership. Likewise, data do not offer evidence of a direct relationship between nativity, duration in the U.S., levels of English proficiency, current or future homeownership in Mexico, and housing discrimination on the one hand and the transition to homeownership on the other.

Conclusion

Latinos from Mexico comprise two-thirds of all Latinos in the U.S., a huge potential market of home buyers. In this chapter, we provided details on the demographic and socioeconomic characteristics of prospective and recent Latino home buyers of Mexican origin and documented the various obstacles they face on the path to homeownership. Unlike many average Americans who own their homes and despite strong aspirations for homeownership, a great number of Mexican-origin Latinos have not been able to claim their piece of the American dream. Where do the challenges lie? We found that Latino home buyers of Mexican origin are predominantly immigrants with low levels of income, education, and knowledge about the home buying process.

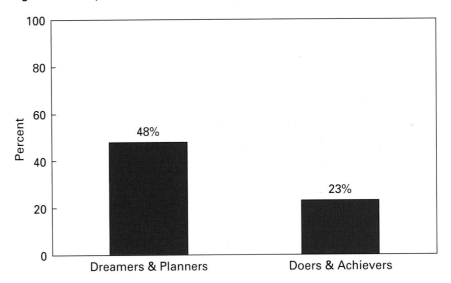

Figure 9.20 Proportion of the unbanked by segment.

Latinos of Mexican origin face financial barriers to homeownership. Most dreamers and planners have moderate incomes yet tend to live in urban areas where housing is very expensive. They are on the verge of being priced out of the housing market. They also find it extremely difficult to save for the down payment and closing costs. This implies that homeownership differentials between Latinos of Mexican origin and members of other ethnic groups, in particular white non-Hispanics, are largely explained by the lower levels of income Latinos of Mexican origin command. To the extent to which levels of income account for the likelihood of owning a house, this difference in level of homeownership is a class issue.

Information barriers are noteworthy. A large number of prospective home buyers of Mexican origin—new immigrants in particular—are not informed about how to qualify for a mortgage and whether financial institutions will even offer them one. Furthermore, they do not know where to turn to get reliable information. Difficulty finding a trusted advisor on home buying is a significant barrier in the transition to homeownership.

Two immigration-related factors depress homeownership rates among Latinos of Mexican origin. One is immigration status. It appears that a significant number of dreamers and planners (and even some doers and achievers) are undocumented immigrants. These individuals might obtain a mortgage if they are lucky enough to find a lender who is willing to accept identification other than a social security number, i.e., an individual taxpayer identification number issued by the Internal Revenue Service for tax purposes. But such cases would be rather isolated. Until they establish legal residency in the U.S., owning their piece of the American dream will continue to elude untold numbers of undocumented immigrants.

The other significant factor related to immigration is relationship to a financial institution. A surprisingly large number of prospective Latino home buyers of Mexican origin are unbanked, a significant barrier to homeownership. Although a segment of the unbanked is comprised of undocumented immigrants without identification normally acceptable to U.S. financial institutions, the remaining portion of the unbanked would largely constitute those who are distrustful of the banking system and/or used to operating in a cash economy.

Note that other barriers to homeownership—such as English proficiency, remittance of assets to Mexico, housing discrimination, and current or planned homeownership in Mexico—were found to be significant barriers to U.S. homeownership in other studies but failed to be supported by our data. We did not find evidence that this is a function of multicollinearity among various cultural factors included in the model we used. Although these factors may have some part to play in determining the transition to homeownership, their roles appear to be indirect or secondary.

The potential is great, therefore, for increasing the rate of homeownership among Latinos of Mexican decent by working to erode these specific barriers. To do this successfully, we believe that both public and private institutions must take into account the reality of the Mexican-origin Latino experience.

Acknowledgments

This chapter draws on data from a research project that was supported by the Freddie Mac Corporation. We greatly benefited from the efforts of many individuals in conducting the earlier project. Our special thanks go to Donald S. Bradley, Brian J. Surette, Louis Tornatzky, and Celina Torres for their research support and assistance throughout the duration of the project.

Endnotes

1. Coulson, N. Edward. Why are Hispanic- and Asian-American home-ownership rates so low? Immigration and other factors. *Journal of Urban Economics* 45:209–27, 1999.

2. Lopez, Manuel Mariano. Su casa no es mi casa: Hispanic housing conditions in contemporary America, 1949–1980. In *Race, Ethnicity, and Minority Housing in the United States*. Jamshid A. Momeni, Ed. New York: Greenwood Press, 1986.

3. *Ibid.*

4. Krivo, Lauren J. Immigrant characteristics and Hispanic-Anglo housing inequality. *Demography* 32:599–615, 1995.

5. Rohe, William M., and Michael A. Stegman. The effects of homeownership on the self-esteem, perceived control, and life satisfaction of low-income people. *Journal of the American Planning Association* 60:173–84, 1994.

6. Lopez-Aqueres, Waldo, Joelle Skaga, and Tadeusz Kugler. *Housing the Latino Population in the 21st Century: The Challenge Ahead.* Los Angeles: The Tomás Rivera Policy Institute, 2002.

7. Bean, Frank D, Stephen J. Trejo, Randy Capps, and Michael Tyler. *The Latino Middle Class: Myth, Reality and Potential.* Los Angeles: The Tomás Rivera Policy Institute, 2001.

8. *Ibid.*

9. *Ibid.*

10. Myers, Dowell, John Pitkin, and Julie Park. *California Demographic Futures: Projections to 2030, by Immigrant Generations, Nativity, and Time of Arrival in U.S.* Los Angeles: University of Southern California, School of Policy, Planning, and Development, 2005.

11. Coulson, N. Edward. Why are Hispanic- and Asian-American homeownership rates so low? Immigration and other factors. *Journal of Urban Economics* 45:209–27, 1999.

12. Gyourko, Joseph, and Peter Linneman. Analysis of the changing influences on traditional households' ownership patterns. *Journal of Urban Economics* 39:318–41, 1996.

13. Krivo, Lauren J. Immigrant characteristics and Hispanic-Anglo housing inequality. *Demography* 32:599–615, 1995.

14. Painter, Gary, Stuart Gabriel, and Dowell Myers. Race, immigrant status, and housing tenure choice. *Journal of Urban Economics* 49:150–67, 2000.

15. Coulson, N. Edward. Why are Hispanic- and Asian-American homeownership rates so low? Immigration and other factors. *Journal of Urban Economics* 45:209–27, 1999.

16. Gyourko, Joseph, and Peter Linneman. Analysis of the changing influences on traditional households' ownership patterns. *Journal of Urban Economics* 39:318–41, 1996.

17. Krivo, Lauren J. Immigrant characteristics and Hispanic-Anglo housing inequality. *Demography* 32: 599-615, 1995.

18. Lopez, Manuel Mariano. Su casa no es mi casa: Hispanic housing Conditions in contemporary America, 1949–1980. In *Race, Ethnicity, and Minority Housing in the United States*. Jamshid A. Momeni, Ed. New York: Greenwood Press, 1986.

19. Painter, Gary, Stuart Gabriel, and Dowell Myers. Race, immigrant status, and housing tenure choice. *Journal of Urban Economics* 49:150–67, 2000.

20. California Association of Realtors. 2000 California existing single-family housing market annual historical data summary. *Real Estate Research Report,* March 2001.

21. Joint Center for Housing Studies of Harvard University. *The State of the Nation's Housing*. Cambridge, MA: Harvard University Press, 2001.

22. Kotkin, Joel, Thomas Tseng, and Erika Ozuna. *Rewarding Ambition: Latinos, Housing, and the Future of California*. Malibu, CA: Pepperdine University, Davenport Institute, 2002.

23. Lopez-Aqueres, Waldo, Joelle Skaga, and Tadeusz Kugler. *Housing the Latino Population in the 21st Century: The Challenge Ahead.* Los Angeles: The Tomás Rivera Policy Institute, 2002.

24. Coulson, N. Edward. Why are Hispanic- and Asian-American homeownership rates so low? Immigration and other factors. *Journal of Urban Economics* 45:209–27, 1999.

25. Krivo, Lauren J. Immigrant characteristics and Hispanic-Anglo housing inequality. *Demography* 32:599-615, 1995.

26. Lopez, Manuel Mariano. Su casa no es mi casa: Hispanic housing conditions in contemporary America, 1949–1980. In *Race, Ethnicity, and Minority Housing in the United States*. Jamshid A. Momeni, Ed. New York: Greenwood Press, 1986.

27. Gyourko, Joseph, and Peter Linneman. Analysis of the changing influences on traditional households' ownership patterns. *Journal of Urban Economics* 39:318–41, 1996.

28. Painter, Gary, Stuart Gabriel, and Dowell Myers. Race, immigrant status, and housing tenure choice. *Journal of Urban Economics* 49:150–67, 2000.

Jongho Lee, PhD, is an Assistant Professor, Department of Political Science, Western Illinois University, Macomb, Illinois.

Harry P. Pachon, PhD, is a Professor, School of Policy, Planning, and Development; and President, Tomás Rivera Policy Institute, University of Southern California, Los Angeles.

Source: James Rojas.

CHAPTER 10

Barriers Confronting Latinos

Jorge Velasco

The Rio Grande City region of Texas where I live, located near the southern border of Texas with Mexico, has experienced the pioneering of "owner finance" builders. This alternative financing mechanism allows home buyers with little credit history or a blemished credit history to purchase homes directly from builders. Once the builder has financed the mortgage note, he or she can either hold this note for some period or sell it to investors in the secondary market. Using this mechanism, builders have sold over 5,000 houses in less than three years.

However, their sales representatives, financial intermediaries, and customer service have been, in some cases, so poor that they have ruined their brand in the market. Some builders who did not understand how to sell houses to Latinos have had to leave the market. To reach Latinos, it makes sense to understand Latinos.

The greatest obstacle that builders face in selling their homes to Latinos is that a significant portion of this target market doesn't understand how home financing works and doesn't know they can afford to buy and care for a home. I will describe the financial and cultural walls separating many Latino families from the purchase of a house based on my experiences selling more than 2,000 homes to the Latino market. I offer solutions for the housing industry to consider while formulating sales techniques and outreach to prospective Latino home buyers. Builders, real estate agents, and financiers must help Latino clients understand home equity, property value, and how easy the home purchasing process can be.

Source: James Rojas.

Looking at Latinos

The image of Latinos in the housing industry is varied. For some, Latinos are represented by the immigrant who crossed into this country a few months ago and has decided to bring his family over in the near future. After securing employment, the family may start thinking about buying a house. To others, Latinos are progressive young couples who are bilingual and bicultural. They want a second house for recreational purposes.

Although both of these groups exist, perhaps they are at the opposite ends of a continuum, with many variations on these stories in between. Where individuals fall along this continuum might be determined by which immigration generation they belong to and their levels of assimilation of American society.

First Generation Profile

- Living in the United States for less than 5 years
- Illegal or legal status
- Migrant worker or career professional
- Low degree of assimilation to American culture
- Prefer to conduct business in Spanish
- Jealously guard the values they learned in their countries
- Prefer to interact with people who know their language and culture
- Maintain close ties to family members back home

Home builders, housing officials, and financiers who have Latino employees or who can speak Spanish have the best chance of reaching first-generation clients. This group identifies better with people whose value scale is similar to theirs than more-assimilated Latinos. Perhaps the most important characteristic is the habit of developing relationships first and then doing business later.

Traditionally, banks don't service the low-end market in the countries they left. Credit is very tight and not accessible by low-wage workers. Therefore, first-generation immigrants tend not to rely on financial institutions to solve short-term financing needs. Research shows that Latinos as a group are the "least bankable" segment in U.S. society (see Chapter 9, The Path to Homeownership Among Latinos of Mexican Origin). It takes longer for them to develop a credit history that will in turn provide access to home loans.

Second Generation Profile

- Living in the U.S. for more than 5 years but less than 15 years
- May have come to the U.S. as children
- Assimilated through the educational system
- Bilingual

Second-generation immigrants are more familiar with financial institutions and mortgage brokers. They also have a better understanding of the way credit works and feel less intimidated at the prospect of purchasing a home.

Third Generation Profile

- Born in the U.S.
- Fully assimilated
- Fluent in English
- Have different levels of proficiency in Spanish
- Highly influenced by their Latino parents and grandparents

Source: James Rojas.

Third-generation Latinos in the U.S. are financially stable and educated enough to buy a house using traditional financing and brokerage options. Regardless, when considering buying a new house, they still view the process as a dream rather than a business transaction.

Bridging Barriers to Reach Latino Home Buyers

The varying levels of sophistication about banking procedures, mortgage loans, and house financing methods have created barriers for Latinos who otherwise might purchase a house tomorrow. The smart builder, financier, or realtor will understand those barriers and address them as they work with Latinos.

Barrier #1: Understanding the Credit System

Some first-generation Latinos have left their countries for good. Several family members start pooling their resources to rent a house or large apartment. As they progress and earn more money, they can rent their own apartment or once again pool their resources with other family members to buy a house. Once they become more financially fit, they look for a chance to own a house on their own. This process can take anywhere between two to six years.

For this group, the dream of owning a home may be the highest of priorities. Once they have decided to stay here, they seek the place where they would spend the rest of their "family life," the time that kids and parents will live together under the same roof. The drive to provide this place for their family is strong and can be a higher priority than becoming financially fit. Sometimes, they will stretch their finances well beyond the comfort zone to own property.

In contrast, the second generation realizes that institutions dictate the way you can buy or finance a house. They learn to live within the system while understanding the ramifications of maintaining a good credit record. At the same time, they understand how real estate brokers, sales people, and developers operate. They know how to shop for the best opportunities to acquire a house at favorable terms. For them, owning a home means they have "made it" and are successful by their parents' standards.

Finally, Latinos born in the U.S. understand the business and financial system as well as anyone. They understand credit beyond the basics and know how to work with banks and other financial intermediaries to obtain financing. For this group, owning a home is a way to improve cash flow, build equity, and optimize taxes.

Barrier #2: Reaching the Dreamers

When you are born in America, you become part of a social security system. You build a credit history from your early adulthood years. Owning a home is no different from owning a car.

For first-generation immigrants, the notion of owning a home in their own countries is so difficult to conceive, for lack of financial resources and credit options, that they can't imagine owning a home in America. Still, they dream on. Home builders can reach this group through marketing and advertising in Latino media.

Once persuaded to buy a house, this Latino group will use 100% of their resources to buy a home. They don't move into a house thinking that they will upgrade to a better home within the next 5 years. They expect to stay in that house for the next 20 years and, in some cases, for the rest of their lives.

The second generation is more familiar with the credit system. When ready, buying their first house is the end of a phase in their lives where they were dependent on other family members for support. It is the beginning of their independence. This is a strong selling point for home builders.

Barrier #3: The Young and the Uninformed

Owning a house for some families has meant devoting 30 or 40 years working toward that goal. For some Latinos in their mid-20s, it is inconceivable to think they can own a house before age 30. Why would it take, for them, only 10 years of work to own their own home when it took their parents a lifetime?

This is a self-imposed limitation that home builders can counter with billboards about how easy it is to own a home, classified ads about people willing to finance a house regardless of credit history, and real estate agents explaining financial procedures. It takes several interactions from different sources to persuade people who aren't consciously shopping for a house. They don't consider contacting a real estate broker to help them find a house or working with a bank or mortgage broker to find out how much they can afford to spend on a house. This market is difficult to reach using conventional marketing approaches because they are not really in the market.

However, using "guerrilla" marketing— a combination of low-cost, high-impact advertising e.g., flyers and business cards with short memorable messages— and an intelligent "counseling" approach to help them understand how simple it is to start the process toward homeownership can help capture this segment. There is also an added benefit. Once these Latinos trust you and become convinced that you or your company is really out to help them, their informal network can be so strong and large that you earn a windfall of referrals. One of the largest single-family builders in the South Texas Valley had the experience of a customer who brought 10 more home buyers into the same neighborhood.

It can be inferred from this example that Latinos rely heavily on the opinions and experiences of their friends, relatives, and acquaintances. To them, what is most relevant is that their next-door neighbor was able to buy a house. What is credible to them is that their brother, who is in a similar financial situation, just bought a new house. If someone they know and relate to was able to purchase, they also can. Home builders should document success stories of Latinos who didn't know they could afford a home and communicate those stories through Latino media.

Source: Christine B. Charlip.

Barrier #4: Cash Culture

More than likely, first-generation Latinos grew up in a cash culture. Until recently, banks in Mexico and other Latin American countries didn't cater to middle- or low-income citizens. It wasn't profitable. In some Latin American countries, citizens need over $1,000 just to open a bank account. Access to credit is even more out of reach.

Therefore, education about what credit is and how it should be used is vital. Ask questions and present scenarios that help you know what they still need to learn and how they will react to problems. Counsel them on how to act responsibly. Sometimes, access to credit is abused simply because of lack of understanding.

First- and second-generation Latinos, in many cases, don't believe they can actually purchase a house merely by just investing a small down payment and then making monthly payments. They struggle to believe that a $60,000 home can be bought by putting down $3,000 and financing the rest at a fixed rate for 30 years by paying around $500 each month. Therefore, it is critical that home sellers trying to reach this market effectively must walk them through the obstacles that have been created in their own minds.

Some of these preconceptions are the result of what their ancestors experienced when trying to buy their own piece of land. Most first-generation Latinos saw their own parents buy a small tract of land and pay for it all at once with their life savings. Once owned, their parents would start to save again to build on the land. The absence of credit from the banking system, as well as a lack of government programs supporting homeownership, made this process longer and more difficult than it is in the U.S.

When a family sees an ad for an $80,000 house, they believe that they cannot afford it. Why? Because trying to buy that home with no financing would mean eight years of working nonstop to maximize savings. Often, this obstacle is enough to stop them from exploring potential access to financing.

Barrier #5: Securing Financing for the "Impossible House"

Frequently, when potential buyers are approached about buying a home, they reject the notion because of the complexities associated with the process. First, they are not shopping for a house with a real estate agent. This means that they rely on the opinions and judgments of their relatives and friends. Second, once they decide to buy a house, the financing process becomes a challenging and threatening prospect. They get discouraged and quit the search.

Home builders should assure their Latino customers that financing a home is comparable to buying a car. It is easier than getting credit card financing because of the collateral. But even builders who provide owner financing have a difficult time convincing customers that the approval process is not difficult, and they may grow suspicious of anyone suggesting otherwise.

Barrier #6: Lack of Trust

In doing business with the Latino buyer, trust is an important consideration. This trust is not necessarily a function of performance, at least not at the beginning. First- and second-generation Latinos want to know more about the person they are dealing with prior to doing business with them.

A builder's track record may be an important consideration for buyers in choosing who to work with, but it is subordinate to the intuition of the Latino buyer. This creates a problem for Latino buyers because their intuition is biased and not always logical. Trust is not necessarily correlated to the track record and experience of the financial intermediary or real estate broker.

Latinos prefer to deal with small operators and tend to be suspicious of large companies with a large sales force. Therefore, larger companies that may be very serious about trying to serve this community frequently have more problems capturing their business than the mom and pop operators.

Essentially, Latinos develop relationships first and do business later. This takes more time, but for sales people it is worth the extra effort. Agents who have performed a service for one Latino family have a high likelihood of referral business.

Establishing trust with a home builder is critical, especially for immigrants. First-generation home buyers have traditionally been abused by unscrupulous business people in their own countries and may have been victimized already in the U.S.

Their lack of familiarity with the business culture makes them vulnerable to fraud, although the amount of fraud they have

Source: James Rojas.

experienced as a group is hard to track. Latinos tend not to complain to the Better Business Bureau or other consumer protection agencies when they experience abuse.

To reach this group, builders, financial intermediaries, banks, real estate brokers, and other housing industry professionals must pay close attention to the training they provide for their sales force who is serving Latino communities. Managers need to be able to help their sales force understand the reluctance of some Latino home buyers.

Research shows that customers will forgive most businesses' failures as long as the customer perceives that the business representative cares about them. This is important to Latinos because they rely heavily on relationship building and trust.

When you have difficulties delivering a product or service to them, you need to communicate the bad news immediately. Sales reps need to show sensitivity toward their customers' frustration and acknowledge their concerns. Once you have done this, you can then correct the failure and feel reasonably certain that they will continue to do business with you.

Even when things are going smoothly, it helps to add an extra dose of tender loving care. Remember, once you have won a Latino family's trust, you will have their loyalty and that of their children and perhaps that of their children's children . . . as long as you keep caring about them.

Barrier #7: Families Pool Resources

It is common for first-time Latino home buyers to finance the purchase of a house with other family members and with other families. Some underwriters see this as a negative and deny financing.

A trio of Latino families may, for example, locate financing, buy together, and then establish a good credit history independent of one another. They will eventually qualify for a house on their own.

The Latino market will continue growing in number and volume. Therefore, in order to capture these customers for the long term, builders and financial intermediaries need to identify ways to work with family consortiums.

Barrier #8: Getting Burned

In the South Texas Valley, several builders I know have marketed to Latinos by both building and financing their houses. However, one builder cheated his customer by providing a substandard product financed at a predatory rate. Once the customer faced quality problems, their recourse was to stop paying their mortgage. They believed that would directly affect the builder.

It turns out that this was a tactic used by the builder to foreclose the house and recycle it in the market. This builder didn't actually have the required financial strength to carry the mortgage note. When the customer stopped paying, it was not the builder who faced the loan delinquency but the mortgage note investor.

In general, when an investor gets burned, he stops buying mortgage notes receivable or demands a higher yield for their investment. When this happens, the builder needs to discount the instrument at a higher rate and reduce its net income. The long-term consequence is that quality continues deteriorating until the company has ruined its reputation.

Unfortunately, by this point, many customers have ruined their credit history as well. They will hunt for a home without the financial strength or credit qualifications and without trusting builders or financial intermediaries. Everyone suffers.

Barrier #9: Con Artists

Financial intermediaries are accustomed to underwriting credit risk using standard criteria developed decades ago. The Latino market is a new force that is often pushed to take credit from hard money lenders, predatory lenders, or other intermediaries who jump at the opportunity of foreclosing on the homes at the first sign of financial difficulty. Some cities have a network of fraudulent individuals who take advantage of this market.

As a builder, if you want to serve this niche and help them solve their housing needs, it is critical that you take a long-term approach. This customer is typically a young family that is buying a first house earlier in life (between ages 32 and 36). The likelihood of buying their "dream" home within the next 10–12 years is high.

Those builders also operating as financiers need to be aware that helping strengthen the credit history of their clients and increasing their clients' awareness of how the credit scoring system and how underwriting works will significantly increase the odds that that family will be refinancing with them. It makes it more likely that the builder will sell them or members of their families another home.

Conclusion

It is critical that builders focus on providing the best quality home, regardless of whether this segment has good credit scores or not. Latinos are brand loyal. They have long memories. They will call on you again and refer you to family members and friends.

Source: Christine B. Charlip.

Jorge Velasco is president and CEO of Qualitas Homes International based in McAllen, Texas. A native of Mexico, he brings over 15 years of experience in understanding and catering to the Latino market in different industries. He is involved in the building and financing of home and business projects across the Rio Grande Valley and in Dallas, Houston, and San Antonio.

Civano, Arizona, a master-planned community focused on sustainable energy practices. *Source:* Moule & Polyzoides Architects and Urbanists.

CHAPTER 11

Outlines for the Future

Richard A. Eribes, PhD

The admonition to "live in the moment" was probably constructed to shift our thinking from the struggles of the past as well as to dampen our anxiety about the future. But, in the back of our minds, we know that the future is unfolding before our eyes.

We take comfort in the "knowable," something we can get our arms around. The previous chapters of this book paint a picture of current conditions that result in both challenges and opportunities in the building of housing and communities for Latinos. This information will help us become more efficient in our line of business, but we should not stop there. We hope that this book encourages the building industry to take a forward-thinking leadership role in housing people of all communities.

The story of the Latino in America is a story of rapid and accelerating change. The building industry is capable of using these forces to create desirable housing futures. The first part of this chapter focuses careful attention on the changing demographics and what that means for regions and communities. The second part addresses current miscalculations and provides course corrections to help us reach sustainable building scenarios in our communities.

Compelling Demographics

In the 1970s, there were 6.5 million Latinos in the U.S. This represented about 3% of the nation's 203 million total population. By 2010,

Source: Christine B. Charlip.

it is estimated there will be nearly 44 million Latinos in the U.S.[1] and by 2050, they will make up 25% of the U.S. workforce.[2]

With $1 trillion in annual purchasing power by 2008,[3] Latinos will be the future American home owners. The growth of Latino home-ownership will account for 19% of the total increase nationwide by 2010. This amounts to an increase of 2.2 million Latino households.

Regions of Growth

Traditionally, Latinos have been concentrated in the Southwest and Florida. However, much of the recent growth has occurred in areas where there have been few Latinos in the past. The emerging population distribution has been a function of the job opportunities. Interestingly, the workforce demand has often not been in the farming sector but instead in light industry.

During the last decade, the Latino population has grown by approximately 214% in the east central region of the country (Kentucky, Tennessee, Alabama, Mississippi) to a population of 203,802.[4] This is a relatively small number compared with the nearly 3.7 million Latinos in the Pacific region (Washington, Oregon, California, Alaska, Hawaii) but illustrative of how Latinos are settling throughout the country.

The highest rate of growth during the last 10 years has taken place in North Carolina (+394%) followed by Arkansas (+337%). California remains the state with the largest concentration; one-third (10,966,556) of the state's population currently is identified as Latino.

Twenty-two states have experienced at least a doubling of their Latino population during the period between 1990 and 2000. They include: Indiana, Wisconsin, Minnesota, Iowa, Kansas, Nebraska, South Dakota, Delaware, Virginia, North Carolina, South Carolina, Georgia, Kentucky, Tennessee, Alabama, Mississippi, Arkansas, Oklahoma, Utah, Nevada, Washington, and Oregon.

Of these 22 states with rapid Latino growth, 14 are also losing single adults from the pool of 25- to 39-year-old college graduates (Utah, South Dakota, Nebraska, Kansas, Oklahoma, Iowa, Arkansas,

Wisconsin, Mississippi, Alabama, Delaware, Indiana, Kentucky, South Carolina).[5] Because of the combined in-migration of Latinos and the out-migration of largely white, college-educated, young adults, the housing demand in these states bears continued tracking.

It is possible that these states will show a dramatic proportional increase in the Latino population in the next census. The demand for housing and homeownership that naturally accompanies movement into the middle class can be expected to result in an increase of 2.2 million families searching for housing. This demand will affect home builders and others in the housing industry across the country.

In 2001, the total number of single-family housing building permits authorized in the U.S. numbered 950,227. For multifamily housing permits, the figure was only 292,713. This represents both a tremendous challenge and a tremendous opportunity to the building industry: A challenge with regard to the capacity to produce housing at this high rate during a period of material scarcity, escalating costs, and labor shortages in the building trades,[6] and an opportunity because of the huge market segment that has until recently been largely ignored.

Builders and other industry intermediaries who wish to market to this population will need to adjust traditional marketing methods. In some cases, they may need a complete overhaul. In the past three years, real estate ads aimed at Latinos have grown 50%.[7] Home-buying counseling programs are increasingly being offered by nonprofits, and financial institutions are developing services with Latinos in mind.

However, some habits die hard. We can expect that home builders will attempt to sell the same products to this different market in the same way that financial institutions have simply promoted translated versions of old services. It would be very cost effective if this was truly possible, but deep cultural differences suggest this is not a blueprint for success.

Future Growth Scenarios

At the local level, which communities will likely experience an increase in housing demand from Latinos? If we look to the year 2025, we can expect that the largest Latino populations will be found in California, Texas, Florida, New York, Illinois, Arizona, New Jersey, New Mexico, and Colorado, in that order. The U.S. Census projects that these nine states will have a collective population of slightly over 49 million Latinos in the next 20 years.[8]

Affordable housing, child care, and a communal garden promenade come together to create an elder-friendly community in San Ysidro, California. *Source:* Estudio Teddy Cruz for Casa Familiar.

We also know that virtually all Latinos (91.3%) live within metropolitan areas,[9] and there is little reason to believe that this will change regardless of the growth of Latinos throughout the South and Midwest. Comparing the current top ten Latino markets[10] with our list of nine Latino growth states for the year 2025, we can conclude that the cities of Los Angeles, New York, Miami/Fort Lauderdale, San Francisco/Oakland/San Jose, Chicago, Houston, San Antonio/Victoria, McAllen/Brownsville, Dallas/Fort Worth, and San Diego will remain large housing markets into the future.

Other cities recognized for their celebration of Latino culture are Denver, Tampa, Sacramento, El Paso, Albuquerque, and Tucson.[11] Home builders in these municipalities should closely monitor population rates in their areas.

Finally, four states that have demonstrated tremendous growth in their Latino population and simultaneously constructed a substantial number of housing units between 2000 and 2003 are Georgia (+142,886 units), North Carolina (+91,940 units), Nevada (+88,898 units), and Virginia (+52,988 units). The majority of this building activity is found in the vicinity of Atlanta, Georgia; Charlotte and Raleigh, North Carolina; Las Vegas, Nevada; and the edge of Virginia abutting Washington, DC, as well as Richmond, Virginia. This last set of cities bears watching as the Latino housing market grows in scale and produces new home building opportunities nationwide.

Community Needs

Housing is more than shelter. It is a package of resources often at the heart of a decent life. It is widely recognized that housing providers are essentially in the community-building business. The future success of this industry will center on its ability to coordinate and organize a multitude of public and private community opportunities. More attention must be placed on the quality of the neighborhood than on the amenities of the individual housing unit. What, therefore, must housing industry leaders and government planners recognize?

Schools

Latinos are the youngest cultural minority in the country. They have large families and are heavy consumers of public education. They also believe completely in the power of education to transform lives. They often look for housing and neighborhoods that deliver on this dream.

Good public education is desired by 39% of prospective Latino home buyers. Quality education does not mean large, crowded, intercity schools, but rather neighborhood schools within walking distance. Unfortunately, the trend across the country does not favor increased investment in education or investment in the existing deteriorating stock of public school facilities. State legislators are increasingly hostile to bilingual education and public services.

At the local level, where housing provision takes place, the market recognizes that neither the Spanish language nor culture can be legislated away. Builders will need to recognize the political climate of their communities and work with local governments in the provision of accessible schools and school sites.

Mixed-Use Development

When developing with Latinos in mind, it makes sense to create mixed-use neighborhoods with a range of housing types, shops, and services incorporated into the master plan. It is time to green light zoning ordinances that allow for this type of development (Figures 11.1 and 11.2).

Latino cultural preferences favor compact neighborhoods, outdoor public places, multigenerational families, and commercial shopping in close proximity to housing. This form of Latino new urbanism can be found in countless communities.[12] The reasons for this can range from purely economic to a lack of enforcement by local zoning and building officials. Clearly, it is an opportunity to rein in sprawl, promote walkable cities, contain land costs, and reduce air pollution.

In addition to our goal of meeting housing demand, we should utilize culturally appropriate strategies to make residents fall in love with their new neighborhoods. It is unlikely that Latinos will abandon the cultural values of cooperation for one of competition simply because they are more financially secure. New mixed-use neighborhoods can respect this tradition.

Figure 11.1 Bernal Gateway, San Francisco, California, is a mixed-use project that wraps clusters of housing with a neighborhood adult school and a child care center at street level for community use.

Source: Pyatok Architects, Inc.

Figure 11.2 In San Jose, California, this mixed-use public-private partnership combines senior housing at Mubuhay Court with the Northside Community Center, creating a village setting.

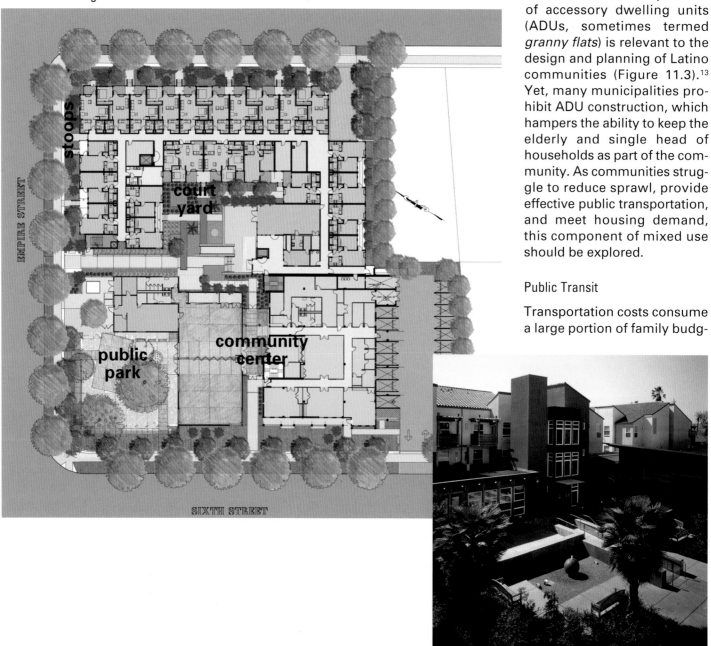

One particular land use deserves specific attention in this discussion. The incorporation of accessory dwelling units (ADUs, sometimes termed *granny flats*) is relevant to the design and planning of Latino communities (Figure 11.3).[13] Yet, many municipalities prohibit ADU construction, which hampers the ability to keep the elderly and single head of households as part of the community. As communities struggle to reduce sprawl, provide effective public transportation, and meet housing demand, this component of mixed use should be explored.

Public Transit

Transportation costs consume a large portion of family budg-

Source: David Baker & Partners.

Figure 11.3 Two examples of municipality-supported accessory-dwelling unit plans, from the cities of Santa Cruz (A), and Watsonville (B), California.

Site Plan

These illustrations show the overall site layout for the Prototype. Below is the "base case" option. To the right are variations of a reversed plan and rotated plan to address access from an alley.

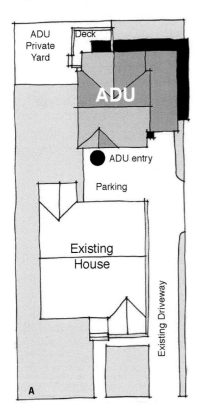

A

Reverse Plan Option

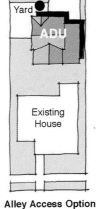

Alley Access Option

Accessory Units and Alley Sites

These infill opportunity sites are located in traditional neighborhood of smaller Bungalow and Victorian houses. These RM-2 sites offer opportunities to add small accessory units in rear yards or alleys. The concepts for these sites feature:

- Small accessory buildings in scale with neighborhood lots and buildings
- Hiding views of parking from the street
- Design that is in character with the existing historic houses

Sketch of Rear Yard Unit

Sketch of Alley Units

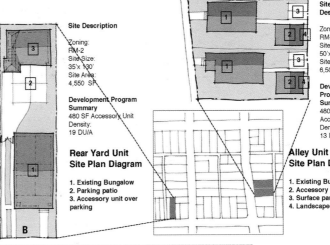

Site Description

Zoning:
RM-2
Site Size:
35' x 130'
Site Area:
4,550 SF

Development Program Summary
480 SF Accessory Unit
Density:
19 DU/A

Rear Yard Unit Site Plan Diagram

1. Existing Bungalow
2. Parking patio
3. Accessory unit over parking

Site Description

Zoning:
RM-2
Site Size:
50' x 130'
Site Area:
6,500 SF

Development Program Summary
480 SF Accessory Unit
Density:
13 DU/A

Alley Unit Site Plan Diagram

1. Existing Bungalow
2. Accessory unit
3. Surface parking
4. Landscaped 5' setback

B

Source: City of Santa Cruz, California.

Source: City of Watsonville, California.

ets, especially for middle class families. This is easy to comprehend by just driving through "anywhere" suburbia. Three-car garages dominate the frontage of many American homes, making it difficult to maintain the functional attribute of the front porch and the supervision of children playing in the street.

Suburban development at the periphery of the metropolitan area makes this condition a reoccurring vision. Assuming the average cost of owning and maintaining an automobile is approximately $8,000

Figure 11.4 Del Mar Station, Pasadena, California, a transit-oriented development bisected by light rail.

Source: Moule & Polyzoides, Architects and Urbanists.

per year, it is obvious that housing can become much more affordable if we assist in exploring transportation alternatives to the automobile in our developments.

Latinos tend to use public transportation where it has been made available, for example the Richmond Station in Richmond, California, has intermodal connections to BART, AMTRAK, and AC transit bus service (Figure 11.4). New developments should seek close-in locations on existing transit lines. These opportunities can provide support for transit-oriented commerce and help anchor community centers with mixed-use development. Related consequences include smaller housing lots (less demand for auto parking), higher densities, less air pollution, more time spent with the family rather than commuting, and perhaps even better health. Transit-oriented residential neighborhoods will increasingly be desirable by all populations in the future.

Community Services and Churches

The ultimate success of any housing development depends at least in part in the integration of new neighborhoods into the service provision fabric of local government. The current wisdom questions the capacity of local jurisdictions to provide primary and secondary education, police and fire protection, and water and sewer service. These questions are especially persistent when housing projects are targeted at Latino populations. Yet, analysis suggests that in the typical case, a new single family home easily pays for itself in less than three years.[14]

Additionally, reality finds that Latinos utilize social services at rates below that for which they are eligible. This is particularly true of immigrant newcomers.[15] There are many potential reasons for this, including fear, cultural tradition, language difficulties, and hostility. One possible explanation is the role that churches play in these communities. Often the church is the glue that binds the social fabric of Latino communities together. Churches can also provide services at a much smaller scale than can be efficiently provided by the public sector.

Latinos have adopted a great diversity of religious expression in America. It can no longer be assumed that they are of the Catholic faith, but they continue to be a religious culture. Sixty-two percent of third-generation Latinos remain Catholic.[16]

At a time when government at all levels is moving away from the direct provision of social services, churches remain important foundational institutions for this community. Churches are the principle demonstration of Latino organizational capacity.[17] In a progression of community influence, Latinos tend to organize themselves first into churches followed by businesses, politics, social clubs, and finally schools.

The church clearly provides an introduction to participatory democracy, to Spanish language social services, and to family assistance and recreation. Furthermore, the provision of locations within community master plans for churches can anchor the provision of public open space, as is the case in the traditional plaza setting. This locus of mixed use, including social institutions, multifamily residential, and local commercial space, should be viewed as value added to this market segment. It is this similarity with the New England commons, so important to the new urbanism model, that can help energize the Latino new urbanism community.

Civic Space

By designing a compact neighborhood with modestly sized lots, some of the land can be utilized as shared open space (Figure 11.5). This often leads to the provision of public parks for recreation and neighborhood gathering. This is extremely important for Latino communities, which heavily use these amenities for social interaction, cultural reinforcement and maintenance, recreation, sports, and relaxation.

A particular class of open space for Latinos is the plaza or placita. Every city and town in Latin America has one, and it is a type of an enduring cultural icon around which housing developments can be designed (Figure 11.6). The placita can be the element

Figure 11.5 Daybreak Grove, Escondido, California, is a 13-unit project inspired by the Latin American plaza as the focus of community life, with kitchens oriented to the shared courtyard.

Source: Davids Killory Architecture.

Figure 11.6 A traditional placita in Trinidad, Cuba (A), and the next generation of passageway as gathering place, Chess Park in Glendale, California (B).

Source: Corky Poster.

Source: Tom Bonner for Rios Clementi Hale Studios.

that allows the integration of housing, commerce, transportation, education, and spirituality.

Building the Future by Examining the Past

It seems counterintuitive that, during a period of widespread robust home sales, we would find ourselves in the midst of a housing crisis. This crisis is a product of a nation where those with modest incomes are significantly underhoused. Housing prices have continued to rise throughout the country because of the growing gap between the supply and demand of "entry-level homes." The national average price of new construction of single-family homes in 2004 was $238,100. This is a 71% increase over the decade, and a 76% increase in the West where many Latinos live.[18] On the Texas border, for example, only one house is built for every two that are needed.[19] This gap has been further exacerbated everywhere by the fact that incomes have not kept pace with the costs of housing.

On the demand side, there are 2.5 million households with children living in substandard housing and another 770,000 living in severely substandard housing. In 1996, there were an estimated 3.5 million homeless adults and children over the course of the year. Add to this a shortfall of 1.8 million affordable units for working families.[20]

During the 1990s, 13.6 million units were added to the national housing supply. For the Latinos who compete for this supply, the situation is particularly difficult because their numbers have grown by 56%, or 12.6 million, during those 10 years. By 2010, an additional 21.6 million Latinos will be added to the demand side. It is not difficult to understand that Latinos could utilize the entire annual addition of 1.2 million single-family and 314,000 multifamily units that were completed in 2001.[21]

In my experience, there are two problems. First, we have not been watching the demographic data closely enough. Second, we have made some poor decisions about the way we build our communities.

Zoning Choices

Across the country, zoning is the primary regulation utilized by local government to protect property values and enforce exclusion. Collectively, we have enormous resources invested in continuing to use this development tool. Unfortunately, we have known for some time that zoning regulations do not work to protect the health and safety of communities.[22] Together with building ordinances, zoning has impeded construction innovation, made infill development extremely difficult, and encouraged sprawl. Pollution, gridlock, and dying central business districts are increasingly choking low-density cities.

We have treated residential areas as too delicate to withstand active, enthusiastic, and robust use. We have opted for isolated and comatose neighborhoods. We now find ourselves responding to a Latino population that requires much more from their neighborhoods. Of this we are frightened, but in the end, we will be thankful. The future of all our cities will benefit from this new market for active, fully integrated, multipurpose communities.

Home Builders

The building industry must continue to explore ways to reduce the cost of housing. The size of the average merchant-built house continues to rise even as land becomes scarcer and land prices continue to escalate. In the 1970s, home builders were delivering 1,500-square-foot homes. Today, homes tend to be in the range of 2,600 to 3,000 square feet. If we are indeed in the midst of a housing crisis, perhaps it is valuable to ask why it makes sense to build one 3,000-square-foot house rather than two 1,500-square-foot houses. It has already been established that reasonable higher densities have many community-wide benefits (Figure 11.7).

Figure 11.7 Casitas de las Florecitas, San Ysidro, California, a first-time home-ownership project of 1,300-square-foot homes.

Source: Harry Connolly and Casa Familiar, Inc., developer.

Figure 11.8 Sustainable living starts with community master planning that is compatible with the local environment, climate, and culture, such as the community of Civano, Arizona.

Source: Moule & Polyzoides, Architects and Urbanists.

Figure 11.9 The homes of Civano come with a guarantee concerning heating and cooling expenses.

Source: Author.

Of course, a smaller unit also utilizes less energy. Regardless of the size of the unit, efficient energy design can offer substantial benefits to the family budget. Savings vary depending on the climate where the housing is built. For instance, in a desert location, the monthly savings in energy costs between a 1,500- and a 3,000-square-foot home can amount to $112 per month or over $1,300 per year.

There are many recent examples to draw from, two of which are in Arizona. The community of Civano was built on 800 acres outside of Tucson (Figure 11.8). Utilizing a coordinated system of sustainable practices to design an entire affordable development, Civano was able to demonstrate a reduction in community energy use by one-third and a nearly 50% reduction in the use of water (Figure 11.9).

Even though the Arizona Public Service Environmental Showcase House, built in Phoenix, is 2,640 square feet, energy use was reduced by 60% over the typical energy-efficient home (Figure 11.10).[22] This amounted to a savings of approximately $3,300 per year simply through the inventive use of traditional construction practices and materials. Water use was also reduced by 55%.

Home builders may even find themselves becoming active facilitators in the real estate sector. Home builders with increasing Latino populations in various parts of the country, including Tucson, Arizona; Madison, Wisconsin; and Indianapolis, Indiana, are experimenting in the home trade-in market. In this marketing strategy, home builders accept the home buyers' existing homes as trade-ins toward a new home. The home builder then takes the responsibility for the resale.

The home building industry must advocate for increased densities, mixed-use development, including ADUs, and the provision of public transit to reduce reliance on the automobile or the industry will have missed an opportunity to assume a leadership role in the Latino housing market.

Local Government

In return, local governments must listen to those interested in more than just protecting their property values. The comprehensive finan-

Figure 11.10 Creative design can produce significant energy savings as demonstrated by the Arizona Public Service Environmental Showcase Home.

Source: Jones Studio, Phoenix, Arizona.

cial health of a community must remain our focus. The current approach will only lead to a collapse of the housing market and a restriction of the residential mobility that so many Americans enjoy.

Today, communities continue to overemphasize the automobile and make public transportation difficult by insisting on high-count parking regulations. Without public transportation, we are now a nation of three-car owners. It costs approximately $8,000 per year to own and maintain an automobile.[24] This represents a major financial investment for any family. Our communities are now forcing many Latino families to choose between a house payment or a car payment. According to the Automobile Club of Southern California, the average family in 2001 spent about 18% of their household income, although many families in the region spent close to 25% of their income, on transportation.[25] This is more than is spent on food, health care, or clothing. This is not the way to house our nation.

The engineering of our residential streets must rediscover common sense. In Latino neighborhoods, the street is a desired and inhabited extension of the living unit. To encourage pedestrian-oriented neighborhoods requires smaller, pedestrian-scaled streets (Figure 11.11). Streets are also the most expensive part of community infrastructure. Narrow streets represent considerable initial cost savings and substantial long-term savings in maintenance and repair expenses.[26]

Figure 11.11 Street scale and pattern are part of the open networks of neighborhoods at Civano.

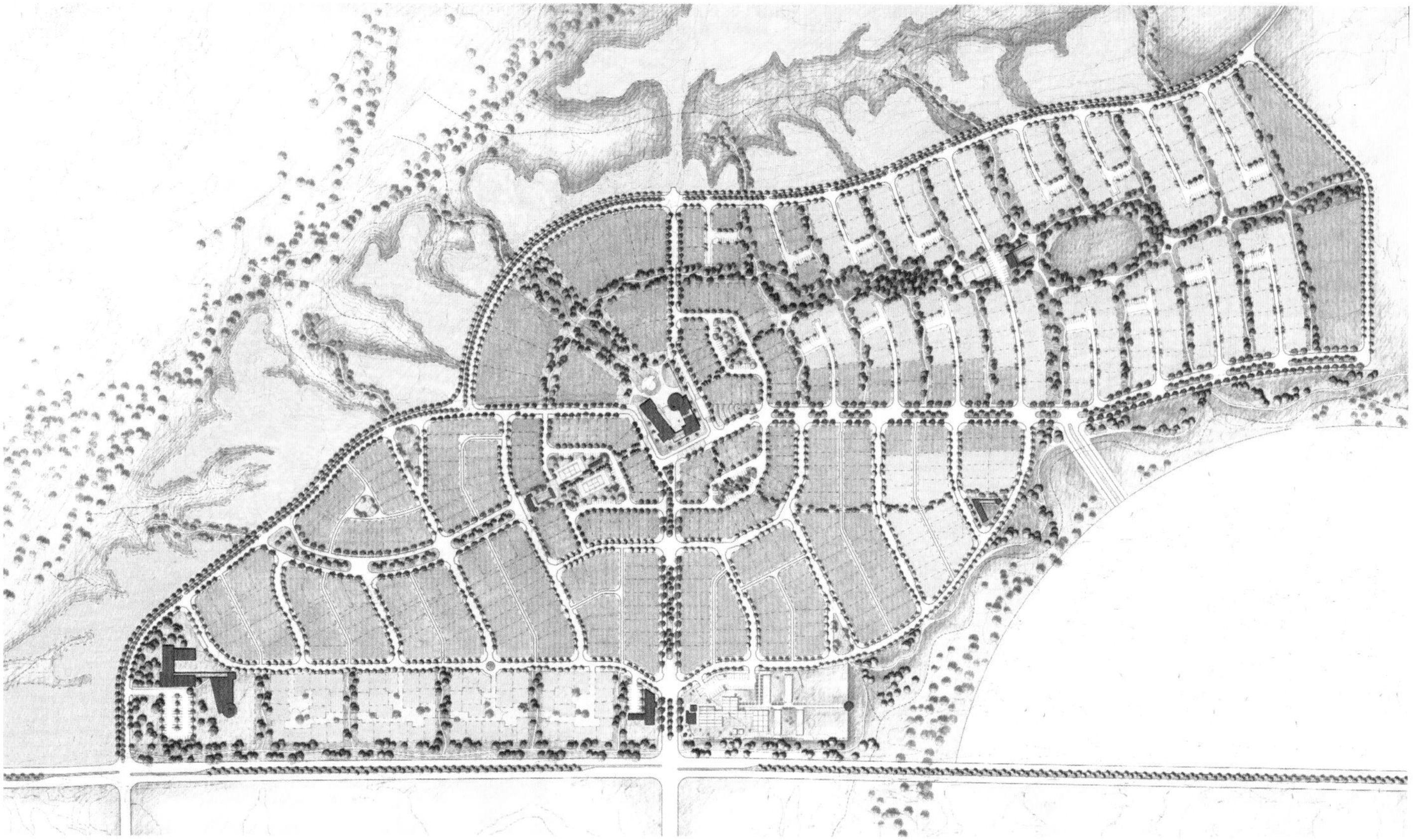

Source: Moule & Polyzoides, Architects and Urbanists.

The development approval and permit process needs to be streamlined. In many communities, the time for complete project approval borders on the ridiculous, extending beyond a year in length. This lag translates into higher housing costs or, worse, poorer quality construction. Who benefits when housing costs more than it should, is of poorer quality, fails to meet current demand, and takes longer to be placed on the tax rolls of the municipality?

Financial Institutions

Financial institutions need to improve access to the purchase of housing. With the anticipation of Latinos having $1 trillion in annual purchasing power by 2008,[3] this is a tremendous new market for the financial industry. We have already seen change in this sector with the re-examination of down payment requirements, an increase in financial counseling services, and the adoption of innovative mortgage financing programs. Still needed is a review of the appraisal process and its impact on first-time home buyers.

Home Buyers

Change is only possible if all members of this complex system of housing provision recognize the role they have to play and decide to work cooperatively. Home buyers should view themselves as active participants in transforming the nation's housing to meet the needs of Latinos. Certainly, the desire is present. The Tomás Rivera Policy Institute found that 84% of Latinos share the common American desire to own their home.[27]

Because the U.S. housing market revolves around credit and financial reliability, potential home buyers need to seriously consider the difficulties created by their "unbanked" status and "cash-only" existence.[28] Potential home buyers must take advantage of homeownership and credit counseling educational programs offered by mortgage lenders, community organizations, local governments, and real estate agents. This assistance is increasingly available in both Spanish and English.

Homeownership suggests a commitment to the community. Potential home buyers can prepare for this by getting involved in the political, social, educational, and spiritual aspects of their communities. Responsiveness of the housing sector to Latinos' needs will depend not only on individual initiative but also on collective behavior. It's vital to register to vote and to exercise this privilege.

Latinos will want to seek builders who are knowledgeable about starter homes.[29] If buyers demand quality, durability, and sustainability, the long-term costs of maintenance and upkeep will far outweigh the initial costs. Housing that offers flexibility of use and future expandability as integral components of the design will increase significantly in value.[30]

Finally, it is also important to recognize that homeownership is one of the only stable forms of wealth accumulation.[31] Compare this to automobiles, which create few "opportunity costs" beyond transportation and build little wealth. Over ten years, for every $10,000 invested in a home, an owner can build $4,730 in equity, but the same amount spent on an automobile yields only $910.[32]

Reforming informal passages into landscape and pedestrian corridors invites development of businesses and mixed uses. *Source:* Estudio Teddy Cruz for Casa Familiar.

Conclusion

The tremendous demand by Latinos for housing is only now coming to light even though the trends have been before us for some time. The first requirement to solve a problem is to recognize and define the issue. The information gathered in this book is one step in that direction.

It is clear that the normal way of doing business between home builders and Latino clients will need adjustment and invention. Change is needed not only in the behavior of home builders but also in the methodology of financial institutions, local governmental agencies, and home buyers themselves.

We must think about using resources in ways that sustain them. This involves thinking simultaneously about economic, environmental, and social values. Sustainable design honors the cultural heritage of the local community, conserves and regenerates our natural environment, advances affordable and healthy living, and supports economic well-being.

In some ways, it is inevitable that our decisions will overvalue cost reduction and the lowest initial price. We would not have a housing industry without this value. However, the concept of sustainability would tell us that it is not solely about lowest price but also about value added.

In the simplest terms, everything in a home owner's life is rent. Your house mortgage is rent, your car payment is rent, your utility bill is rent, your entertainment budget is rent, your food bill is rent, and your health care costs are rent. Additionally, rent is perpetual, and a builder's decisions will affect the long-term cost and long-term value of homes purchased today.

What can we do to reduce rent, think long-term, and act sustainably? First, understand the local environment and climate and then plan with nature rather than trying to overcome it through the use of costly technology.

Next, simplify. One of the most significant cost reduction decisions we can make is to plan modestly sized building lots. This leads to house designs appropriately scaled to modestly sized building sites. The design should reflect efficient and multiple-use function, encour-

The F10 House, Chicago, designed by EHDD Architecture, strives to reduce life cycle environmental impact by a factor of 10, features a solar chimney for light, heating, and cooling. *Source:* Doug Snower Photography.

age natural ventilation, and provide for future expansion. All of these factors add value to the housing unit and reduce both the short-term and long-term costs to the buyer.

Evaluate the true long-term economic, social, and environmental costs of the project. Many building decisions have low initial costs and substantial long-term operating and maintenance costs. This is best understood in the area of energy usage. It is clear that larger houses use more energy. But construction decisions can substantially reduce the long-term energy use.

The use of green building materials when combined with natural ventilation can also substantially increase interior air quality. For a population like Latinos, who suffer from respiratory illnesses at a much higher rate than the general population,[33] this is certainly value added to the project that can be marketed.

Finally, it is important to recognize that dwellings are the building blocks of our communities and that, in the end, they are only the means to great neighborhoods.

Home builders are frontline witnesses to a transformation of the American housing landscape. The entire nation as well as the Latino community benefits from their ideas, innovations, and investments.

Endnotes

1. Lee, Jongho, Louis Tornatzky, and Celina Torres. *El Sueño de su Casa: The Homeownership Potential of Mexican-Heritage Families*. Los Angeles: The Tomás Rivera Policy Institute, 2004, p. 2.

2. Weber, Harry R. "Major Retailers Hiring More Hispanics to Cater to Burgeoning Market." The Associated Press: *The State*, Columbia, South Carolina. Sunday, February 20, 2005.

3. *Ibid.*

4. Millard, Ann V., and Jorge Chapa. *Apple Pie and Enchiladas: Latino Newcomers in the Rural Midwest*. Austin: University of Texas Press, 2004.

5. Jones, Tim. "States Struggle to Stem Brain Drain." *Chicago Tribune,* February 20, 2005.

6. Creno, Glen. "Housing Boom Drains Pool of Skilled Labor." *The Arizona Republic*, September 12, 2004.

7. Fleishman, Sandra. "Homing in on Hispanic Buyers: Spanish Is Becoming a Language of Both Sales Pitches and Protections." *Washington Post*, December 4, 2004, p. F1.

8. U.S. Census Bureau. "Projected State Populations, by Sex, Race, and Hispanic Origin: 1995–2025." Accessed at http://www.census.gov/population/projections/state/stpjrace.txt.

9. U.S. Census Bureau. "American Community Survey 2003 Multi-Year Profile." June 2003. Accessed at http://www.census.gov/acs/www/Products/Profiles/Chg/2003/ACS/index.htm.

10. "Top 40 Hispanic Markets." *Coloquio, The Electronic Newsletter of the Hispanic Community of Baltimore–Washington, DC, Metropolitan Area.* Accessed at http://www.coloquio.com/english/hcities.html.

11. Terry-Azios, Diana A. "Top Ten Cities for Hispanics." *Hispanic Magazine.com.* July–August 2001. Accessed at http://www.hispanicmagazine.com/2001/julaug/Features/toptencities.html.

12. El Nasser, Haya. "New Urbanism Embraces Latinos." *USA Today,* February 16, 2005.

13. Andrews, James H. Not your grandmother's granny flat. *Planning* 71(3): 8–9, 2005.

14. National Association of Home Builders. "The Local Impact of Home Building in a Typical Metropolitan Area Comparing Costs to Revenue for Local Governments." October 2005. http://www.nahb.org/fileUpload_details.aspx?contentTypeID=3&contentID=35601&subContentID=28003.

15. Millard, Ann V., and Jorge Chapa. *Apple Pie and Enchiladas: Latino Newcomers in the Rural Midwest.* Austin: University of Texas Press, 2004.

16. Espinosa, Gaston, Virgilio Elizondo, and Jesse Miranda. *Latino Religions and Civic Activism in the United States.* New York: Oxford University Press, 2005.

17. Millard, Ann V., and Jorge Chapa. *Apple Pie and Enchiladas: Latino Newcomers in the Rural Midwest.* Austin: University of Texas Press, 2004.

18. U.S. Census Bureau. "Characteristics of New Housing." 2004. Accessed at http;//www.census.gov/const/www/charindex.html.

19. Housing: Homes of Our Own. In *Windows on State Government: Bordering the Future.* Accessed at http://www.window.state.tx.us/border/ch07/ch07.html.

20. Cisneros, Henry G., Jack F. Kemp, Nicolas P. Retsinas, and Kent, W. Colton. *Opportunity and Progress: A Bipartisan Platform for National Housing Policy.* Cambridge, MA: Joint Center for Housing Studies of Harvard University, 2004.

21. U.S. Department of Housing and Urban Development. Office of Policy Development and Research. "U.S. Housing Market Conditions, Historical Data. New Privately Owned Housing Units Completed 1969–Present." 2001. Accessed at http://www.huduser.org/periodicals/ushmc/ winter2001/hist dat04.htm.

22. Babcock, Richard, and Fred P. Bosselman. *Exclusionary Zoning: Land Use Regulation and Housing in the 1970's.* New York: Praeger, 1973.

23. Pijawka, K. David, and Kim Shetter (Eds.). *The Environment Comes Home: Arizona Public Service's Environmental Showcase Home*. Tempe, AZ: Herberger Center for Design Excellence, 1995.

24. "The Cost of Car Ownership." *Livable Places*, Los Angeles. Accessed at http://www.livableplaces.org/policy/carownerhip.html.

25. *Ibid.* The estimated cost of utilizing public transit in Southern California is $696 per year.

26. *Building Better Neighborhoods: Creating Affordable Homes and Livable Communities*. St. Paul: Greater Minnesota Housing Fund, 2001.

27. Lee, Jongho, Louis Tornatzky, and Celina Torres: *El Sueño de su Casa: The Homeownership Potential of Mexican-Heritage Families*. Los Angeles: The Tomás Rivera Policy Institute, 2004, p. 7.

28. *Ibid.*, p. 14–16.

29. *Building Better Neighborhoods: Creating Affordable Homes and Livable Communities*. St. Paul: Greater Minnesota Housing Fund, 2001.

30. *Ibid.*

31. Bradley, Donald. *Serving the Mexican-Heritage Household: Are There Lessons From the Mexican Housing Market?* Presented at AREUEA and CREUES International Real Estate Conference, Cancun, Mexico, 2000.

32. "The Cost of Car Ownership." *Livable Places*. Accessed at http://www.livableplaces.org/policy/carownerhip.html.

33. Hunninghake, Gary M., Scott T. Weiss, and Juan C. Celedán. Asthma in Hispanics. *American Journal of Respiratory and Critical Care Medicine* 173:143–63, 2006.

Richard Eribes, PhD, is a Professor of Architecture and former Dean of the College of Architecture and Landscape Architecture, University of Arizona, Tucson. He has published and lectured extensively on U.S. housing and community development trends.

CHAPTER 12

Preferences of Latino New Home Buyers

Michael Carliner

The recent growth in the number of Latino home buyers has already shifted the mix of new housing production somewhat to reflect the requirements and preferences of Latino households. There will be many more Latino home buyers in the years ahead. Latinos represent about 18% of the young adult population now approaching home buying age but make up just 9% of all those age 40 and older. With homeownership rates for Latinos lower than for the population as a whole, there is also greater potential for a rise in the Latino ownership rate than for the overall rate. Moreover, immigration has been higher since 2000 than during the 1990s.

Many of the differences between the housing demands of Latino households and other households reflect differences in demographic characteristics such as age, household size, and number of children. The lower incomes typical among Latino households shape their demands as well, if not their desires. There are also some statistically significant differences between the preferences of Latino households and those of other households even after adjusting for demographics, income, location, and whether they are first-time or repeat buyers.[1]

Whether driven by differences in demographics or by culturally rooted differences in lifestyles or aesthetics, the differences between the preferences of Latino home buyers and preferences of other home buyers—shown by buying patterns, surveys, and focus groups—are not radical. Moreover, preferences among home buyers within the broad Latino universe, and even within separate ancestry group and subcultures, are quite heterogeneous.

As an example, one of the distinctions found in the National Association of Home Builders (NAHB) surveys between Latino home buyers and other home buyers has been a greater preference for distinctly separate living, dining, and family rooms. But 27% of Latino survey respondents, like 31% of all respondents, indicated that they want a home with the kitchen completely open to the family room. And 30% of Latino respondents, like 37% of all respondents, would be willing to buy a home with no living room in exchange for having more space elsewhere in the home.

Features such as pastels and archways have been cited elsewhere as Latino preferences. The information gathered in our surveys and government statistics regarding the characteristics of homes occupied by Latinos does not extend to questions such as favorite colors or architectural styles, but for those characteristics that have been covered in surveys and construction statistics, the evidence suggests that Latinos generally wish to have housing much like that of non-Latinos who are similarly situated. On average, however, Latino households are rather different from non-Latino households.

Similarities between the preferences of Latinos and the preferences of other households with similar demographic and economic characteristics do not mean that there are no distinct Latino housing demands. The size and character of Latino households are the result of choices, not just random, involuntary circumstances. Housing and living arrangements are joint preferences.

Table 12.1 shows some of the key characteristics of Latino households and of all households, as indicated by the 2003 American Housing Survey (AHS). The AHS is conducted every two years by the U.S. Census Bureau for the Department of Housing and Urban Development. In addition to data covering all (owner and renter) households, the table shows owner households, as well as those who purchased new or existing homes in 2001 or later (i.e., in the 2.5–3 years prior to the survey).

The questions in the AHS include whether a home owner has ever owned a home before and whether the home had ever been occupied prior to the current household moving in. Other surveys usually do not identify first-time buyers and do not include an equally direct measure of whether the home was bought new.

Table 12.1 2003 American Housing Survey

	All				Latino			
			Home Buyers				**Home Buyers**	
	Households	**Owners**	**New**	**Existing**	**Households**	**Owners**	**New**	**Existing**
Number (thousands)	105,836	72,234	2,585	10,503	11,037	5,106	219	1,068
Age								
<25	5.7%	1.8%	4.2%	6.1%	8.5%	2.5%	5.7%	6.7%
25–34	17.4%	12.5%	31.2%	32.7%	27.2%	19.0%	42.7%	35.1%
35–44	21.3%	21.3%	28.7%	27.0%	25.2%	27.3%	26.8%	32.1%
45–54	20.6%	23.1%	15.7%	17.5%	17.8%	22.3%	13.9%	15.7%
55–64	14.6%	17.3%	10.4%	9.6%	10.3%	14.1%	5.0%	7.0%
65+	20.4%	24.0%	9.8%	7.1%	11.0%	14.9%	5.9%	3.4%
Median	**47.7%**	**51.2%**	**39.6%**	**38.9%**	**40.6%**	**45.5%**	**35.5%**	**32.7%**
Household Type								
Married	**51.3%**	**62.7%**	**75.0%**	**57.1%**	**52.7%**	**67.4%**	**72.5%**	**67.6%**
w/ children	23.3%	26.9%	42.5%	31.7%	34.4%	41.2%	52.1%	48.0%
2+ children	4.9%	5.4%	9.3%	6.3%	9.7%	11.8%	15.2%	13.2%
Other Family, Female	**12.2%**	**9.0%**	**6.3%**	**10.3%**	**18.0%**	**12.0%**	**7.7%**	**11.8%**
w/ children	7.2%	4.2%	3.5%	7.0%	11.4%	6.0%	4.0%	8.9%
Other Family, Male	**4.1%**	**3.4%**	**2.3%**	**4.5%**	**7.7%**	**5.8%**	**7.2%**	**7.9%**
w/ children	1.9%	1.5%	1.7%	2.5%	3.1%	2.4%	5.1%	3.0%
Nonfamily	**32.3%**	**24.9%**	**16.4%**	**28.0%**	**21.6%**	**14.7%**	**12.7%**	**12.6%**
Living alone	26.6%	21.4%	12.1%	21.0%	15.8%	12.5%	11.2%	9.1%
Other	5.7%	3.5%	4.3%	7.0%	5.8%	2.2%	1.5%	3.5%
Other Relatives in HH	**20.8%**	**22.8%**	**13.2%**	**15.5%**	**32.3%**	**36.1%**	**22.6%**	**27.6%**
Parent	1.8%	1.8%	2.3%	2.4%	4.0%	4.8%	3.9%	**5.2%**
Brother/sister	1.9%	1.3%	1.3%	2.0%	5.2%	3.1%	2.3%	4.5%
Adult child	14.9%	17.5%	8.1%	8.6%	19.6%	25.9%	12.0%	13.1%
Grandchild	2.6%	2.8%	1.5%	1.6%	4.7%	6.1%	3.6%	2.6%
Other relative	3.7%	3.8%	2.1%	4.0%	9.2%	9.1%	4.2%	10.1%
Nonrelatives in HH	**5.7%**	**3.5%**	**4.3%**	**7.0%**	**5.8%**	**2.2%**	**1.5%**	**3.5%**
Education of Householder								
LT HS diploma/GED	17.4%	14.5%	6.3%	10.3%	40.9%	35.6%	15.2%	31.1%
Bachelor's Degree	17.4%	18.6%	27.5%	23.6%	9.0%	11.4%	20.8%	13.8%
Additional Degree	9.5%	11.1%	12.9%	12.4%	3.9%	5.4%	10.4%	6.7%
Citizenship								
Native	89.2%	91.8%	89.6%	87.2%	52.9%	57.0%	67.4%	49.8%
Naturalized	5.3%	5.4%	6.2%	6.5%	17.0%	22.8%	12.6%	19.8%
Noncitizen	5.5%	2.9%	4.2%	6.3%	30.2%	20.1%	20.0%	30.4%
First Time Owner		44.6%	29.5%	45.4%		62.9%	43.9%	62.4%
Household Income								
Mean	62,608	75,130	89,710	74,433	46,625	63,691	74,833	60,182
Median	40,124	51,160	69,000	54,000	32,800	45,200	64,944	44,500
Home Value								
Mean		192,052	250,624	190,594		184,136	256,086	188,406
Median		135,000	190,000	135,000		130,000	200,000	140,000

Source: 2003 American Housing Survey (HUD/Census Bureau), tabulated by NAHB
Note: Home buyers are owners who moved in 2001 or later

The AHS data show that Latinos who buy newly built homes are, in many respects, not typical of all Latino households. New home buyers are generally better educated and have higher incomes, despite being younger, and they are more likely to have children. There are similar differences between non-Latino home buyers and other non-Latino households.

The AHS for 2003 effectively sampled about 1 in 2,000 of the U.S. population. It only included about a hundred interviews with Latinos who bought new homes, so the detailed characteristics of Latino new home buyers shown in Table 12.1 could be subject to significant random sampling error. Table 12.2 shows similar information based on the 5% public use sample from the 2000 Census. Home buyers were identified as those owning homes that they moved into in 1999 or in the first 3 months of 2000. New home buyers were those who also reported that their homes were built during that period. The results from the 2000 Census generally mirror and confirm the demographic profile of Latino new home buyers indicated by the 2003 AHS.

The data from 2000 indicate, however, that Latinos represented 6.7% of new home buyers in 1999–2000, whereas the AHS indicates a share of 8.5% for purchases during 2001–2003. Data from a third Census Bureau data set provide evidence that the difference is not due to sampling error, but that there has been rapid growth in the Latino share of new home purchases. The American Community Survey (ACS) indicates that the Latino share of purchases of recently built homes increased from 7.5% in 2001 to 8.7% in 2004.

Latino householders (owners and renters) in general, and Latino buyers of new homes in particular, are younger than non-Latinos. The median age of Latino new home buyers at the time of the 2003 AHS was about 35.5 years, suggesting a median age of about 34 at the time of purchase. Non-Latino buyers were typically 4 years older. Moreover, only about 11% of Latino new home buyers were aged 55 or older, compared to about 20% of non-Latino new home buyers. Among all new home buyers, less than 30% were first-time buyers, but among Latinos buying new homes, it was a first-time purchase for 44%.

More existing homes are sold each year than new homes, and first-time buyers, especially, are more likely to buy an existing home than a new home. Among Latino first-time home buyers in the AHS, only 13% bought newly built homes, whereas among Latino home buyers

Table 12.2 2000 Census

	All				Latino			
			Home Buyers				Home Buyers	
	Households	Owners	New	Existing	Households	Owners	New	Existing
Households (thousands)	**106,741**	**70,732**	**1,763**	**5,547**	**10,432**	**5,103**	**131**	**554**
1 Person	25.7%	20.3%	12.1%	19.4%	14.3%	11.2%	9.4%	8.6%
2 Person	32.5%	35.6%	35.4%	32.8%	20.6%	21.7%	21.0%	19.0%
3 Person	16.5%	17.1%	19.4%	18.1%	18.7%	18.2%	18.8%	17.8%
4 or More	**25.2%**	**27.1%**	**33.2%**	**29.6%**	**46.5%**	**48.9%**	**50.8%**	**54.6%**
5 or More	**10.9%**	**11.2%**	**13.5%**	**12.9%**	**27.2%**	**28.6%**	**27.7%**	**33.1%**
In Single-Family Home	**71,733**	**60,896**	**1,427**	**4,440**	**5,870**	**4,330**	**103**	**429**
1 Person	18.8%	18.2%	10.9%	16.1%	10.3%	10.2%	9.2%	6.9%
2 Person	34.3%	35.9%	36.0%	32.8%	20.2%	21.6%	22.3%	17.8%
3 Person	17.8%	17.5%	19.5%	19.0%	18.4%	18.4%	19.0%	17.6%
4 or More	**29.1%**	**28.3%**	**33.5%**	**32.1%**	**51.1%**	**49.9%**	**49.5%**	**57.6%**
5 or More	**12.5%**	**11.7%**	**13.1%**	**14.0%**	**30.4%**	**29.1%**	**25.5%**	**35.3%**
Rooms:								
7 or More	28.9%	40.1%	46.6%	35.8%	12.7%	22.1%	27.8%	21.0%
9 or More	8.1%	11.5%	16.7%	10.2%	2.5%	4.6%	8.0%	4.7%
In Single-Family Home	71,733	60,896	1,427	4,440	5,870	4,330	103	429
7 or More	40.7%	44.6%	52.9%	42.7%	20.6%	24.5%	32.4%	25.4%
9 or More	11.4%	12.8%	19.9%	12.3%	4.0%	5.0%	9.6%	5.5%
Householder Citizenship:								
Native	88.7%	91.5%	91.1%	87.7%	53.4%	59.9%	61.6%	47.9%
Naturalized	5.7%	5.6%	4.7%	5.7%	18.0%	21.4%	17.5%	19.3%
Noncitizen	5.6%	3.0%	4.2%	6.5%	28.6%	18.7%	21.0%	32.8%
Householder Age:								
Under 25	5.1%	1.3%	4.6%	6.5%	7.8%	2.5%	6.1%	8.8%
25–34	17.1%	11.7%	28.6%	30.3%	25.5%	17.6%	38.0%	36.6%
35–44	22.6%	22.6%	28.0%	27.8%	26.2%	27.3%	29.0%	30.2%
45–54	20.2%	22.9%	18.6%	17.1%	18.2%	22.2%	15.5%	14.6%
55–64	13.6%	16.3%	11.2%	9.4%	10.5%	14.1%	7.1%	6.0%
65+	21.5%	25.2%	9.0%	8.7%	11.8%	16.3%	4.4%	3.8%
Median	**47.5**	**51.2**	**40.5**	**39.2**	**41.0**	**46.1**	**36.9**	**36.2**

who had owned homes before, 23% bought new homes. Those shares are slightly lower than the corresponding shares for non-Latinos. Of Latinos buying existing homes, 62% were first-time buyers.

Among all households, as well as among Latino households, slightly more than half are headed by married couples. But nearly 70% of Latino married couples in 2000 had children under age 18 in their households, compared to 46% of non-Latino married couples. In addition, the reported number of Latino single parents is relatively high.

New home buyers are more likely than existing home buyers, long-time owners, or renters to have children under 18 in the household. Among all households buying new homes in 1999–2000, slightly less than half included children, but among Latino households buying new homes, nearly two-thirds included children.

Compared to other households where children are present, larger shares of Latino households have 3 or more children under 18. Among Latino new home buyers in 1999–2000, the share with 3 or more children was 19%, whereas only 10% of all new home buyers' households had 3 or more children. Because Latino home buyers were younger, on average, their children were also generally younger than those of other home buyers. The presence of young children is one of the key influences on the preferences of Latino home-buying households.

As the AHS data in Table 12.1 show, Latino home-buying households are also more likely to include other relatives, such as adult children, parents, and siblings. The presence of these other adults has different, equally profound, influence on Latino housing choices.

Overall, among Latino households buying new homes in 1999 or early 2000, more than half consisted of 4 or more people, and nearly 27% included 5 or more. Among all new home buyers, only a third included more than 3 people, and just 13% consisted of 5 or more.

Households consisting of people living alone have become more common in U.S. society over the past several decades. In general, Latinos are much less likely to live alone than non-Latinos. It is notable, however, that among Latino singles purchasing homes in recent years, a relatively large share bought new homes. The growing number of non-Latino singles buying homes is more heavily concentrated in the existing home market.

Although only slightly more than half of Latino householders are native-born U.S. citizens, well over 60% of Latino new home buyers were born in the U.S. As of 2000, the homeownership rate for U.S.-born Latino householders was nearly 58%, compared to a 42% rate for foreign-born Latino householders. Most of the homeownership gap between U.S.-born Latinos and non-Latinos can be attributed to the younger ages of Latinos. After adjusting for differences in the age

Source: © Corbis.

distribution, the homeownership rate for U.S.-born Latinos is only about 3 percentage points below the national average. Thus, the potential for an increase in homeownership is much greater for foreign-born Latinos. Whether immigrants will become a larger share of Latino home buyers will depend, however, on future rates of immigration, the legal status of past and future immigrants, the economic progress of immigrants, and the ability of the financial and housing industries to reach the immigrant population.

In 2003, NAHB conducted the latest in a series of surveys measuring consumer preferences regarding new homes. For the first time, the survey included supplementary samples to distinguish preferences of major ethnic and racial groups.[2]

Questionnaires were sent to more than 5,000 households, selected from panels maintained by National Family Opinion (www.mysurvey.com), a firm specializing in household surveys. The sample was chosen to include home owners and renters distributed by income, age, region, and household type in specified proportions, intended to reflect likely new home buyers. Of the 2,923 respondents, 212 identified themselves as Hispanic/Latino, including 48 who were foreign born.

The respondents in the Latino subsample had age, income, regional, and household-type characteristics similar to the overall survey sample. This provided a more direct measure of the influence of ethnicity, rather than the effects of differences in average age or income. On the other hand, the Latinos in the survey may have been too atypical of the overall Latino population to be representative. The median income of Latino households in the survey was well above the median of $32,800 for all Latino households, although it was close to the $64,944 median income of Latino households buying new homes that was reported in the 2003 AHS.

With the survey organized so that age and income were controlled, the true differences in the preferences of the typical Latino home buyer and of those in the overall market would be a combination determined by ethnicity and differences in age and income. The differences between Latinos and others shown by the survey include the effects of household size and other characteristics to the extent that those are not correlated with age and income.

The 2003 NAHB survey, as well as earlier surveys, found that larger households with more children are more concerned with having

Source: © Corbis.

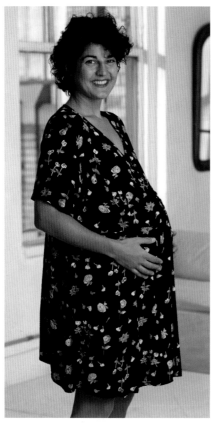

Source: © Corbis.

space than with luxury amenities. There are many other patterns, not all of which are intuitively obvious, associated with larger households and/or more children. For example, having a dining room ranks higher for families with more children, although this preference may not be due to regular use of the dining room for family meals.

The implications of more young children include a priority on living in a good school district and having a neighborhood playground. Families with young children also tend to prefer homes where the family room and yard are visible from the kitchen and where the master bedroom is close to the other bedrooms. Families with older children and, presumably, those with other adult relatives in the household prefer to have the master bedroom away from other bedrooms, to have more bathrooms, and to have good soundproofing.

With or without children, younger households are more likely than older households to prefer two-story homes. They are more likely to say they want a home office, even though they are less likely than older households to report working at home.

One consequence of the larger number of people in Latino households is a greater interest in the secondary bedrooms. Although about half of all households indicated that they wanted four or more bedrooms in NAHB's 2003 preference survey, for many of them "bedroom" was almost a euphemism. On average (based on data collected in earlier NAHB surveys), most home buyers would only use one or two bedrooms regularly for sleeping. The other bedrooms would be used as guest rooms, home offices, or hobby/sewing rooms or for storage. Among Latino households, bedrooms would be used as bedrooms. That difference was reflected in focus groups, where Latinos complained that, although the master bedrooms in new homes were impressive, the other bedrooms were inadequate.

When asked in the 2003 NAHB survey what they would be willing to sacrifice in order to make a house more affordable, only 24% of Latinos, compared to 29% of non-Hispanic whites, would accept a smaller house, but a larger share of Latinos than non-Hispanic whites would accept a smaller lot (32% vs. 29%) (Table 12.3). Among Latinos as well as other respondents, younger households and those with children were less likely to accept a smaller house or a smaller lot and instead would be willing to have some parts of the house initially left unfinished or to commute farther.

The survey asked where home buyers would like to have the washer and dryer located in their new home. Latinos were more likely than others to say that laundry facilities should go in the garage or basement rather than near the bedrooms or kitchen (Table 12.4). In focus groups, this was explained by concerns about noise disturbing sleeping children or intruding on meals.

Although the majority of Latinos, like other home buyers, indicated a preference for a family room adjoining the kitchen, fewer Latinos wanted the kitchen to be completely open to the family room (Table 12.5). Furthermore, 24% of Latinos, compared to 15% of non-Hispanic whites, wanted the kitchen and family room in completely separate areas of the house.

Latinos were more likely than other home buyers in each region to indicate a preference for a stucco exterior (Tables 12.6A and Table 12.6B). However, except for those in the west, Latinos were more likely to say that they preferred brick rather than stucco, even at higher cost. Of course, in responding to a survey, it is easy to say that you would be willing to spend an extra $20,000 for brick. When it comes to actual purchases with real money, brick may be less of a priority.

Latinos were less willing than other survey respondents to buy a house without a living room in order to get additional space elsewhere in the home (Table 12.7). Moreover, they were more interested in having a fireplace in the living room. Most other respondents wanted a fireplace, but non-Hispanic whites were more likely to want it in the family room. Latinos were also more likely to prefer a wood-burning fireplace to a gas fireplace. The desire for a living room with a fireplace is partly attributable to the fact that more of the Latinos in the survey (and in the marketplace) were first-time home buyers. Households who have owned homes before are less likely to feel the need for either a living room or a fireplace.

Another set of questions presented choices between pairs of alternatives. Those "either–or" questions produced some of the sharpest differences between

Table 12.3

What would you be prepared to accept in the home to make it more affordable for you?

	Latino	White	African American	Asian
Unfinished spaces that you could finish at a later date	37	43	37	36
Smaller lot	32	29	23	41
Farther away from shopping, entertainment, etc.	28	34	26	23
Smaller house	24	29	23	28
Longer commute to work	23	21	23	19
Fewer amenities (i.e., no fireplace, no garage, etc.)	13	15	11	11
Other	7	6	6	8
Less expensive material	5	5	7	7

Table 12.4

Where would you like to have your clothes washer and dryer in a new home?

	Latino	White	African American	Asian
Basement	22	13	30	21
Near bedrooms	22	35	21	25
Kitchen area	20	26	23	25
Other	19	18	11	11
Garage	18	7	15	18

Table 12.5

Which of the following kitchen–family room arrangements, all equal in size, would you prefer to have?

	Latino	White	African American	Asian
Visually open, but with a half wall	31	37	31	44
Completely open	27	34	24	29
Completely separate areas of the house	24	15	28	12
Side-by-side, but with a full wall	10	7	8	8
Oversized kitchen, no family room	8	7	9	8

Table 12.6A

What material would you prefer for the front exterrior of your home, assuming the additional costs?

	Latino	White	African American	Asian
Brick (add 5K)	40	43	60	42
Stucco-cement (add 1K)	23	12	10	19
Stone (add 10K)	15	13	10	17
Vinyl siding	8	16	11	7
Aluminum siding	6	5	8	7
Wood (add 500)	5	8	1	5
Cement fiber (add 500)	2	2	1	4
Other	1	2	0	0

Table 12.6B

What material would you prefer for the other three sides of your new home, assuming the additional costs?

	Latino	White	African American	Asian
Brick (add 15K)	36	33	49	30
Stucco-cement (add 3K)	29	17	14	25
Vinyl siding	14	25	17	17
Stone (add 25K)	7	5	4	9
Aluminum siding	5	6	11	7
Wood (add 1K)	5	10	2	8
Cement fiber (add 1K)	2	3	4	4
Other	1	1	0	0

Table 12.7

Evaluate how various designs and features would influence your purchase decision?

	Latino	White	African American	Asian
Woodburning Fireplace				
Essential/Must have	13	16	21	11
Desirable	47	37	40	39
Indifferent	19	23	23	35
Do not want	20	24	17	14
Gas Fireplace				
Essential/Must have	7	12	11	6
Desirable	37	38	38	51
Indifferent	29	29	31	34
Do not want	26	21	20	10

Latinos and non-Hispanic whites found by the survey. Latinos were much less willing to merge dining and living rooms (Table 12.8). Echoing the responses noted above, regarding willingness to buy a home without a living room in order to get more space elsewhere, the explicit choice of a larger family room with no living room versus living and family rooms of equal size found Latinos favoring the equal-size option by more than 2 to 1, whereas half of non-Hispanic whites chose each alternative. Most Latinos also rejected the idea—popular among non-Hispanic whites—of putting the master bedroom on the first floor of a two-story home. Most Latinos over age 45, however, liked the idea of a first-floor master bedroom, reflecting differences among age-groups for other ethnic populations.

For a number of the "either–or" questions where Latinos differed from non-Hispanic whites, the responses of Asians and African Americans were similar to those of Latinos. But the share of Latinos prepared to trade off bedroom space for a larger master bath was similar to that for non-Hispanic whites. African Americans and (perhaps surprisingly) Asians were much more uniform in choosing bedroom space over bathroom space.

Latinos were more interested than other prospective home buyers in having a patio, fenced yard, and in-ground lawn sprinklers. In one focus group of recent home buyers, several Latino participants complained that the standard patio provided with their homes was inadequate. One participant said that for most homes they looked at, "They tell you it's a patio, but it's just a big stepping stone." The interest in front porches was about the same between Latinos and non-Hispanic whites, and Latinos were somewhat less interested in decks or trees.

Only 64% of the Latinos in the survey currently lived in single-family detached homes, compared to 70%

of all respondents (Table 12.9A and Table 12.9B). However, the 74% share of Latinos saying they preferred to live in a single-family home matched the overall share.

Other surveys have also found strong preferences for single-family detached homes among Latinos, including a 2001 survey of California households conducted by the Public Policy Institute of California. That survey found 60% of Latinos and 65% of all Californians were currently living in single-family homes. When asked where they would "most prefer" to live, 85% of Latinos and 84% of all respondents selected single-family detached homes.[3]

Looking beyond the individual home, the NAHB survey asked what community amenities would "seriously influence you to move to a new community, realizing that these features, in varying degrees, increase the cost of the home or homeowner association fees." This was followed by a list of 19 facilities or features (plus a place to write in others). More than half of all respondents, including Latinos, indicated that parks and walking/jogging trails would attract them (Table 12.10).

More than a third of Latinos also identified playgrounds, public transportation, convenience stores, exercise rooms, and a gated community with a security guard as attractions. The shares of non-Hispanic whites reporting that they would be influenced by each of those features were lower. Only 5% of Latinos said they would be influenced by the presence of soccer fields—the same share as for other respondents.[4]

Compared to non-Hispanic whites, a larger share of Latinos in the NAHB survey indicated a preference for living in a central city or close-in suburb, and

Table 12.8

Within the same amount of money space, which of the following would you choose?

	Latino	White	African American	Asian
Two full master bedroom suites plus one standard bedroom OR One full master bedroom suite plus three standard bedrooms	26/74	26/74	23/77	32/68
A much larger family room and no living room OR Family room and living room about equal size	32/68	50/50	20/80	32/68
Larger than average kitchen and smaller living area space OR Typical kitchen and living area spaces	34/66	34/66	30/70	38/62
A bigger house with fewer amenities OR a smaller house with high quality products and amenities	41/59	35/65	42/58	45/55
An open living room/dining room OR Distinct and separate dining and living rooms	41/59	58/42	36/64	53/47
Master bedroom on the first floor in a two-story home OR Master bedroom on the second floor in a two-story home	42/58	59/41	46/54	41/59
More space in master bedroom and less space in the master bath OR Less space in master bedroom and more in the master bath	69/31	66/34	79/21	81/19

Table 12.9A

Which type of home do you currently live in?

	Latino	White	African American	Asian
Single family detached	64	72	61	73
Townhouse/single family attached	10	9	12	11
Multifamily	11	9	14	8
Mobile home	5	5	2	0
Other	12	6	10	8

Table 12.9B

Which type of home would you like to buy?

	Latino	White	African American	Asian
Single family detached	74	75	69	76
Townhouse/single family detached	10	11	13	14
Multifamily	5	5	12	4
Mobile home	3	2	0	0
Other	8	6	5	5

Table 12.10

Please indicate all of the following community amenities that would seriously influence you to move to a new community, realizing that these features, in varying degrees increase the cost of the home or home owner association fees.

	Latino	White	African American	Asian
Park Area	56	53	56	55
Walking/jogging trails	53	57	54	59
Convenience/Drug store	48	37	50	42
Outdoor swimming pool	45	40	35	46
Exercise room	40	32	49	39
Public transportation	38	25	46	46
Security guard at gate	38	27	42	44
Playgrounds	36	26	34	36
Lake	33	35	32	31
Card-operated gate w/no guard	20	17	19	24
Clubhouse	20	24	28	24
Business center	18	12	21	21
Billiard room	15	9	13	11
Daycare center	14	8	21	17
Baseball or softball field	11	8	11	11
Tennis courts	11	13	19	25
Basketball courts	11	8	20	12
Other	8	10	7	9
Racquetball courts	7	5	6	7
Soccer field	5	5	4	6

Table 12.11

In what type of area would you prefer to buy your new home?

	Latino	White	African American	Asian
Central city	13	5	15	12
Suburban (close in)	36	28	36	49
Outlying suburban	31	37	38	30
Rural	20	29	11	9

fewer wanted a home in a rural area (Table 12.11). Compared to African Americans and Asians, however, a larger share of Latinos said they would prefer to live in a rural area. The shares indicating that they preferred to buy a home in a central city were 13% for Latinos, 5% for non-Hispanic whites, 15% for African Americans, and 12% for Asians.

The household structure of Latino home buyers is similar in many ways to that of the average U.S. household of the 1950s, before the baby bust of the late 1960s made families with more than two children a rarity and before the surge in divorce rates in the 1970s and reduced marriage rates raised the nonfamily share of U.S. households. The housing preferences of Latinos also mirror previous non-Hispanic home buyer preferences. Perhaps over time the households and preferences of Latinos will become even more indistinguishable from the mainstream. At the same time, however, the designs and ideas of Latinos will influence the broader home-buying public.

Endnotes

1. For a multiple-regression discrete-choice model, see Carliner, Michael and Gopal Ahluwalia. "Housing Preferences of Immigrants and Minorities." Presentation to American Real Estate and Urban Economics Association 13th Annual International Conference, July 30, 2004. Available at http://www. areuea.org/conferences/papers/46/412.pdf.

2. National Association of Home Builders and Freddie Mac. *Consumer Preferences Survey*. Washington, DC: Builder Books, 2004. Available at www.BuilderBooks.com.

3. Baldassare, Mark. *PPIC Statewide Survey: Special Survey on Land Use*. San Francisco: Public Policy Institute of California, November 2001, p. 1. See also PPIC surveys for November 2002 and November 2004 for other measures of housing preferences.

4. The survey results contrast with the suggestions that soccer fields are a defining characteristic of Latino requirements. For example, see Garcia, Robert, Erica Flores, and Elizabeth Pine. *Dreams of Fields: Soccer, Community, and Equal Justice*. Los Angeles: Center for Law in the Public Interest. Report on Sports in Urban Parks to the California Department of Parks and Recreation, December 2002. Available at www.clipi.org/pdf/dreamsoffields.pdf.

Michael Carliner is Staff Vice President for Economics at the National Association of Home Builders, Washington, DC. Responsible for economic analysis and forecasting, his expertise extends to demographic trends, consumer preferences, use of building materials, and housing finance.

Storytelling by elders such as this beloved abuelo not only transmits Latino culture across generations but cements the bonds of Latino families. *Source:* Fernando Pagés, Brighton Construction Company, Lincoln, Nebraska.

INDEX

N

National Association of Hispanic Real
    Estate Professionals (NAHREP),
    35, 39, 45–46
National Association of Home
    Builders (NAHB), 131, 210,
    215–16, 219
National Council of La Raza (NCLR),
    7, 9, 20
    NCLR Homeownership Network, 39
New urbanism, Latino, 101–5, 107,
    115, 120–24, 135–37, 151, 193,
    197

P

Paint, 25, 54, 81, 82, 84. *see also*
    Color
Parks, 24, 77, 90, 93, 96, 103–4,
    110–12, 113, 118, 121–22,
    137–38, 197, 219
Patio, 8, 19, 22, 27, 56, 69, 82, 93,
    102–3, 106, 107, 121, 141, 218
Pew Hispanic Center, 34–35, 46
Playroom. *see* Family room
Plazas, 24, 77, 90, 96, 103, 108, 110,
    111–13, 121–22, 197
Porch, 51, 62, 64, 69, 70, 91, 93-84,
    104, 105, 107–8, 120, 142–3, 195,
    218

S

Schools, 25–27, 35, 37, 77, 79, 84, 96,
    117, 135–36, 146, 192–93, 197
Sight lines, 19, 67, 68, 84, 216
Single family, 1, 61, 63–66, 105, 116,
    119, 121, 129–30, 134–35,
    137–38, 144, 191, 198, 213,
    218–19

Streets, 23, 26, 27, 106, 113, 118,
    120–21, 138, 201–2
    streetscape(s), 108–9, 139, 42–43
Storm water management, 136,
    142–45
Suburb(an), 1, 10–11, 14–15, 63, 71,
    90, 96, 104–6, 109, 114, 120–21,
    123, 219–20
    sprawl, 101–2, 116
Social space(s), 11, 18–19, 22–23, 27

T

Tomás Rivera Policy Institute, 34–35,
    37–38, 45–46, 119, 202
Transportation, 23, 24, 27, 35, 37, 90,
    97, 130, 136, 148, 155, 194, 196,
    198, 201, 203, 219–20
Transit-oriented developments, 81,
    120, 148, 196

U

Unbanked, 170–72, 202

W

Workforce housing, 7, 11, 16, 21, 134

Y

Yard space, 19, 22, 27, 62, 64, 66–67,
    69, 92, 93, 102, 105, 107, 137,
    141, 216, 218

Z

Zones, house of a, 92-93
Zoning, 78, 129, 136, 141, 146–48,
    193, 198–99